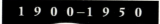

AFRICAN AMERICAN

LIFE

IN THE RURAL SOUTH

1 9 0 0 – 1 9 5 0

AFRICAN AMERICAN LIFE

IN THE RURAL SOUTH

1900–1950

Edited by

R. DOUGLAS HURT

UNIVERSITY OF MISSOURI PRESS

Columbia and London

Copyright © 2003 by
The Curators of the University of Missouri
University of Missouri Press, Columbia, Missouri 65201
Printed and bound in the United States of America
All rights reserved
First paperback printing, 2011
5 4 3 2 1   15 14 13 12 11

Library of Congress Cataloging-in-Publication Data

African American life in the rural South, 1900–1950 / edited by
R. Douglas Hurt.
          p. cm.
Includes bibliographical references and index.
     ISBN 978-0-8262-1960-2 (pbk: alk. paper)
     1. African Americans—Southern States—History—20th century.
2. African Americans—Southern States—Social conditions—20th
century. 3. African American farmers—Southern States—History—
20th century. 4. Agriculture—Social aspects—Southern States—
History—20th century. 5. Sharecropping—Southern States—
History—20th century. 6. Southern States—History—1865–1951.
7. Southern States—Race relations.8.Southern States—Rural
conditions. I. Hurt, R. Douglas.
E185. 6 .A257 2003
975 .0049607301734—dc21

                                                            2003002150

   ∞™
     This paper meets the requirements of the
American National Standard for Permanence of Paper
for Printed Library Materials, Z39.48, 1984.

Text designer: Elizabeth Young
Cover designer: Kristie Lee
Typesetter: The Composing Room of Michigan, Inc.
Printer and binder: The Maple-Vail Book Manufacturing Group
Typefaces: Dante, Frutiger57

Contents

AFRICAN AMERICAN
LIFE

IN THE RURAL SOUTH

1 9 0 0 – 1 9 5 0

Introduction

The condition of African Americans in southern agriculture at the turn of the twentieth century is well known. It is a depressing story of degradation, poverty, and hopelessness for the men, women, and children who lived in desperation and without alternatives. The textile mills and mines did not welcome them, the segregated schools provided little opportunity for upward mobility, and the employment possibilities created by the First World War lay in the distant and unknown future. At that time, 90 percent of the African American population lived in the South, and 83 percent resided in rural areas, primarily on farms. The goal of "forty acres and a mule" remained beyond their reach, if not their dreams, even though black landowners had slowly increased to about 13 percent of African American farmers. These black farmers held 13.5 million acres in the South, but their holdings paled in comparison to whites, who owned more than 100 million acres in 1900.

At the turn of the twentieth century, tenancy in the South bound most of the 707,364 black farmers to the land through the crop lien and furnishing merchant system. At that time, about 75 percent of all black farmers were tenants, usually sharecroppers. With more than half a million black farmers captive to the trinity of cotton, tenancy, and poverty, they were a desperate people with little hope. African American tenants usually farmed about fifty acres, settled their accounts at the end of the year, and remained in debt and bound by a continuing contract that required them to remain on the land and work off their debt to the landowner or furnishing merchant. African American farmers also lived within tightly configured boundaries marked by racism more than fences or county lines. Their lives differed little from those of their parents and grandparents who endured slavery and the pre–Civil War plantation system. Little wonder, then, that many African American farmers left for northern cities when World

War I created employment opportunities that lured them like a new promised land.

By 1910, 89 percent of the nation's black population still lived in the South and constituted 35 percent of the region's population; 73 percent of those African Americans resided in the countryside. Twenty-three percent of those farmers owned a total of more than 15 million acres. But African American farmers—landowners, tenants, and sharecroppers—soon began leaving the land for better opportunities in the towns and cities. Pulled by city jobs and pushed by the boll weevil, between 1910 and 1920 approximately half a million African Americans left the rural South, more than all the black migrants who had headed north during the previous forty years. African American farmers who stayed essentially had few alternatives other than to cast their fate with another landowner who offered more and better credit, improved living conditions, and respectful treatment. Yet "anti-enticement" laws and violence limited their freedom to move and improve their lives. Some African American farmers fled the land and became part of the great ebb and flow of migrant agricultural workers along the East Coast, thereby exchanging one form of rural poverty and degradation for another. At best, the cities within the South offered a mean and lowly sanctuary and escape from the land.

Moreover, between 1910 and 1930, more than 1.5 million African Americans, mostly farmers, left the South, pushed by the boll weevil, poverty, and want and pulled by industrial jobs outside the region. Between 1910 and 1920, 10.4 percent or 200,400 African Americans left Alabama and Mississippi alone for the promise of a better life beyond the South; an additional 2 million departed from the region between 1930 and 1950. Still, in 1920, more than 920,000 black farmers lived in the South, of which approximately 24 percent owned land, and their farms averaged seventy-seven acres. Put differently, 76 percent of African American farmers remained tenants, of whom approximately 50 percent were sharecroppers. Compared to white farmers, the average value of their farms remained low. In 1910, African American farms, including livestock, averaged $799 in value; the figure was $1,588 a decade later. White-owned farms averaged $2,140 and $3,911 in value for the same periods. Consequently, the African Americans who remained on the land during the 1920s confronted enduring poverty.

By the early 1930s, the agricultural programs of the federal government, particularly under the Agricultural Adjustment Acts, encouraged landowners to release their tenants, black and white. Only the
Southern Tenant Farmers' Union gave hope to a relative few who literally bet their lives that their conditions would improve when they
joined the organization. Still, the number of African American farmers
peaked in 1935, fifteen years before the climax of the white agricultural population in the South. Despite the Great Migration of African
American farmers from the countryside during the first third of the
twentieth century, by 1940, 77 percent of the U.S. black population still
lived in the South, and 64 percent lived in rural areas. On the eve of
World War II, African American farmers remained locked in the sharecropping system, with landowners composing only about 20 percent of
the total. Few earned more than two hundred dollars per year; most received less than half that amount in cash for their labor.

World War II encouraged more African American farmers to leave
the land, and more than one million blacks departed the South during
the 1940s. Pushed by wretched agricultural conditions and pulled by
war industries that offered jobs with high and regularly paid wages,
more African Americans fled the land, often to the North, but also to
southern cities. During the 1940s, Congress crippled, then terminated,
the Farm Security Administration. This agency had been the last hope
for farmers, especially black, who could not qualify for operating loans
through traditional credit institutions such as banks. Federal farm programs, however, continued to aid the large-scale landowners at the ex-
pense of sharecroppers, whom they continued to release from their
employment. After World War II, the mechanization of southern agriculture proceeded rapidly. White landowners increasingly adopted the
mechanical cotton picker, released their tenants and sharecroppers, and
hired some back as day laborers who earned cash wages.

By the mid–twentieth century, African Americans had little opportunity to remain on the land as farmers given their nearly insurmountable problems. Discrimination was a fact of life for black farmers who
attempted to purchase land or acquire loans for operating expenses.
Most African American farm families still resided in unpainted houses
that were little more than shacks. Virtually all lived without indoor
plumbing or window screens. Few of these farmers had more security

than an annual oral contract with the landowner. Moreover, African American farmers who owned their land produced too little on too few acres to earn a satisfactory living. Few black farmers could acquire the capital through savings from the sale of cotton, tobacco, or other commodities to purchase land, expand their production, and earn a profit. As a result, black migration from the countryside continued. Few opportunities existed for African American farmers to seek off-the-farm employment and, thereby, use outside income to keep their farms viable. Once the children of African American farmers left the land for better job opportunities and a higher standard of living in the towns and cities, usually in the North, they seldom returned.

By 1950, only 25 percent of southern farmers were African American. At that time, approximately 536,000 African American farmers remained in the South, of whom 195,000 were sharecroppers. Thereafter, the rush from the farms continued. Seven in ten African American farmers did not own the land that they plowed, planted, and harvested. During the 1950s, nearly 2.5 million African American farmers left the South. Black farmers who remained in the region were more likely to be tenants than landowners. By 1960, African American farmers had become nearly irrelevant.

While African American farmers struggled in poverty, the federal government did little to aid them. Agricultural policies were made far away in the halls of Congress, but they were executed from local offices, frequently by the county agent, whose loyalty went to the planter class. Federal officials refused to permit African American farmers to participate in a host of economic programs designed to help white farmers stay on the land and operate efficient, profitable farms. At best, they extended only parsimonious aid to African American farmers through the county agent and home demonstration systems of the Extension Service. Race, of course, influenced this denial of equal access to government programs. Although racism proved a nearly insurmountable hindrance to African American farmers throughout the South during the first half of the twentieth century and played a major role in preventing black farmers from acquiring land of their own, it also proved particularly insidious when it influenced the application of federal agricultural policy and determined the participants of government farm programs.

African American rural life, however, is more than just the story of southern agriculture. Indeed, the history of African American rural life involves far more complexity than analysis of tenancy, sharecropping, and landownership. Simply put, rural does not necessarily mean agricultural. While historians and educated readers of American history know the general parameters of African American agricultural history from slavery to the mid–twentieth century, they know considerably less about black rural life beyond the context of farming, particularly in the twentieth century. The purpose of this collection of essays, written by leading scholars of southern history, then, is to provide a window to the rural African American past during the first half of the twentieth century to enable better historical understanding beyond the discussion of sharecropping, cotton, and poverty.

Louis M. Kyriakoudes begins this collection by discussing African American migration within the South. He cogently demonstrates that long before and throughout the Great Migration beyond the South, rural black southerners were on the move, seeking and often finding opportunities in towns and cities. Racism proved as strong as economic opportunity in fostering mobility for black farm families as they moved frequently to better their condition. Yet while rural African Americans moved frequently, they usually relocated within their immediate vicinity or county. Kyriakoudes also challenges the consensus opinion that landowners held their sharecroppers in continuing contracts that essentially made them peons. Instead, he argues that planters usually wrote off continuing debts, because they had no hope of collection. He also reminds that World War II stimulated southern urbanization, which pulled many African American farmers from the land in the same way that wartime jobs in northern cities did.

Ted Ownby in an arresting essay forcefully addresses the anti-agrarianism of Booker T. Washington, W. E. B. Du Bois, Richard Wright, and Zora Neale Hurston. He compares and analyzes the autobiographical works of Washington, Du Bois, Wright, and Hurston in relation to the concept of agrarianism and farm life. Each writer, among others, portrayed rural life from different perspectives. Washington emphasized the moral lessons and self-reliance to be learned from farm work. Du Bois considered any benefits of farm life ruined by tenancy and white oppression. Wright believed that farming ensured only

degradation, toil, and poverty for his people. Hurston was more am-
bivalent about the rural South, reflecting only about the rich folk life
that it spawned while shunning any mental attachment to the land.
These and other autobiographers ultimately believed that farm life im-
poverished the mind, broke the spirit, and ensured abject poverty, and
they saw no reason to remain on the land.

Lois Myers and Rebecca Sharpless use oral history interviews to
demonstrate the cultural ingenuity of landless country people and to
discuss the most important institution for rural African Americans—
the church. It has been said, with much truth, that the South has never
been more segregated than it is today at eleven o'clock on Sunday
mornings. Indeed, in the rural South the black churches, primarily Baptist and Methodist, have given African Americans a place to meet, pray,
and socialize free from the control of whites. The black churches have
been instrumental in offering hope to a downtrodden people and have
provided a place for self-expression and personal achievement, particularly because the poor education of its members, to say nothing of
racism, prevented them from participating in the social and political
world of the white community. Whites considered the African American churches benign, even useful, social institutions, and were more
likely to provide financial help to the church than to any other black
institution. The church, then, provided not only salvation but also social experience as well as the opportunity for some blacks to enter a
professional class as pastors, while the buildings became symbols of
stability and community. When African Americans left the countryside
for the towns and cities, the rural black churches often went with them.

Melissa Walker discusses the fluidity of race relations in the rural
South as opposed to the relative rigidity of segregation in the cities by
studying the formal and informal separation of blacks and whites in the
countryside. She observes that racial and class hierarchies, shaped by
the landlord-tenant relationship, were both fixed and fluid as well as dependent on local customs. With interracial relationships, that is, place,
dependent more on behavior than space, the separation of the races relied on mutually understood boundaries for acceptable behavior by
African Americans. As long as blacks accepted a position of inferiority,
white paternalism, and economic inequality, they often had considerable latitude in dealing with whites. African Americans, however, sel-

dom mixed with whites socially in public. Walker notes that some blacks also welcomed separation, if not segregation, for their own protection and to avoid dealing with whites, whom they feared, on a daily basis. Certainly, Jim Crow in the rural South was a policy of segregation built on nuance as well as force.

Valerie Grim broadly surveys African American rural culture during the first half of the twentieth century and illustrates the profusion of customs and practices of rural black southerners. She particularly examines the ways blacks created a separate culture that represented their interests. She discusses the importance of daily activities from the preservation of vegetables and hog killing time to church- and school-sponsored events that promoted literacy and the arts. She notes the importance of the church in the spiritual as well as social lives of African Americans, particularly through events such as baptisms, weddings, and funerals. The country store also served as the cultural hub for rural African Americans, and the men and women who met on its porch observed their own protocol, for both good and ill. The acquisition of telephones and radios also affected African American rural culture by bringing it into greater contact with the outside world. She argues that all social events and technological acquisitions must be given meaning within the context of African American rural culture.

William P. Browne provides a broad overview of the plight of African American agriculture during the twentieth century. By emphasizing that the Farm Security Administration served as the only federal agency that could help small-scale, subsistence black farmers, he argues that the U.S. Department of Agriculture circumvented that aid by developing agencies such as the Agricultural Adjustment Administration and various credit and loan programs designed to aid commercially oriented white farmers. Moreover, he notes the fundamental racism on which USDA policies were based until the late twentieth century. As a result, the federal government, primarily represented by the USDA, intentionally ignored black farmers because it considered them nonentities in production agriculture. Confronted with a negligent, if not hostile, federal government, African American farmers had little choice but to migrate to the cities, no matter the employment situation there. At best, African American farmers received only scant justice near the end of the twentieth century after litigating for the receipt of the financial aid that the federal government had denied them as a result of blatant discrimination relating to a host of programs since the 1930s.

Jeannie Whayne discusses the efforts of African American county and home demonstration agents to improve the agricultural practices and health and nutritional needs of black farm men and women while negotiating the world of white policy makers and supervisors. She argues that these black agents became skilled negotiators, with the most successful achieving improved conditions on black farms while avoiding any challenge to the racial status quo. Yet by improving economic conditions, even in a rudimentary way, for African American farmers, the Extension Service inevitably encouraged black farmers to think about economic independence, which, in turn, challenged customary relationships between black sharecroppers and white planters. African American extension agents always tread a narrow path between the worlds of white planters and black farmers while working to improve the daily lives of African American farm families. When World War II changed the economic order, black extension agents became as superfluous as African American farmers.

Peter Coclanis and Bryant Simon analyze the manner in which African Americans used strategies of exit and voice, that is, self-expression and loyalty, to deal with the reality of life in the rural South. Exit from the farms, or at least the threat of it, whether to the North or to another farm in the South, gave some blacks an alternative or hope for a better life. In reality, many blacks could not afford to leave either their farms or the South. Many African Americans who remained in the region attempted to gain greater freedom within the Jim Crow system by seeking political enfranchisement or participating in the Southern Tenant Farmers' Union. Some used music, particularly the "Blues," to protest and give expression to their condition, and challenged the expectations and unwritten rules of whites in subtle but consistent ways. To the extent that rural African Americans showed loyalty to whites, they did so as a subterfuge to gain what they wanted in a world where racial violence was a fact of life.

Overall, these essays show that African Americans were not always or entirely helpless victims who lived in a rural world circumscribed by racism, degradation, and violence. Although the harsh realities of space, place, and race dictated the parameters of their lives, African

Americans took responsibility for negotiating the complex world of the rural South during the early twentieth century. While they often seemed little more than passive supplicants in a world beyond their control, they took initiative, that is, agency, for their lives in a variety of subtle ways to create order, gain dignity, and win freedom—all to achieve a better life in the rural South.

The intent of this collection of essays, then, is to be suggestive, varied, and eclectic. Each author helps us think about African American rural life in different contexts and new ways. Although African American history during the early twentieth century has been largely confined to telling the story of production agriculture within the cotton plantation system or tobacco South, and while late-twentieth-century black history has largely been confined to their urban experience, the rural history of African Americans is rich, important, and largely understudied. Consequently, this collection of essays is designed to encourage further study and discussion of an important but little-known aspect of the American past.

I am grateful for the help that I received from my research assistant Leah Tookey.

"Lookin' for Better All the Time"

Rural Migration and Urbanization in the South, 1900–1950

LOUIS M. KYRIAKOUDES

Sometime around the year 1900 Samuel Dean, a black sharecropper's son, left his family farm in the Bedford County community of Flat Creek, Tennessee, for the county seat of Shelbyville. Not making enough money in Shelbyville, Dean soon moved to Nashville, where he found work in a feed mill. Dean punctuated his stay there with a stint in the meatpacking plants of St. Louis, followed by a brief foray to Akron, Ohio, during World War I before returning again to Nashville. When asked by a Works Progress Administration interviewer in the 1930s why he had moved to so many places so frequently, Dean responded, "I was lookin' for better all the time."[1]

Dean's "lookin'" and the numerous moves he undertook complicate our view of the early-twentieth-century southern rural exodus we call the Great Migration. The migration that swept black southerners to the cities of the North and West was just one portion of a broader black and white exodus from southern agriculture. Dean's story suggests that the frequent moves of black and white southerners created migration patterns of great complexity. Highly mobile rural southerners moved across the rural South, seeking greater opportunities in the region's tenancy-dominated agriculture. Others poured into southern cities or left the region altogether for the urban North, seeking greater economic opportunity and an escape from

---

1. Samuel Dean Narrative, November 2, 1938, Nashville, Tennessee, Federal Writers Project Papers, Southern Historical Collection, University of North Carolina, Chapel Hill.

what James Weldon Johnson once characterized as "the tremendous shore of southern barbarism."[2]

Historians have examined carefully the pull of northern migration. The very visible and dramatic arrival of large numbers of black southerners in Chicago, New York, Philadelphia, and Pittsburgh has ensured that the chief emphasis of scholarship on the Great Migration would lie with these important destinations.[3] Yet by looking carefully at migration patterns among those rural southerners, white and black, who remained in the region, we can sort out some of the less visible changes in the relationship between rural labor markets and agriculture to understand how migration fit into the life strategies of rural black southerners. By doing so, we can understand not only those who left, but also those who chose to stay behind.

Early-twentieth-century observers understood that the cityward migration of black and white southerners marked the beginning of a profound demographic shift in the region. Around the turn of the century, Howard University mathematics professor and pioneering African American demographer Kelly Miller noted that the "general drift of the [Negro] population at large [is] towards overcrowded [urban] centers." In 1906 journalist Ray Stannard Baker, visiting an Atlanta bursting with blacks and whites fresh from southern farms, noted that "the opportunities of the city have attracted the black people, just as they have the whites, in large numbers." Twenty years later, Chapel Hill regionalist T. J. Woofter, Jr., similarly observed that "both

2. James Weldon Johnson in 1923, quoted in James R. Grossman, *Land of Hope: Chicago, Black Southerners and the Great Migration,* 16.

3. The literature on the Great Migration is large. The more notable works include Grossman, *Land of Hope;* Carole Marks, *Farewell—We're Good and Gone: The Great Black Migration;* Peter Gottlieb, *Making Their Own Way: Southern Blacks' Migration to Pittsburgh, 1916–1930;* Kimberley L. Phillips, *Alabama North: African-American Migrants, Community, and Working-Class Activism in Cleveland, 1915–45.* Earl Lewis, *In Their Own Interests: Race, Class, and Power in Twentieth-Century Norfolk, Virginia* is notable in its examination of migration to a southern city. Important bibliographic and historiographic guides are: Frank Alexander Ross and Louis Venable Kennedy, *A Bibliogrpahy of Negro Migration* (New York: Columbia University Press, 1934); Joe William Trotter, Jr. ed., *The Great Migration in Historical Perspective: New Dimensions of Race, Class, and Gender;* and Alferdteen Harrison, ed., *Black Exodus: The Great Migration from the American South.*

in the South and the North the trend of the Negro population is definitely cityward."[4]

The migration of black southerners to northern cities operated as one element in a much larger rural exodus by both blacks and whites. Baker believed that black migrants were "responding to exactly the same natural laws that control white farmers." Writing in 1920 as the war-era wave of black migration northward was nearing completion, Woofter argued that "there are very few counties in the South where the colored and white people do not move in the same direction in response to the same situations." Black observers were quick to point out that racial oppression drove blacks from the South's farms and the region. Separating race oppression from economic motives creates a false distinction. The patterns of race oppression were so deeply interwoven into the economic context of the sharecropping system as to be inseparable. The oppressiveness of the southern racial caste system as it developed after Reconstruction directly supported the economic subjugation of black workers both in industry and agriculture. The contours of the sharecropping system, with its promotion of excessive cotton cultivation and inefficient credit and marketing institutions, sapped the meager returns of small southern farmers, black and white. William J. Edwards, an Alabama-based African American educator, acknowledged the plight of black southerners, but concluded that race oppression "may be all classed as the secondary cause of this great exodus." Hardship drove rural blacks to a life in cities. "These people are hungry, they are naked, they have no corn and had no cotton; so they are without food and clothes. What else can they do but go away in search of work?" wondered Edwards in 1918, during the midst of the Great Migration's first wave.[5]

4. Kelly Miller, "The City Negro," *Southern Workman* 31 (April 1902): 217–18; Ray Stannard Baker, *Following the Color Line: American Negro Citizenship in the Progressive Era* (1908; reprt., New York: Harper and Row, 1964), 46; T. J. Woofter, Jr., *Negro Problems in Cities* (Garden City, N.Y.: Doubleday, Doran and Co., 1928), 29.

5. The origins of the southern sharecropping system are examined in Ronald L. F. Davis, *Good and Faithful Labor: From Slavery to Sharecropping in the Natchez District, 1860–1890* (Westport, Conn.: Greenwood Press, 1982); Gerald D. Jaynes, *Branches without Roots: Genesis of the Black Working Class, 1862–1882* (New York: Oxford University Press, 1986); Jay R. Mandle, *The Roots of Black Poverty: The South-*

In fact, moving was a central feature of late-nineteenth and early-twentieth-century southern rural life. Southern tenant farmers and sharecroppers—black and white—had always been highly mobile, seeking better land and better terms. Some black farmers, moved by the "pioneering spirit," as Carter Woodson described it, went west. Most famous was the well-organized movement of the "exodusters," which left Nashville in 1879 for Kansas.[6] Texas, Oklahoma, Arkansas, and the Mississippi Delta continued to draw black southerners searching for lower farm rents and higher wages. Writing of his youth in South Carolina during the 1880s, William Pickens recalled that his parents were "farmers of the tenant or day-labor class and were ever on the move from cabin to cabin, with the proverbial unacquisitiveness of the 'rolling stone.'" In 1888 Pickens's father contracted with a labor agent to move the family from their home in South Carolina to the Arkansas Delta, "where the soil was fertile and wages high." Moving west offered little relief. Mired in debt to finance the move, Pickens's father sharecropped and worked as a logger to keep his family fed. Failing to get ahead in the Arkansas Delta, he moved the family again to a farm near Little Rock. Despite "no less than twenty removals of our family" before Pickens reached the age of eighteen in 1899, his father was unable to extricate them from the grinding poverty of the sharecropping regime. The West beckoned, but opportunities were not forthcoming.[7]

Well into the twentieth century, seasonal farm labor migration patterns carried young black men to work the wheat harvests of Texas and Oklahoma. These young men would head west, following the annual

---

ern Plantation Economy after the Civil War (Durham, N.C.: Duke University Press, 1978); Roger Ransom and Richard Sutch, *One Kind of Freedom: The Economic Consequences of Emancipation* (Cambridge, England: Cambridge University Press, 1977), 81–105. See also T. J. Woofter, *Negro Migration: Changes in Rural Organization and Population in the Cotton Belt,* 14; Baker, *Following the Color Line,* 78; William J. Edwards, *Twenty-Five Years in the Black Belt* (Boston: Cornhill Co., 1918), 96; Neil Fligstein, *Going North: Migration of Blacks and Whites from the South, 1900–1950.*

6. Carter Woodson, *A Century of Negro Migration* (New York: Russell and Russell, 1969), 120–21.

7. William Pickens, *The Heir of Slaves: An Autobiography* (Boston: Pilgrim Press, 1911), 7–8, 11, 22–23.

harvest as the crop ripened. Most would return to their homes in the South at the end of the season, but many "remain[ed] as wage hands the following year," working as hired farm help. On the East Coast, the advent of the 1920s farm depression sent southern blacks on the road as migrant laborers, working the fruit and vegetable crops in the burgeoning truck farms of Florida and New Jersey.[8]

The structure of the sharecropping system compelled black southerners to move frequently. Sharecropper contracts were year-to-year, and changing farms could offer the hope of any number of improvements: lower rents, the chance to farm more productive land, access to healthier workstock and better implements, better housing, or less demanding or more honest landlords. Typical was Athey Pierce, an Alabama sharecropper who testified before congressional investigators that he had recently moved from one farm to another because "the man wouldn't have the house fixed up . . . every time it rained everything in the house would get wet."[9] Tenant and sharecroppers, black and white, would engage in the annual search for something better.

Hosea Hudson, the Birmingham labor activist, knew well sharecropping's peripatetic ways. Hudson recalled of his youth in the Georgia Black Belt that "we were always moving, always in the hope of finding a landlord who would not take advantage of us." From 1903 to 1918, when Hudson married and struck out on his own, his family moved at least nine times. In 1903, when Hudson was only five years old, their landlord seized not only the family's cotton crop but also their hogs and cows to settle an outstanding debt. The family then moved to a nearby plantation, "stayed one year, made a crop and moved on." Hudson's family moved again in 1906, every year from 1909 through 1913, and again in 1916 and 1917. Along the way, Hudson's family farmed for two black landlords, who treated them no better than their white counter-

8. C. O. Brannen, "Relation of Land Tenure to Plantation Organization," USDA, *Bulletin* no. 1269 (Washington, D.C., October 1924), 44–45; Cindy Hahamovitch, *The Fruits of Their Labor: Atlantic Coast Farmworkers and the Making of Migrant Poverty, 1870–1945*, 113–16.

9. U.S. House of Representatives, "Hearings before the Select Committee to Investigate the Interstate Migration of Destitute Citizens: Interstate Migration," 76th Cong., 3d sess., pt. 2, Montgomery Hearings, August 14, 15, and 16, 1940 (Washington, D.C.: Government Printing Office, 1940), 442.

parts, and his grandmother's white half brother. Despite the many moves, Hudson recalled, the family "hardly ever succeeded in bettering our condition."[10]

While mobility among tenant farmers and sharecroppers could be quite high, contemporary social surveys confirm that its spatial scope was quite limited. A 1926 study of black farmers in Southampton County, Virginia, found that virtually all tenant farmers had changed farms at some point in their lives, with an average of four years and three months passing between each move. Despite the high farm-to-farm mobility, Southampton County tenants rarely ventured from their immediate locality: 81 percent did not change their church, school, or "trading center" upon moving. Another 1924 study of tenant farmers across ninety-three southern plantation counties found similar levels of farm-to-farm mobility among both blacks and whites. Among black farmers, 39.6 percent remained on their farms one year or less, with more than three-quarters changing farms within a four-year period. Whites were even more eager to move. Fifty-three percent of white tenants moved within a year and 83 percent did so within four years. Depression-era mobility patterns resembled those of the 1920s. T. J. Woofter's expansive survey of 5,060 farm families residing on 646 cotton plantations found that white sharecroppers averaged 4.4 years on a farm, while their black counterparts averaged 5.6 years.[11]

The logic of sharecropping shaped these localized mobility patterns. Since credit markets were local, for the poorest tenants—those owning neither tools nor workstock—a reputation for skill and hard work could be their only capital asset. Hence, many tenant farmers tended

10. Georgia and Florida were the only two southern states where the landlord's statutory lien applied against not only the tenant's crops but also "against all property possessed by the tenant." See Brannen, "Relation of Land Tenure to Plantation Organization," 60–61; Hosea Hudson, *Black Worker in the Deep South: A Personal Record* (New York: International Publishers, 1972), 1–16.

11. W. S. Scarborough, "Tenancy and Ownership among Negro Farmers in Southampton County, Virginia," USDA, *Bulletin* no. 1404 (Washington, D.C.: April, 1926), 24, especially Table 2; Brannen, "Relation of Land Tenure to Plantation Organization," 74, Appendix D, Table 3; T. J. Woofter, *Landlord and Tenant on the Cotton Plantation,* Works Progress Administration, Research Monograph V (Washington, D.C.: Government Printing Office), 110.

to stay in the same general vicinity where they were well known among those who acted as the gatekeepers to credit in the sharecropping system: local landlords and furnishing merchants. The converse was true as well. Tenant farmers who wanted to escape a reputation for intractability, ineptitude, or for challenging established patterns of racial subservience had an incentive to move farther away, to where they were not known.[12]

The high turnover among sharecroppers did not generally lead to debt peonage in the classic sense of restrained mobility. Those who have argued that debt peonage tied black sharecroppers to particular landlords, thus leading to the "metamorphosis of slavery," have overstated their case. Sharecroppers moved too frequently. When an indebted sharecropper sought a new farm, the merchant or landlord who held his debt sought to levy personal property, as in the case of Tom Glenn's seizure of the livestock of Hosea Hudson's family. When there was no property to seize, landlords wrote off the debt.[13]

Landlords and furnishing merchants were inclined to write off bad debts because the usurious interest rates they charged sharecroppers for the credit necessary to acquire their annual "furnish" of seed, fertilizer, other supplies, and provisions provided little incentive to carry heavily indebted sharecropper families from year to year. Roger Ransom and Richard Sutch's study of late-nineteenth-century sharecropping estimated that in the 1880s the annual interest rate sharecroppers

12. Gavin Wright, *Old South, New South: Revolutions in the Southern Economy since the Civil War*, 97–98.

13. Arguments in favor of the immobility of tenant and sharecropper labor by coercion can be found in Jonathan M. Wiener, *Social Origins of the New South, Alabama, 1860–1885* (Baton Rouge: Louisiana State University Press, 1978), 69–73 and Crandall A. Shifflett, *Patronage and Poverty in the Tobacco South* (Knoxville: University of Tennessee Press, 1982), xii; William Cohen, "Negro Involuntary Servitude in the South, 1865–1900: A Preliminary Analysis," *Journal of Southern History* 42 (February 1976): 31–60. Cohen modifies his argument in the more recent *At Freedom's Edge: Black Mobility and the Southern White Quest for Racial Control, 1861–1915*. Pete Daniel, "The Metamorphosis of Slavery, 1865–1900," *Journal of American History* 66 (June 1979): 88–99; Pete Daniel, *The Shadow of Slavery: Peonage in the South, 1901–1969*, 3–81; and Daniel A. Novak, *The Wheels of Servitude: Black Forced Labor after Slavery* (Lexington: University Press of Kentucky, 1978); Woofter, *Landlord and Tenant on the Cotton Plantation*, 61.

paid on their furnish averaged 59.1 percent, but ranged anywhere from 44.2 to 74.6 percent. Not much had changed by the 1930s, when T. J. Woofter found interest rates ranging from 50 to 75 percent. Another depression-era cotton plantation survey concluded that sharecroppers' annual interest rates "remained two to three times as high" as what the landlords and merchants were themselves paying for short-term credit.[14]

Thus, as Hosea Hudson's case indicates, mobility did not translate into improving conditions for the great mass of sharecroppers and tenants. The constant shifting from farm to farm did little to undermine the fundamentals of the sharecropping system as too many farmers sought to farm too much cotton, remaining mired in debt, even as the landlords for whom they labored changed from year to year. The sharecropping system operated as a treadmill, circulating landless farm families within fairly well-established local migration networks while offering them little by way of improvement in their economic prospects.

This treadmill was only disrupted when a series of economic and demographic shocks beset the rural South in the 1910s and continued through World War II, disrupting sharecropping's mobility patterns and sending blacks and whites pouring out of the rural South on their way to cities in the South and North. The Great Migration has been viewed by demographers as the result of a series of "push" and "pull" factors operating together to prevail upon black southerners to move. Students of the migration have long stressed the economic pushes of low agricultural incomes, high rates of tenancy, and limited opportunities to ascend the agricultural ladder to join the ranks of the farmowning. The short-term shock of boll weevil infestation in the heart of

---

14. Ransom and Sutch, *One Kind of Freedom,* 130, 237–43; Woofter, *Landlord and Tenant on the Cotton Plantation,* 62; William C. Holley, *The Plantation South, 1934–1937,* Works Progress Administration, Research Monograph 22 (Washington, D.C.: Government Printing Office, 1940), 27–28.

Ransom and Sutch, *One Kind of Freedom,* 126–48, attribute these high interest rates charged tenants and sharecroppers to the furnishing merchant's "territorial monopoly," which insulated him from competition and allowed such usury. This view has been challenged in Louis M. Kyriakoudes, "Lower-Order Urbanization and Territorial Monopoly in the Southern Furnishing Trade: Alabama, 1871–1890," *Social Science History* 26 (spring 2002): 179–98.

the plantation belt devastated cotton crops and also increased production costs as outlays for insecticide were added to the sharecropper's furnish. The cessation of European immigration in 1914 and wartime employment demands drew black and white southerners to the urban North, thus beginning the Great Migration.[15]

In addition to these economic pushes and pulls, which operated across both races, albeit unequally, there was the powerful push of race subjugation. Blacks fleeing the rural South fled exclusion from the political process, injustice in the courts, abysmal schools for their children, and a social order where deference to whites in all spheres of public life was expected and enforced with violence. Demographers Stuart Tolnay and E. M. Beck have found a reciprocal relationship between the out-migration of blacks from southern counties and the incidence of lynching in the 1910s and 1920s. Tolnay and Beck find that blacks were most likely to migrate from areas where racial violence was most prevalent. More interesting, however, is their finding that high black out-migration tended to reduce future levels of racial violence. Thus Tolnay and Beck confirm what other scholars have also found, that black migration tended to result in less oppressive conditions as white employers responded in their own interest to localized labor shortages.[16]

While the World War I–era African American migration northward was highly visible, it was not so massive as to disrupt or depopulate the rural South, which before World War II was a thickly populated region. Southerners were a highly fecund people who exhibited the highest fertility in the nation. As indicated by Table 1, the ratio of children

15. The classic demographic formulation of the push-pull model remains Edward G. Ravenstein's two essays: "The Laws of Migration," *Journal of the Royal Statistical Society* 48 (1885): 167–227 and "The Laws of Migration," *Journal of the Royal Statistical Society* 52 (1889): 241–301. The best contemporary restatement of Ravenstein's work is Everette S. Lee, "A Theory of Migration," *Demography* 3, no. 2 (1966): 47–57. The timing of the Great Migration is explored in William J. Collins, "When the Tide Turned: Immigration and the Delay of the Great Black Migration," *Journal of Economic History* 57 (September 1997): 607–32.

16. Stewart E. Tolnay and E. M. Beck, "Racial Violence and Black Migration in the American South, 1910 to 1930," *American Sociological Review* 57 (February 1992): 103–16; James R. Grossman, "Black Labor Is Best: Southern White Reactions to the Great Migration," in Harrison, ed., *Black Exodus*, 51–71.

୧୬   Table 1. **Child-Woman Ratio,**
         South and Non-South, 1910–1950

	1910	1950
South	560	462
Non-South	401	397

South is defined as the eleven former Confederate states plus Kentucky.

Child-Woman ratio indicates children under age 5 per all women, ages 15–49 x 1,000.

Source: Steven Ruggles and Matthew Sobek et al., "Integrated Public Use Microdata Series: Version 2.0" [Computer File] (Minneapolis: Historical Census Projects, University of Minnesota, 1997).

younger than five per one thousand women ages fifteen to forty-nine, a standard indicator of fertility, substantially exceeded the national average during the first half of the twentieth century. Consequently, the rural population of the South grew steadily, rising from 17.8 to 22.7 million during the period from 1900 to 1940. Only after the massive rural out-migration of the World War II decade did the region's rural population level off and begin a slow decline, falling to 22.5 million by 1950.[17]

Observers in the 1930s and 1940s blamed much of the poverty that beset the rural South on the region's swelling rural population. Rupert Vance wrote on the eve of World War II that "population increase in rural low-income areas has meant a general lack of opportunity," a situation made much worse in the depression decade when migration to urban areas slowed. Howard Odum put it more bluntly, stating that the region's population "is undoubtedly too large." Sociologist Gunnar Myrdal echoed Vance and Odum by pointing to "overpopulation and soil erosion" as chief causes of rural poverty.[18] Pre–World War II south-

17. Donald B. Dodd and Wynelle S. Dodd, *Historical Statistics of the South, 1790–1970* (Tuscaloosa: University of Alabama Press, 1973).

18. Rupert B. Vance, *Rural Relief and Recovery,* Works Progress Administration, Social Problems No. 3. (Washington, D.C.: Government Printing Office, 1939), 9–

Table 2. Total Farmland per Rural Population in the South, 1900–1950

1900	18.1 acres
1910	15.7 acres
1920	14.7 acres
1930	13.8 acres
1940	14.2 acres
1950	15.3 acres

Source: Donald B. Dodd and Wynelle S. Dodd, *Historical Statistics of the South, 1790–1970* (Tuscaloosa: University of Alabama Press, 1973).

erners did seek to squeeze into an increasingly crowded agricultural sector. One indicator of this population pressure on southern agricultural resources is the declining ratio of farmland to the region's rural population, which declined steadily from 18.1 acres per rural dweller in 1900 to only 13.8 acres per rural dweller in 1930, nearly a one-quarter decline, as indicated in Table 2.

More recently, the economic historian Gavin Wright has developed a sophisticated formulation of the effect of high rural population densities on southern agriculture. Wright argues that the South, from emancipation through the Great Depression, was characterized by a "regional labor market" in which southern workers and their low wages were isolated from broader national pressures. The northward migration of the 1910s and 1920s did little to integrate southern labor

10; Howard W. Odum, *Southern Regions of the United States* (Chapel Hill: University of North Carolina Press, 1936), 461, 462; Gunnar Myrdal, *An American Dilemma: The Negro Problem and Modern Democracy*, 231. The overpopulation case is made more thoroughly in Rupert B. Vance and Nadia Danilevsky, *All These People: The Nation's Human Resources in the South* (Chapel Hill: University of North Carolina Press, 1945). See also Clarence H. Danhof, "Four Decades of Thought on the South's Economic Problems," in Melvin L. Greenhut and W. Tate Whitman, eds., *Essays in Southern Economic Development* (Chapel Hill: University of North Carolina Press, 1964), 15–21.

markets with the rest of the nation, and southern wages actually declined compared to the national average in the 1920s and 1930s. Only the mobilization for World War II began the process of breaking open the South's regionally isolated, low-wage labor market.[19]

Wright's argument is useful for understanding the overall contours of rural out-migration and its relationship to southern urbanization. The constant circulation of sharecroppers and tenants from farm to farm is symptomatic of an isolated, regional labor market. Identifying the demise of the regional labor market in the wartime mobilization of the 1940s helps explain the timing of truly massive black and white migration from the countryside. It also draws attention to the factors that pulled southerners out of the countryside. While sustained rural out-migration had proceeded since the First World War, it was the World War II–generated boost in southern urbanization along with the end of depression conditions in northern and western cities that provided enough "pull" to begin alleviating the region's high rural population densities. In other words, the attraction of jobs in the North was not sufficient enough to affect the overall size of the southern rural population. Urban development within the region also was necessary before there would be significant declines in the southern rural population.

Long the most rural region in the country, the South began to urbanize at substantial rates after 1880. Yet, as Table 3 shows, in 1900 only 15.5 percent of the region's population resided in cities and towns of twenty-five hundred or more inhabitants. By 1950, 42.9 percent of all southerners lived in cities and towns, and the total urban population reached nearly seventeen million. The portion of southerners living in large cities—metropolitan places of fifty thousand or more residents—was, however, much lower, rising to just 28.2 percent of the population.[20]

19. Wright, *Old South, New South*, 7–8, 200–207, 238.
20. Don H. Doyle, *New Men, New Cities, New South: Atlanta, Nashville, Charleston, Mobile, 1860–1910* (Chapel Hill: University of North Carolina Press, 1990), 3–7, 76–79. The definition of a metropolitan area used here is the same as the 1950 census definition of a "Standard Metropolitan Area," which is "a county or group of contiguous counties which contained at least one city of 50,000+ residents. To be part of an SMA, a county either had to contain the 50,000+ city, or had to be

Table 3. **Urban and Metropolitan Population, 1900–1950**

Census Year	Urban Total (1,000s)	Pct.	Metropolitan Total (1,000s)	Pct.	Whites (1,000s)	Pct.	Blacks (1,000s)	Pct.
1900	3,281	15.5	1,495	7.1	976	7.2	518	6.9
1910	4,989	20.2	2,628	10.6	1,820	11.1	807	9.8
1920	6,965	25.3	4,170	15.1	3,044	15.9	1,127	13.5
1930	10,006	31.9	—	—	—	—	—	—
1940	11,994	34.6	7,083	21.8	5,394	22.4	1,689	19.9
1950	16,949	42.9	10,243	28.2	8,068	29.1	2,175	25.4

"Urban" indicates population residing in places of 2,500 or more. "Metropolitan" indicates population residing in cities of 50,000 or more, or in counties contiguous to such cities and which were metropolitan in character.

There is no data for the 1930 metropolitan status.

Source: "Urban" figures, Donald B. Dodd and Wynelle S. Dodd, *Historical Statistics of the South, 1790–1970* (Tuscaloosa: University of Alabama Press, 1973); "Metropolitan" figures, Steven Ruggles and Matthew Sobek et al., "Integrated Public Use Microdata Series: Version 2.0" [Computer File] (Minneapolis: Historical Census Projects, University of Minnesota, 1997).

Data from the second half of the Great Depression show the differing propensities of black and white farmers to migrate (Table 4). Among all working-age blacks and whites residing on farms, blacks were more likely than whites to have moved during the period from 1935 to 1940. However, whites were more likely to have moved across county and state lines. Blacks who remained in the South were more likely to have moved within their county, replicating the localized, circular migration patterns of sharecropping. Those blacks who left the region are not reflected in these statistics. Overall, blacks were more likely to leave the South altogether.

Southern cities exerted a much stronger pull on whites than blacks during the World War II decade, even as blacks were more likely to

metropolitan in character and integrated with a central city." See Steven Ruggles et al., "Metarea" in "Data Dictionary," Integrated Public Use Microdata Series: Version 2.0 [Computer File] (Minneapolis: Historical Census Projects, University of Minnesota, 1997).

Table 4. **Migration Status of Farm-Dwelling Southerners,**
Ages 15–65

Migration Status, 1935–1940	Blacks	Whites
Same House	34.9%	43.2%
Same State and County, Different House	54.1	43.6
Same State, Different County	5.1	6.4
Contiguous Different State	1.3	1.8
Noncontiguous State	0.2	0.7
Abroad	0.7	0.8
Not Reported/Missing	3.7	3.5
Total	100	100

Source: Steven Ruggles and Matthew Sobek et al., "Integrated Public Use Microdata Series: Version 2.0" [Computer File] (Minneapolis: Historical Census Projects, University of Minnesota, 1997).

leave the rural South and the region as a whole. In the 1940s, the southern black metropolitan population grew by only 29 percent, while the white urban population swelled by 50 percent. Forward survival ratio estimates of net migration to the metropolitan South (Figure 1) show that during the 1940s, the rate of white migration to larger southern cities stood at nearly twice that of blacks.[21] Yet black migration from the nonmetropolitan South stood at a rate more than twice that of whites. Clearly, the attraction of jobs in the urban North and West pulled much harder on southern blacks than southern whites.

The emphasis on urbanization pulling southerners out of the countryside helps place in context the demographic effects of the depression-

21. The forward survival rate method calculates an expected population for age cohorts over the course of a census decade based on national survival ratios and subtracts it from the actual population enumerated at the end of the decade. The method is more fully discussed in Donald J. Bogue et al., *Techniques of Estimating Net Migration* (Chicago: Community and Family Study Center, University of Chicago, 1982), 15–30; Everette S. Lee et al., *Population Redistribution and Economic Growth, United States, 1870–1950*, vol. 1, *Methodological Considerations and Reference Tables* (Philadelphia: American Philosophical Society, 1957), 15–34.

Figure 1. **Estimated Net Migration Rates to the Metropolitan and Non-Metropolitan South, 1940–1950**

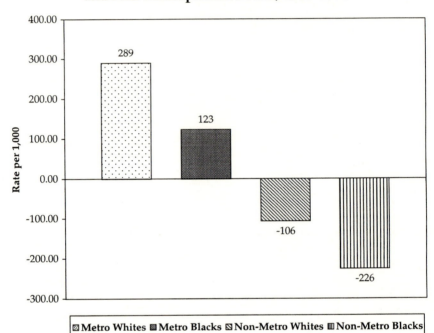

Source: Steven Ruggles and Matthew Sobek et al., "Integrated Public Use Microdata Series: Version 2.0" [Computer File] (Minneapolis: Historical Census Projects, University of Minnesota, 1997).

era crop-reduction and subsidy programs of the Agricultural Adjustment Administration (AAA). Landlords rarely shared crop-reduction subsidies with tenants and sharecroppers. Planters instead began increasingly to rely on wage hands and to use their subsidy checks to finance investments in farm machinery, even before the arrival of a reliable cotton harvesting machine in the late 1940s. Sharecroppers understood this process. In 1939, a black Alabama tenant complained: "I don't believe there's going to be any tenant farmers any more. . . . The landlords will just hire help and you can work it or let it alone which means that most of them will work at any price to keep from starving." In 1940, another black Alabama tenant reported that the AAA "just

Table 5. **Occupations for Farm-Dwelling Black Male Heads of Households, U.S. South, 1910–1920; 1940–1950**

Occupation	1910	1920	1940	1950
Professional and Technical	0.2%	0.3%	0.2%	0.3%
Farmers and Farm Managers	94.2	86.2	67.8	71.5
Managers, Officials, and Proprietors	0.1	0.1	0.1	0.2
Clerical and Kindred	0.0	0.0	0.1	0.2
Craftsmen	0.2	0.4	0.7	0.9
Operatives	0.2	0.4	1.4	3.5
Service Workers	0.0	0.2	0.6	0.6
Farm and General Laborers	4.9	12.0	25.0	16.6
Other/Blank etc.	0.2	0.6	4.2	6.2
Total	100.0	100.0	100.0	100.0
Black Male Heads of Household Dwelling on Farms	46.7	52.5	41.8	27.1

Source: Steven Ruggles and Matthew Sobek et al., "Integrated Public Use Microdata Series: Version 2.0" [Computer File] (Minneapolis: Historical Census Projects, University of Minnesota, 1997).

plowed up my best cotton and ruined it . . . [and] I ain't got nothing for it yet."[22]

These sharecropper's complaints are supported by the occupation data for black, farm-dwelling male heads of households in Table 5. In 1900, nearly all farm-dwelling black men worked as farmers, the vast majority under some form of tenancy arrangement. Farm laborers were rare; only 2.3 percent worked as farm or general laborers. By 1940, however, nearly one-quarter of farm-dwelling male household heads were working as laborers, and only about two-thirds described them-

22. Jack Temple Kirby, *Rural Worlds Lost: The American South, 1920–1960* (Baton Rouge: Louisiana State University Press, 1987), 51–79. Mary Hines and Family Narrative, f. 2 AL-2, p. 10, Federal Writers Project Papers, Southern Historical Collection, University of North Carolina, Chapel Hill; U.S. House of Representatives, *Interstate Migration*, 443.

selves as farmers. The shift to wage work on southern farms was well underway for rural blacks, and these rural wage workers can be considered potential migrants, cut loose from the sharecropping system, but not yet urban dwellers.

By 1950, even as mechanization investments by southern landowners intensified, the portion of farm-dwelling blacks working as laborers declined sharply. What lay behind this sharp drop in the portion of southern black male heads of households living on farms? This figure fell from a high of 52.5 percent in 1920 to only 27.1 percent in 1950, with the greatest drop occurring the 1940s (Table 5). Consequently, the ratio of farmland to population increased sharply (Table 2) as heavy rural out-migration, for the first time, began to reduce the size of the southern rural population. By 1950, migration to cities within and beyond the South had broken the isolating barriers that had kept millions of rural southerners, black and white, on an endless agricultural treadmill.

Thus, the region's migration patterns in the first half of the twentieth century were complex as black and white southerners strove to better their condition through moving. Rural southerners seemed to be in constant motion, changing farms often, sometimes from year to year. Their opportunities were shaped by interaction of changes in the rural economy and the availability of work in cities within and beyond the region. Only when mobilization during World War II opened up jobs for black and white southerners in northern cities and spurred heavy increases in urbanization within the South did migration have a significant impact upon the size of the southern rural population.

The author gratefully acknowledges the support of the National Institute of Child Health and Human Development training grant and the Carolina Population Center, University of North Carolina at Chapel Hill in the completion of this essay.

"A Crude and Raw Past"

Work, Folklife, and Anti-Agrarianism in Twentieth-Century African American Autobiography

TED OWNBY

Could African American autobiographers in the early twentieth century be agrarians? If so, what kind of agrarianism did they build into their understanding of themselves and other African Americans? Did Richard Wright speak for other African American autobiographers when he said years of sharecropping had stripped his father of his basic humanity?

Beginning in the 1700s and increasing in the antebellum period, African American writers used autobiographies to put individual faces on broad social problems, to reject stereotypes of many kinds, and to serve as political documents. By the early twentieth century, writing one's life story was firmly established as a vital genre among African American writers. Yet, how did writers in that autobiographical tradition interpret, neglect, or reject the idea, so common among African Americans in the late 1800s and early 1900s, that they had a right to land in the South? After emancipation, expecting to own land and claiming rights to it combined to form one of the great narratives of African American life. In political discussions during and after Reconstruction, freedpeople consistently said they deserved southern land because their labor had made it valuable. Adding to that agrarian promise were religious notions that God's chosen people would reach the Promised Land some day, perhaps after considerable suffering.[1]

1. Among the works on African American autobiography that have influenced this paper are Henry Lewis Gates, "Introduction," in Gates, ed., *Bearing Witness: Selections from African-American Autobiography in the Twentieth Century*, 1–9; William L. Andrews, *To Tell a Free Story: The First Century of Afro-American Autobiography*; William L. Andrews, ed., *African-American Autobiography: A Collection of Criti-*

How did African American writers in the early twentieth century—the time when chances for owning land were declining—describe their own relationship to farm life, the land, and the rural community? In the past few years, literary scholars have urged us not to see agrarianism at the center of southern writing, and of course they are right in stressing that the Vanderbilt Agrarians claimed too much credit for themselves for defining the content and questions of southern culture.[2] It is easy

---

cal Essays; James Olney, ed., *Autobiography: Essays Theoretical and Critical* (Princeton, N.J.: Princeton University Press, 1980); Sidonie Smith, *Where I'm Bound* (Westport, Conn.: Greenwood Press, 1974); David L. Dudley, *My Father's Shadow: Intergenerational Conflict in African American Men's Autobiography;* Joanne M. Braxton, *Black Women Writing Autobiography: A Tradition within a Tradition;* V. P. Franklin, *Living Our Stories, Telling Our Truths: Autobiography and the Making of the African-American Intellectual Tradition;* David G. Nicholls, *Conjuring the Folk: Forms of Modernity in African America* (Ann Arbor: University of Michigan Press, 2000); Deborah E. McDowell and Arnold Rampersad, ed., *Slavery and the Literary Imagination, Selected Papers from the English Institute, 1987* (Baltimore: Johns Hopkins University Press, 1989); Arlyn Diamond, "Choosing Sides, Choosing Lives: Women's Autobiographies of the Civil Rights Movement," in Margo Culley, ed., *American Women's Autobiography: Fea(s)ts of Memory* (Madison: University of Wisconsin Press, 1992), 218–31; James Olney, "Autobiographical Traditions Black and White."

The key work on Reconstruction and freedpeople's ideas about land continues to be Eric Foner, *Reconstruction: America's Unfinished Revolution, 1863–1877* (New York: Harper and Row, 1988). On theories of rights to land, see also Julie Saville, *The Work of Reconstruction: From Slave to Wage Labor in South Carolina, 1860–1870* (New York: Cambridge University Press, 1994); Gerald David Jaynes, *Roots without Branches: Genesis of the Black Working Class in the American South, 1862–1882* (New York: Oxford University Press, 1986). On the idea of the Chosen People, see Lawrence W. Levine, *Black Culture and Black Consciousness: Afro-American Folk Thought from Slavery to Freedom;* William H. Wiggins, *O Freedom! Afro-American Emancipation Celebrations* (Knoxville: University of Tennessee Press, 1987); Eddie S. Glaude, Jr., *Exodus! Religion, Race, and Nation in Early Nineteenth-Century Black America* (Chicago: University of Chicago Press, 2000).

2. Patricia Yaeger, *Dirt and Desire: Reconstructing Southern Women's Writing;* Michael Kreyling, *Inventing Southern Literature* (Jackson: University Press of Mississippi, 1998); Richard Gray, *Southern Aberrations: Writers of the American South and the Problem of Regionalism* (Baton Rouge: Louisiana State University Press, 2000). Gray tended to stress issues of the garden myth, pastoralism, and agrarianism in *Writing the South: Ideas of an American Region, with a New Afterword.*

to see that African Americans would reject white southerners' ideas of agrarianism. The notions of ease, place, hierarchy, independence, and family security so essential to white agrarian writers in the South were much more problematic for African Americans, whose work in the soil offered little ease, independence, or security. The tradition of African American autobiography had long said that farming somebody else's land was a trap, and ideas of folklife could be a more subtle trap if they helped confirm impressions that black southerners were basically happy out singing in the fields. African American writers had known at least since Frederick Douglass wrote in 1845 that ideas about folklife could be dangerous. Douglass, realizing that many people admired the music of African Americans, corrected whites' ideas that slaves sang in the fields because they were happy. Instead, Douglass insisted that slaves sang most when they were most unhappy, and the depth of their music showed the depth of their pain. In that tradition, African American autobiographers over the next several generations depicted themselves as individuals struggling against oppression and its psychological and personal effects by escaping from the place and condition of that oppression.[3]

Instead of simply saying what African American writers did *not* say, it is more important to ask what features of rural life and farm life Booker T. Washington, W. E. B. Du Bois, Richard Wright, and Zora Neale Hurston chose to incorporate into the stories of their lives. Each of the four writers had something positive to say about farm life, or at least rural life, but none portrayed agriculture as offering an ideal life. For Washington, farm life offered lessons people should use for doing other, better things. For Du Bois, the urban northerner who moved to the South and stayed for a good part of his young adult years, farm life was potentially idyllic, but tenancy deprived it of that potential. For Wright, farm life was primarily a hook with devastating consequences, but he admired the communal ways farming people found to survive. Hurston, more than the others, described a happy childhood in a farm

3. Frederick Douglass, *Narrative of the Life of Frederick Douglass, An American Slave*, edited by David W. Blight (Boston: Bedford / St. Martin's, 1993), 47. See also especially Andrews, *To Tell a Free Story*, Robert B. Stepto, *From Behind the Veil: A Story of Afro-America Narrative* (Urbana: University of Illinois Press, 1979), and Dudley, *My Father's Shadow.*

setting, but she did little to connect farm life to the rest of her work. All of them saw tenancy as the serpent in the garden, but none saw that garden as a potential Eden.

Intriguingly, all four also addressed the nature of rural life through some sort of social science. Booker T. Washington and W. E. B. Du Bois were amateur ethnographers, describing the lives of African Americans in the rural South as part of ways of life that differed from the lives the authors had known. Du Bois was also a professional historian and sociologist. In dramatically different works—autobiography and social science documentation—Richard Wright offered contrasting portraits of the experience of rural poor people. Zora Neale Hurston also wrote both autobiography and social science, but her main passion in describing the lives of rural black southerners was through documentary fieldwork. For all four, that double sense of being insiders, sharing essential characteristics with African Americans who worked on farms while also being professional outsiders who were observing rural people, gave their work a twist that was in part emotional, in part analytical.

The great majority of *Up from Slavery* was a call for individual uplift, with Booker T. Washington offering his own life as an example and guide. In his concern for cleanliness, personal propriety, standard English grammar, and enterprise, he urged black readers to give up the ways of life that confirmed and perpetuated their poverty. Thus, he might seem to have had little positive to say about poor farming people.

When Washington first moved to Alabama in 1881 to develop Tuskegee Institute, he went out into the rural areas, in many ways as an activist anthropologist. Though born a slave and raised among farming people, Washington portrayed himself as a stranger when he visited black farm workers near Tuskegee. His language sounds much like the curious words of countless sophisticated outsiders going out among unsophisticated folks with unusual ways. "The most of my traveling was done over the country roads, with a mule and a cart or a mule and a buggy wagon for conveyance. I ate and slept with the people, in their little cabins. I saw their farms, their schools, their churches. Since, in the case of the most of these visits, there had been no notice given in advance that a stranger was expected, I had the advantage of seeing the real, everyday life of the people."[4]

That real, everyday life troubled him. Most families slept in one room, often with unrelated members of the household. Privacy was difficult and often impossible to achieve. Perhaps most troubling, farming people were dirty, and Washington always professed a gospel of cleanliness.

Their diet was fat pork, corn bread, and what he used quotation marks to call "black-eye peas." Using the language of countless travelers who shook their heads over the shortcomings of the locals, he wrote, "The people seemed to have no other idea than to live on this fat meat and corn bread." They fried most of their food in a skillet over a small fire, and eating was performed in the simplest ways, with few or no forks and spoons. For breakfast, "the husband would take his bread and meat in his hand and start for the field, eating as he walked." Women ate directly from the pan. Children ate with their hands.[5]

Washington was troubled to see such large families among black farmers in Alabama. While others might consider such families economically necessary and warmly human, Washington saw them as expensive causes of trouble. Children spent most of their time, like black southerners of all ages, working in the cotton fields. And when food was scarce, according to Washington, the smaller children got the least.

Finally, Washington had little respect for the language of country people. When he quoted vernacular speech, he generally did so to display people's lack of education and their resulting ignorance. The first time we hear someone speak in *Up from Slavery*, a black political figure is trying to teach Washington how to succeed in Alabama. "We wants you to be sure to vote jes' like we votes. We can't read de newspapers very much, but we knows how to vote, an' we wants you to vote jes' like we votes."[6] The man continued that he and other African Americans knew how to vote by watching whites vote and then doing the op-

---

4. Booker T. Washington, *Up from Slavery* (New York: Dell, 1965), 85–86. On the significance of this trip to Washington, see Louis R. Harlan, *Booker T. Washington: The Making of a Black Leader* (New York: Oxford University Press, 1972), 119–21.

5. Washington, *Up from Slavery*, 86.

6. Ibid., 85.

posite. Washington suggested three forms of ignorance here, and each of the three reinforced the others. The most obvious was when the man said he and other African Americans could not read. The second was what seemed to Washington the obvious ignorance of simply voting opposite of how whites vote. One of his frequent suggestions was that blacks and whites should not identify their interests as being naturally in opposition. And the third was the use of vernacular speech—the disagreement of subjects and verbs, the mispronunciation of "just," "the," "exactly," and "then." For Washington, this was not the colorful speech of rural people, or a language specific to Americans with African ancestry; it was ignorance of doing things in ways that would lead out of poverty.

Washington did not call these people "the folk," nor did he treat them as ignorant peasants who had been living the same way for generations. Instead, he stressed that they were victims of an oppressive system that offered few alternatives, benefited when they went into debt for sewing machines, organs, or clocks, and did nothing to educate them for anything but agricultural labor. Washington's primary lesson was *not* that rural people were ignorant of how to succeed in a cash-based economy. His lesson was that they were victims of creditors' control and their own ignorance of alternatives. These "traditions" of fried food, large families, dirt, crowding, and vernacular speech were, for Washington, rooted not in slavery, nor certainly in the nature of rural life. Instead, they were rooted in an unfair social system that would take a particular form of education to overcome.

Like most agricultural reformers of his day, Washington called for farm people to grow their own food. He complained that "their one object seemed to be to plant nothing but cotton," and that they spent their scarce money on food they could (and, he thought, should) have been growing. He worried about this emphasis not on moral grounds that people were naturally better off for the independence gained from feeding themselves, but on the economic grounds that economic forces controlled them more thoroughly when they had to deal with landowners and merchants for their survival. In his second autobiography, *Working with the Hands,* Washington emphasized that he did not wish to encourage or romanticize the life of a simple yeoman. "I have little respect," he stressed, "for the farmer who is satisfied with merely 'making a living.'" Instead, he envisioned a money-making agriculture in which farm families could enjoy "a comfortable dwelling-house, and in it bath-tubs, carpets, rugs, pictures, books, magazines, a daily paper, and a telephone."[7]

Far more clearly than Du Bois, Wright, or Hurston, Washington was an agrarian. Much of his language sounded like the agrarianism of many generations of American elites who paid tribute to farming as the foundation of everything good in the world, especially the foundation of all economic value and personal worth. In criticizing the "superficiality" of African Americans who moved to Washington, D.C., hoping to gain fame, respect, and wealth through politics and political connections, he said he wished farm work could reform their characters. He believed far too many people sought help from the federal government, "very much as a child looks to its mother."[8] Growing up meant rejecting anyone's assistance. "The members of this class had little ambition to create a position for themselves, but wanted the Federal officials to create one for them." This has the ring of fears from the American Revolutionary generation about self-indulgent people who used special privileges to benefit from other people's work. Washington continued, "How many times I wished then, and have often wished since, that by some power of magic I might remove the great bulk of these people into the country districts and plant them upon the soil, upon the solid and never deceptive foundation of Mother Nature, where all nations and races that have ever succeeded have gotten their start,—a start that at first may be slow and toilsome, but one that nevertheless is real."[9] In this Jeffersonian passage, Washington avoided the type of agrarianism common among many postbellum African Americans, who argued that former slaves deserved land that their and their parents' labor had made valuable. Instead, Washington scoffed at people who looked to the federal government for assistance and, as an antidote to ambitions based on special favors, urged people to work hard whether on farms or anywhere else.

7. Booker T. Washington, *Working with the Hands, Being a Sequel to "Up from Slavery" Covering the Author's Experiences in Industrial Training* (New York: Doubleday, Page and Company, 1904), 32. On his rejection of single-crop agriculture on economic grounds, see Washington, *Up from Slavery*, 86; *Working with the Hands*, 49.

8. Washington, *Up from Slavery*, 67.

9. Ibid., 71.

The fascinating thing is that while Washington wanted to teach lessons that would allow poor rural people to lift themselves from poverty, he believed all black southerners needed to know how to work on a farm. He idealized the skills of subsistence farming and urged people to use them to escape poverty. In his agrarian ideal, people seeking economic improvement needed, above all, the work ethic to take care of themselves through their own labor, with no help from anyone. Farm life in itself was not particularly good—or bad—but it helped teach people lessons about uplift.

Washington thought students at Tuskegee Institute needed to relive many of the experiences of the poorest rural people starting farms and homes. It was important for them to have experienced the most grinding forms of labor in order to move on to something else. This was a crucial point for Washington, as he struggled to convince Tuskegee students that manual labor taught them the discipline necessary to develop their own abilities. He even thought it was good training for students to live in crowded, unfinished housing—cleaner versions of the cramped farm people's housing he found so deplorable in his first trip to Alabama. In the early days at Tuskegee, "the cooking was done out-of-doors, in the old-fashioned, primitive style" and most people had to eat with few or no dishes.[10] This was exactly what he found troubling among poor farm folk in rural Alabama, but here it offered students important moral lessons.

Booker T. Washington seems to have adopted the Promised Land idea that people are better off for suffering and surviving. But he saw the Promise not as a collective blessing of land for the Chosen People. Instead, suffering and surviving in the rural South taught individual skills necessary for overcoming poverty. Learning that about 85 percent of people in the Deep South made their living from farms, Washington feared any form of education that encouraged people to think they were too sophisticated to work with their hands. Washington told a story he had heard to illustrate what he feared about the ambitions of too many of the Tuskegee students. A black man working in the cotton fields on a hot Alabama day "suddenly stopped, and looking toward the skies, said: 'O Lawd, de cottom am so grassy, de work am so hard, and

10. Ibid., 117.

the sun am so hot dat I b'lieve dis darky am called to preach!'"[11] For Washington, education was a failure if people pursued it only in order to get out of the sun. He never held up farm life as being the ideal end for most people, but he was offended by people who considered it undignified, and he believed it taught skills people needed to overcome their poverty.

Perhaps the most complex relationship with rural folk, and especially the agricultural roots of rural life for African Americans, appears in the work of W. E. B. Du Bois. Like Washington, Du Bois wanted black southerners to overcome their status as poor and dependent workers, and he believed they had some essential virtues that could benefit the rest of American society. Du Bois, as a well-educated Massachusetts native, felt even more than Washington like an outsider among rural black southerners. Much of his fascination with the rural South came from a few summers he spent teaching schools in rural Tennessee and Georgia. Despite his concern about rural people's forced poverty, poor living conditions, and lack of education, he often wondered if maybe they had something he did not.

When Du Bois moved south in his late teens to attend Fisk University in 1885, neither he nor his parents had worked in the fields. He described rural life in two ways, once through the eyes of a social scientist and once through personal reminiscences about his youth. Of the four authors, Du Bois wrote the most about land, the attempts of black southerners to own it, and efforts by plantation owners and white politicians to keep them from doing so. Du Bois understood the importance of both land and government in the Promised Land story. His *Black Reconstruction*, published in 1935, was one of the first works of scholarship to place the issue of land ownership at the center of Reconstruction. He argued that freedpeople wanted land in part because of their experience as slaves of controlling gardens and livestock. More broadly, he emphasized that they believed land was a right. In postwar political discussions, "Again and again, crudely but logically, the Negroes expressed their right to the land and the deep importance of this right."[12]

11. Ibid., 96.
12. W. E. B. Du Bois, *Black Reconstruction in America: An Essay toward a History of the Part which Black Folk Played in the Attempt to Reconstruct Democracy, 1860–1880* (1935; reprt., New York: Russell and Russell, 1962), 123, 369.

When Du Bois wrote as a sociologist or historian, he described African Americans on southern farms from the tradition of northern abolitionists who traveled the South to argue that racial privilege damaged everyone. Rural Georgia was "the Land of the Unfenced, where crouch on either hand scores of ugly one-room cabins, cheerless and dirty. Here lies the Negro problem in its naked dirt and penury." People lived in a slow and sluggish form of poverty. Du Bois continued in his neoabolitionist vein, describing Georgia as "a land of rapid contrasts and of curiously mingled hope and pain," where a past of slavery too often led to agricultural labor as a new form of enslavement. He interpreted a twenty-two-year-old as a "Poor lad!—a slave at twenty-two."[13]

That interpretation worked to reject ideas that African Americans were shiftless and that their basic natures made it difficult for them to work hard or to learn new skills. As an emerging radical in *The Souls of Black Folk* and a mature radical in *Black Reconstruction* and *Dusk of Dawn*, Du Bois consistently stressed that the causes of black southerners' poverty lay not in their character but in the laws, rules, and economic practices of white landowners. In this scholarly interpretation, African Americans in the rural South suffered from a long series of decisions and policies by people who tried to force them to work as cheap labor. As a scholar, the young Du Bois said that above all, black southerners were victims, and he discussed them with a little pity and a great deal of anger.

But Du Bois, very much like Washington, had mixed feelings when he went out into the field to meet real live black farmers. Just four years after Washington toured rural Alabama, a teenage Du Bois left Nashville to experience the rural South for himself. In *Dusk of Dawn*, he pictured himself as an idealistic innocent going out to meet and teach the poor and ignorant outside of Alexandria, Tennessee. "I determined to know something of the Negro in the country districts. . . . I had heard about the country in the South as the real seat of slavery. I wanted to know it."[14]

---

13. W. E. B. Du Bois, *The Souls of Black Folk* (1903; reprt., New York: The New American Library, 1969), 149, 155.

14. W. E. B. Du Bois, *Dusk of Dawn: An Essay toward an Autobiography of a Race Concept* (New York: Harcourt Brace and Co., 1940), 31.

Du Bois wrote little about his time in rural Tennessee—twelve pages in *The Souls of Black Folk* and just a few paragraphs in *Dusk of Dawn*— but it seems to have affected him in powerful ways. He was saddened but not surprised by the poverty. He described "the hard ugly, drudgery of country life and the writhing of landless, ignorant peasants" and said the experience dramatized "the race problem at nearly its lowest terms." As Manning Marable writes, it was in rural Tennessee where "The crucible of southern black life and labor was opened to DuBois." But Du Bois was struck even more powerfully by something strong and beautiful he found among rural African Americans. He quickly found that, more than pitying rural, uneducated, poor people, he respected and perhaps more importantly loved them. He loved the way they shared communal experiences, and he surely if silently lamented that he had not had such a community in his Massachusetts boyhood. He respected how they shared a "half-awakened common consciousness, sprung from common joy and grief, at burial, birth or wedding, from a common hardship." He wondered if they felt things more deeply than he did. "How hard a thing is life to the lowly, and yet how human and real!"[15]

Like countless educated city people who have gone into the country-side to document and teach the uneducated, Du Bois worried that he might be romanticizing the simple lives of rustic folk. But he pressed on to consider how his stay among poor African Americans in rural Tennessee affected him. First, it helped him question his assumptions about Progress. He had grown up assuming that all of America was on the same road toward a better future, based on more and ever-more application of science to social problems and economic opportunity. "Wealth was God. . . . [E]verywhere the poor planned to be rich and the rich planned to be richer; everywhere wider, bigger, higher, better things were set down as inevitable."[16] His months in rural Tennessee encouraged him to doubt that assumption and to consider other perspectives.

15. Ibid., 31; Manning Marable, *W. E. B. Du Bois: Black Radical Democrat* (Boston: Twayne Publishers, 1986), 10. For a full discussion, see David Levering Lewis, *W. E. B. Du Bois: Biography of a Race, 1868–1919* (New York: Henry Holt, 1993). Du Bois, *Souls of Black Folk*, 103, 108.

16. Du Bois, *Dusk of Dawn*, 26–27.

Du Bois saw and felt the poverty of rural African Americans, but "on the other hand, I heard the sorrow songs sung with primitive beauty and grandeur." He had heard such songs before. They touched him on the rare occasions he heard African American religious music in Massachusetts, and he was there to hear the Fisk Jubilee singers in Nashville. But it was in rural Tennessee where Du Bois first heard the songs in what he called their "primitive" state. He said that in "this little world," most things were "dull and humdrum," except for Sundays, when "the soft melody and mighty cadences of Negro song fluttered and thundered."[17]

Much of the achievement of *The Souls of Black Folk* lay in its combination of questions about conventional American ideas of progress with excitement over the emotional power of African American religious music. Through his time in rural Tennessee, Du Bois gained a connection to the experience of centuries of deep emotions he had not previously encountered. As he described it in his autobiographical writing, his generalizations about the nature of poverty and oppression turned into something more powerful when he got to know poor rural people and heard their music. Social science only took him so far; the emotionally powerful part that went beyond understanding came from listening. He restated Frederick Douglass's rejection of the notion that African Americans sing to show they are happy. Instead, the significantly named "Sorrow Songs" were "the music of an unhappy people, of the children of disappointment." Du Bois concluded his discussion of the Sorrow Songs with an impassioned hope that the Songs breathed "a faith in the ultimate justice of things. The minor cadences of despair change often to triumph and calm confidence. Sometimes it is faith in life, sometimes a faith in death, sometimes assurance of boundless justice in some fair world beyond. But which ever it is, the meaning is always clear: that sometime, somewhere, men will judge men by their souls and not by their skins."[18]

Some scholars of Du Bois have been so interested with his connec-

---

17. Ibid., 31; Du Bois, *Souls of Black Folk*, 102.

18. Du Bois, *Souls of Black Folk*, 267, 274. On the ultimately optimistic nature of *Souls of Black Folk*, see David W. Blight, "W. E. B. Du Bois and the Struggle for American Historical Memory," 49–50.

tion to African culture that they have not studied where he located that connection. It was, in substantial part, in rural Tennessee, outside Alexandria. That was where he first got to know the people whose lives and songs gave him the basis for his conclusions about the ways Sorrow Songs might help transform American life. In the concluding chapter of *The Souls of Black Folk,* Du Bois twice used the same term—"primitive"—that he used to describe the rural people he first met on his trips into the Tennessee countryside.[19] By pairing his respect for poor rural people with the message and experience of the Sorrow Songs, Du Bois seems to have developed his own version of a Chosen People myth that said people who had been down so long had the emotional depth and collective strength to hold out hope for something better. This respect for rural people was not a form of agrarianism. It derived nothing special from owning land or working in soil. But it did suggest that rural people who lived away from centers of learning and sophistication held the deepest potential to change the world.

It is clear that Du Bois shared with Washington a sense that rural life mattered a great deal to African Americans, and to their past and their future. Neither held up simple agrarian ideals of landowning independence or the rural community as something all African Americans should pursue. Writing at the turn of the century, when so many black southerners kept alive the notion of the Promised Land and relatively few had yet started leaving the South, both believed rural life had particular strengths they hoped African Americans would use. For Washington, that strength lay in the lessons farming people could teach about individual self-reliance through difficulty. For Du Bois, it lay in a communal form of beauty that dramatized the promise of a better life. Both, significantly, feared the consequences of losing contact with those strengths.

Two generations later, African American autobiographers were not so sure that rural life had much relevance. The great southern-born autobiographers of the 1940s, Richard Wright and Zora Neale Hurston, had few positive things to say about farm life. Richard Wright's anti-agrarian perspective is well known. As a migration writer, a blues

19. Du Bois, *Souls of Black Folk,* 268, 271.

writer, a writer of personal empowerment and a rejecter of tradition, Wright hated what farm life did to poor people. His angry portrait of the damage farm labor and poverty had done to his father is one of the great anti-pastoral passages in literature. His father left for a distant city when Richard and his brother were young, and Wright did not see him again for twenty-five years. At that meeting, Wright's father was "standing alone upon the red clay of a Mississippi plantation, a sharecropper, clad in ragged overalls, holding a muddy hoe in his gnarled, veined hands." In a passage countless scholars have quoted and analyzed, Wright described his father as "a creature of the earth (who) endured, hearty, whole, seemingly indestructible, with no regrets and no hope." Enduring whole and indestructible and without regrets might seem positive characteristics of people in a rural folk culture. Such language might even fit the white stereotype of blacks as hearty folks who lived for the present, particularly when Wright continued that his father "asked easy, drawling questions" and "laughed, amused" at the answers.[20]

Wright stressed the destructive sides of what poverty and farm life had done to his father's personality. "I stood before him, poised, my mind aching as it embraced the simple nakedness of his life, feeling how completely his soul was imprisoned by the slow flow of the seasons, by wind and rain and sun, how fastened were his memories to a crude and raw past, how chained were his actions and emotions to the direct, animalistic impulses of his withering body." This was not just the physical deprivation of hunger and hard work and back-bending labor. The life of a sharecropper had trapped his father in a system that denied him access to what Wright saw as the most essential elements of humanity—the freedom to imagine and question. Wright's own passions for reading, thinking, and questioning seemed to him impossible for his father. Thus to Wright, a dehumanizing system had done its job.[21]

20. Richard Wright, *Black Boy,* restored text established by the Library of America (New York: Harper Perennial, 1993 [orig. pub., 1945]), 40–41.

21. Ibid., 40. Among the many scholars to concentrate on this passage are George E. Kent, *Blackness and the Adventure of Western Culture* (Chicago: Third World Press, 1972); Blyden Jackson, "Richard Wright: Black Boy from America's Black Belt and Urban Ghetto," in Robert J. Butler, ed., *The Critical Response to Richard Wright* (Westport, Conn.: Greenwood Press, 1995).

That description of his father is so powerful and decisive that it might seem Wright's final word on the subject. People who worked away their lives in powerless positions on other people's farms were barely human, and we should all be incensed at the system and the damage it caused. Yet even in *Black Boy,* Wright wrote occasionally, just a little, in the pastoral tradition. Early in the book, shortly after he announced its themes of danger and alienation, he listed beautiful, pastoral memories of his early experiences. He recalled "the delight" of "seeing long straight rows of red and green vegetables," "the faint, cool kiss of sensuality when dew came on to my cheeks and shins" as he ran down garden paths, "the vague sense of the infinite" as he watched the Mississippi River, "the echoes of nostalgia" as he listened to the sounds of geese. From this pastoral beginning, Wright moved dramatically to the other side of the natural world—death and destruction. "There was the experience of feeling death without dying that came from watching a chicken leap about blindly after its neck had been snapped by a quick twist of my father's wrist." He recalled thirst, hunger, panic, terror, and "the speechless astonishment of seeing a hog stabbed through the heart, dipped into boiling water, scraped, split open, gutted, and strung up gaping and bloody." Scores of southern writers have described hog killings as part of agrarian memories of community interdependence, with hog owners sharing meat in happy holidays of abundance. The pastoral possibilities he raised and denied, so early in the book, were part of the tragic quality—what Robert Stepto calls the "anti-pastoral strain" in *Black Boy*—that stressed that so many rural people went hungry. Maybe the world could be a garden, but not the world of his childhood.[22]

Readers of *Black Boy* may be surprised by the portrait of African American rural life Wright offered just four years earlier in *12 Million Black Voices*. That lyrical, poetic book combined his own word pictures

22. Wright, *Black Boy,* 8–9; Robert B. Stepto, "Literary and Ascent: *Black Boy,*" reprinted in Harold Bloom, ed., *Richard Wright: Modern Critical Voices* (New York: Chelsea House Publishers, 1987), 83. On hunger as the "central motif" in *Black Boy,* see Herbert Leibowitz, "'Arise, Ye Pris'ners of Starvation': Richard Wright's *Black Boy* and *American Hunger,*" in Henry Louis Gates, Jr., and K. A. Appiah, eds., *Richard Wright: Critical Perspectives Past and Present* (New York: Amistad, 1993), 331. On Wright's rejection of ideas of a Southern Eden, see Michel Fabre, *The World of Richard Wright* (Jackson: University Press of Mississippi, 1985), 79–80.

with 147 photographs, mostly by Farm Security Administration photographers, to create shared images of African Americans that praised them for their survival skills, their love of life and each other, and their understanding that things could change.

For much of *12 Million Black Voices,* Wright's portrayal of agriculture labor looked a great deal like the devastation he described in his father, and the hunger described in his own childhood. "Cotton is a drug, and for three hundred years we have taken it to kill the pain of hunger." In freedom as in slavery, too many African Americans worked hard for somebody else, with little incentive or hope. The whole thing was a prison; "our days are walled with cotton." He wrote repeatedly of the "Lords of the Land," emphasizing the limits they placed on African Americans' lives. Too often, he wrote, "when an impulse moves us, when we are caught in the throes of inspiration, when we are moved to better our lot, we do not ask ourselves: 'Can we do it?' but: 'Will they let us do it?'"[23]

But the collective picture celebrated farming people in ways Wright's individual picture in *Black Boy* did not. Despite the oppression and the challenges they faced, African Americans who lived on farms in the South had three great strengths. They had big, adaptable families with various shapes and compositions. Like Booker T. Washington, Wright knew that larger families created larger demand for expenses and a greater challenge to feed them all. But he loved them anyway, in part because more people meant more workers and hence greater hope for the deliverance of the whole family. More broadly, he loved the way the entire black community celebrated life with each new birth. "Some people wag their heads in amusement when they see our long lines of ragged children, but we love them. . . . Like black buttercups, our children spring up on the red soil of the plantations. When a new one arrives, neighbors from miles around come and look at it, speculating upon which parent it resembles. A child is a glad thing in the bleak stretches of the cotton country, and our gold is in the hearts of the people we love, in the veins that carry our blood."[24]

23. Richard Wright, *12 Million Black Voices* (1941; reprt., New York: Arno Press, 1969), 35, 49, 59.

24. Ibid., 59.

Secondly, Wright celebrated the willingness of black farming people to work together. As part of his rejection of the individualistic, consumer orientations of American capitalism, he was attracted to people's willingness to identify their needs with those of a large group. "Our way of life is simple and our unit of living is formed by the willingness of two or more of us to organize ourselves voluntarily to make a crop, to pool our labor power to wrest subsistence from the stubborn soil." Much like Washington, Wright sounded an agrarian tone that there was something fundamentally human about farming: "We live just as man lived when we first struggled against this earth."[25] But for Richard Wright, this understanding of farming offered no lessons to help individual men struggle out of poverty. Instead, it was a communal strength of people who had learned to survive through the necessity of working together.

Finally, Wright, who described his angry rejections of the religion his mother and grandmother offered him in *Black Boy,* offered an appealing description of religious worship in *12 Million Black Voices.* "What we have not dared feel in the presence of the Lords of the Land, we now feel in church. Our hearts and bodies, reciprocally acting upon each other, swing out into the meaning of the story the preacher is unfolding." The sweetness of the service, he said, allowed worshipers to feel "somewhere within our hearts a possibility of inexhaustible happiness" that "drains the gall out of our years." The power of worship and the lingering feelings hold antidotes to the frustration of farm life and the violence African Americans faced in the South. "When the soil grows poorer, we cling to this feeling; when clanking tractors uproot and hurl us from the land, we cling to it; when our eyes behold a black body swinging from a tree in the wind, we cling to it."[26]

The intriguing thing is that the same author who could paint a portrait of individual alienation from family and community in *Black Boy* also idealized group solidarity and survival in *12 Million Black Voices.* He rather scoffed at religion as escapism in his autobiography while holding it up for the strength it offered in his sociological study, and he rebelled against his family and received little help from his community in

25. Ibid., 60.
26. Ibid., 68, 73.

his autobiography but wrote poetically about families and communities in *12 Million Black Voices.* His dichotomy was the reverse of Du Bois, who tended to pity rural African Americans in his scholarship but saw great value in their culture in his autobiographical writing.

At the end of *12 Million Black Voices,* Wright ultimately rejected the folkways of big families and supportive face-to-face communities. Instead of survival strategies, he urged, African Americans needed to envision a new future based on sharing with all working people the fight against employers and exploiters. Wright ultimately believed that to change the world in a dramatic way, African Americans needed more than survival strategies. They needed more than extended, adaptable families to share the burdens of difficult lives, more than interdependent and supportive communities, and more than religious faith and powerful music. They needed, he urged, to question more of the assumptions they had developed about sticking together and helping each other out; survival strategies were fine ways to show people's strength and creativity, but those strategies got in the way of changing the world. Instead, African Americans needed to look beyond themselves and align with other oppressed working people. Only a new kind of rebellion would lead out of the forms of oppression that had trapped his father. For Wright, any kind of agrarian thinking would interfere with those radical possibilities.

Of the four writers, only Zora Neale Hurston included a scene of a southern Eden. As a small child, she and her parents and siblings lived among chinaberry trees and jasmine bushes, with a five-acre garden and a yard full of fruit trees. In her 1942 autobiography, *Dust Tracks on a Road,* Hurston recalled a beautiful, comfortable place, with an abundance that made life pretty easy. Fruit became preserves, and fish were easily available. "We had chicken on the table often; home cured meat, and all the eggs we wanted." Children gathered eggs, boiled them, and were then free to "lay around in the yard and eat them until we were full." Along with the fundamental agrarian ideas of ease and leisure came a childish innocence. "We had a big barn, and a stretch of ground well covered with Bermuda grass. So on moonlight nights, two-thirds of the village children from seven to eighteen would be playing hide and whoop, chick-mah-chick, hide and seek, and other boisterous games in our yard."[27] With plenty of food and an idyllic location, Hurston's mother wanted all of her children to stay around the house.

The startling thing is how irrelevant this agrarianism was to the rest of *Dust Tracks on a Road*. After they made earlier appearances in the autobiography, nature, abundance, and ease hardly appeared as things to enjoy, pursue, recall, or reject. A second definition of agrarianism appeared a bit more, one closer to Richard Wright's understanding in *12 Million Black Voices*. Farmers in the Eatonville area worked together, helping each other, and the resulting experience was both work and play. Hog killing time was celebratory work, with plenty of food at its completion. But that understanding also faded away as Hurston began her story of her own adventures as an anthropologist and traveler.

Zora Neale Hurston, whom scholars and readers often present as a contrast to Richard Wright, shared with Wright a powerful sense of nonconformity. According to their parents, both asked too many questions, and both always asked why, even if the question was uncomfortable. In her autobiography, Hurston recalled that as a girl, she felt certain the moon followed her—and only her—at night. She gained the strength to question things and dream from her mother, who urged her to "jump at de sun."[28] The twist for Hurston was that while her mother urged high hopes and her father urged her not to question things so often or so loudly, it was Hurston's father who left Zora the example of the lure of travel. Rare for someone who so loved her home and yard and family, Zora also loved to travel. But instead of seeing this as a rejection of her background—she was no lonely hero ready to reject her past and family—she believed she had inherited from her father the willingness to move. Her mother, noting that Zora always wanted to go experience new things from the time she could walk, feared that Zora was the victim of a folk hex. Perhaps, her mother worried, an enemy had sprinkled "travel dust" around the Hurston doorstep when Zora was born. But Zora believed she simply inherited the tendency to ramble from her father.[29]

27. Zora Neale Hurston, *Dust Tracks on a Road*, 18, 19, 20.
28. Ibid., 21.
29. Ibid., 32. Arguing that Hurston's individualism was part of African American folk culture is Deborah G. Plant, *Every Tub Must Sit on Its Own Bottom: The Philosophy and Politics of Zora Neale Hurston* (Urbana: University of Illinois Press, 1995).

What is intriguing is that Hurston kept up her fascination with idio-
syncrasy and nonconformity while also putting enormous faith in folk
behavior. Hurston's love of talk on the front porch of the store is legendary. In her autobiography, she described the store porch before she
even got to her own birth. It was thus an essential part of her background, like her parents and grandparents and the town of Eatonville.
One of the most important and also most attractive features of Hurston's
descriptions of porch talk was her appreciation of cultural events in all
their fullness. Like most folklorists, she loved what she was document-
ing. Unlike many of them, she tried hard to record the feeling of being
there, not merely the words. Thus, she did not merely say the stories
were humorous; instead, she wrote, "The porch rocked with laughter."[30]

An important point for understanding Hurston is that the folklife she
found so compelling had no special connection to the land or rural life.
In fact, she did not see being settled and knowing one's community and
family as being particularly conducive to the production and appreciation of interesting, powerful stories, songs, jokes, and the rest. For her,
creativity was always a good thing, and she wanted no past that tied her
to the same people and the same stories. Hurston referred to the same
agrarian joke that Booker T. Washington used about the farming man
who decided he was called to preach as a way to avoid working in the
hot sun, but she used it for different, not particularly agrarian, purposes. First, she did not tell the story herself; she had a storefront full
of storytellers elaborate on the joke in ways that took away its agrarian intent. She described one woman who retold a story about a man
frustrated by "Work, work, work! Everywhere Ah go de boss say hur-
ry, de cap' say run. Ah god a durn good notion not to nary one. Wish
Ah was one of dese preachers wid a whole lot of folks makin' my support for me." He sat down in the shade of a log, and prayed that if God
were *not* calling him to preach, God should lift him up and drop him on
the other side of the log. "You know God never picked 'im up, so he
went off and tol' everybody dat he was called to preach."[31] Other storytellers jumped in and started topping that story, one with a story of

30. Hurston, *Dust Tracks on a Road*, 24.
31. Hurston, *Mules and Men* (1935; reprt., New York: Harper Perennial, 1991),
20.

a mule that kept calling a man to preach so they could both get out of the sun, and then more with some other humorous stories about preachers. Hurston loved all of the stories, and did not retell them, as Washington did, to make moral lessons, certainly not moral lessons about the virtues one could learn from farming.

In fact, several stories in *Mules and Men* included antipastoral themes that Richard Wright might have found appealing, even if he did not choose to laugh at them. One storyteller complained, "There's more work in de world than there is anything else. God made de world and de white folks made work," and two more told stories explaining how African Americans became workers for white people. As many scholars have noticed, the subversive elements in Hurston's stories were often the source of their humor. One of those elements involved her pairing white people's agrarianism with their belief in white supremacy. Hurston quoted "de white man's prayer." "Now, Lord, we want some rain. Our crops is all burning up and we'd like a little rain. But I don't mean for you to come in a hell of a storm like you did last year—kicking up racket like niggers at a barbecue. I want you to come calm and easy. Now, another thing, Lord, I want to speak about. Don't let these niggers be as sassy as they have been in the past. Keep 'em in their places, Lord, Amen."[32]

Compared to Booker T. Washington and W. E. B. Du Bois, farm life was not particularly important to Hurston or Wright. For Wright, it was significant primarily for what it represented about how life should *not* be. Potentially positive features might have been things to remember, but only as part of the process of moving on to other, better realities. Much as rural life was irrelevant to Richard Wright's politics, it was irrelevant to Zora Neale Hurston's anthropology. She recalled an attractive childhood of rural abundance, but it turned out to be so secondary to her main interests that she saw no need to reject it. As a collector and lover of stories and songs, Hurston saw nothing special about the farm as a source of material, and she traveled to lumber camps, cities, and the Caribbean islands looking for the best material. Neither

32. Ibid., 74, 89. See Nicholls, *Conjuring the Folk;* Susan Mersinhelder, "Conflict and Resistance in Zora Neale Hurston's *Mules and Men,"* *Journal of American Folklore* 109 (summer 1996), 267–88.

Hurston nor Wright wrestled much with ideas about the Chosen People, the Promised Land, or Reconstruction-era ideas of a right to land. Neither had seen much of the hope of landowning that was so important to earlier generations of African Americans. Both knew farm life primarily as children, both left the South as teenagers, and both wrote their autobiographies in the early stages of the largest South-to-North African American migration in history. Literary analysts since Ralph Ellison have depicted Richard Wright as a blues writer, for his direct and dramatic confrontation with suffering. It seems useful to consider Hurston a blues writer as well, for she also wrote about life on the road, without nostalgia about rural life. As William J. Maxwell writes, "The most significant relationship to the Great Migration shared by Hurston and Wright was their travel with it."[33] While Hurston returned to the South and Wright never did, both were seeking something other than lives and ideals rooted in rural traditions.

The sense, dramatized by Richard Wright, that African American autobiographers should reject farm life and the culture around it continued into the civil rights years. Neither of the great autobiographies written during the civil rights period, Anne Moody's *Coming of Age in Mississippi* and Maya Angelou's *I Know Why the Caged Bird Sings*, has much that is positive to say about farm life or its effects on social life. Moody wrote in the tradition of Wright's *Black Boy*, pointing out directly and symbolically that agriculture was part of a form of oppression that people were better off leaving behind. Agriculture had failed her family, like it had failed Wright's. Born in southern Mississippi in 1940, Moody grew up when landowning seemed impossible, and the second and largest African American migration to the North seemed to offer the best chance for the future. In her 1968 autobiography, Moody offered two symbolic depictions of farm life and its failures. First, her stepfather Raymond had agrarian visions. "Raymond sat around talking about becoming a big-time farmer, raising lots of kids, making plen-

33. William J. Maxwell, *New Negro, Old Left: African-American Writing and Communism between the Wars*, 157. Also on migration literature, see Lawrence R. Rodgers, *Canaan Bound: The African-American Great Migration Novel* (Urbana: University of Illinois Press, 1997). On Richard Wright as blues author, see Ralph Ellison, *Shadow and Act* (1964; reprt., New York: Vintage Books, 1972); Houston A. Baker, Jr., *Long Black Song: Essays in Black American Literature and Culture*.

ty of money, and being his own man."[34] But the cheap land he was able to rent was not merely bad; it was full of hand grenades and bullets left by an army camp. Thus, working the crop meant literally plowing through a minefield. After that proved less deadly than he feared, Raymond organized the Moody children to start chopping cotton. The night before her first day in the field, Anne Moody had a dream that the sun was so big, hot, and red—"like a big mouth about to swallow us"— that it burned up everything and killed everyone she knew. She dreamed, "I was leaning on my hoe and I was rocking and the sun came down even closer. I was the last one standing and I knew it was coming for me. I quickly glanced at all the dead bodies evaporating around me. And I felt myself crumbling under the heat of the sun." When she woke up sweating and in a panic, she felt too sick to work, but her mother gave her some aspirin and sent her off to the field. At the end of the crop season, the family had made almost nothing, and Moody "was surer than ever that I would never be a farmer."[35]

Along with these searing descriptions of farming as either a minefield or a killing fire, Moody also said farming could be a hook. "Mama and Raymond had been hooked to the soil since they were children, and I got the feeling, especially from Mama, that they were now trying to hook me." Her mother told her sometimes about how much cotton she had picked as a child and "how 'old Mother Nature' took care of things." Her mother loved her vegetable garden and loved to talk about her mustard greens. Anne Moody found it all intriguing, "planting seeds, growing your own food, using the rain and sun and the earth," but she drowned out her mother's agrarian talk with dreams of traveling and chances to try new things. In a conclusion Richard Wright would have found familiar, she decided, "I knew if I got involved in farming, I'd be just like Mama and the rest of them, and that I would never have that chance."[36] Rejecting farm life and the agrarian dreams that accompanied it was one important step in Moody's rejection of the perspective of her mother. Above all, she decided, agriculture was a hook that attracted people with the lure of natural abundance and in-

34. Anne Moody, *Coming of Age in Mississippi*, 80.
35. Ibid., 84, 89.
36. Ibid., 88–89.

dependence, only to require work that wore them out and forced them deeper into a hopeless, powerless debt that shut out all other options.

Maya Angelou was less dramatic about the dangers of farm life, and she wrote less clearly in the Richard Wright tradition of alienation from everyone around her. Her grandmother in Stamps, Arkansas, owned a small store, and, like Zora Neale Hurston, she loved the sounds and friendliness of the store's front porch. But much like Anne Moody, she bemoaned what tenancy, debt, and hard physical labor did to farming people. Angelou's image was one of happy mornings and painful afternoons. People of all ages left the store joking at daybreak and came back beaten down by cotton, the work it required, and the hopelessness it created. In Angelou's memorable phrase, they were "dirt-disappointed." "No matter how much they had picked, it wasn't enough. Their wages wouldn't even get them out of debt to my grandmother, not to mention the staggering bill that waited on them at the white commissary downtown." Writing 125 years after Frederick Douglass published his first autobiography, Angelou repeated a theme from Douglass. Returning in the afternoons, farm workers grumbled "about cheating houses, weighted scales, snakes, skimpy cotton and dusty rows. In later years I was to confront the stereotyped picture of gay song-singing cotton pickers with such inordinate rage that I was told even by fellow Blacks that my paranoia was embarrassing."[37] She was enraged to watch people whose fingers were bloodied by cotton bolls, whose backs and legs ached, and who had to work on with an ever-deepening sense of hopelessness.

One of the fascinating developments since the civil rights movement is the rise of an unabashedly agrarian literature among some African American writers, especially autobiographers. That writing includes very little discussion in the tradition of Richard Wright's *Black Boy* about the damage the land and agricultural poverty could do to people. A new genre one might call the African American pastoral has emerged in the post–civil rights years, as more African American autobiographers have begun to write about strengths in the community lives of farming people. Most obviously, works such as *Growing Up Black in Ru-*

37. Maya Angelou, *I Know Why the Caged Bird Sings* (1968; reprt., New York: Bantam Books, 1970), 7.

ral Mississippi (1992) by Chalmers Archer, Jr., and *Once Upon a Time When I Was Colored* (1989) by Clifton Taulbert portray the strength of rural black communities in the 1940s and 1950s and deemphasize the stories of alienated individuals in the Richard Wright tradition. Much of that strength derived from land, work, and family. Both authors describe extended families and the strength they created. Both have a wistful tone common to pastorals; both authors believe the particularly rural past has lessons that should be useful for people in the present.

Taulbert sometimes seems a contemporary version of Booker T. Washington, urging hope and hard work based on lessons from a rural past. Unlike Washington, however, Taulbert sees the best lessons as neighborliness and interdependence—the traits Richard Wright found attractive but ultimately rejected. Taulbert has built on his autobiographies to teach lessons through a self-help book and foundation, both of which he says are based on the strengths of "porch people" who taught him and took care of him in Glen Allen, Mississippi.[38]

Chalmers Archer, Jr., grew up in the 1930s on what his family called "The Place," a group of rented cabins in Balance Due, Mississippi. The chapter on farm life is called not "Black Boy" but "A Poor Black Farm Kid," and the difference in Archer's and Wright's perspectives is startling. Archer summarizes, "Ann and all, for both kids and young adults, the Place was a wonderful, relatively comfortable, and happy place to be and live." His portrait of rural life, despite references to violence and injustice, emphasizes the abundance of the natural world, good food, relative self-sufficiency, and, above all, community interdependence. In a statement that fit into the long agrarian tradition of southern culture, he concluded his book by responding to questions from friends from Detroit—"sophisticated city kids"—who often asked how hard it had been to live in Mississippi. "'Is life down there in Mississippi bad?' Yes, sometimes very bad, I would reply. 'Are your folks real poor?'" He end-

---

38. Clifton L. Taulbert, *Once Upon a Time When We Were Colored* (New York: Penguin Books, 1989). On Clifton Taulbert's applications of his ideas, see Taulbert, *Eight Habits of the Heart: Embracing the Values that Build Strong Families and Communities* (New York: Penguin USA, 1999), and the Building Community Institute web site at www.cliftontaulbert.com. See also a children's book, Clifton L. Taulbert, with Earl B. Lewis and Cindy Cave, *Little Cliff and the Porch People* (New York: Dial Books, 1999).

ed his book with the agrarian answer: "No, we were not poor." He meant that partly in a literal sense, that his family always made enough food so that they could eat, but he also had a broader meaning that people could rely on each other.[39]

Alice Walker developed her own pastoral vision in the 1974 essay "In Search of Our Mothers' Gardens." Walker wrote that her mother's greatest form of creativity was in gardening. It was not farming, which would most likely have involved working for someone else; instead, it consisted of creating huge and unique flower gardens. Two folk elements characterized Walker's image. Members of their Georgia community repeatedly visited Mrs. Walker's garden to take cuttings and in doing so turned her art into a group creation. Even more intriguingly, Alice Walker imagined that African women hundreds of years earlier had been doing the same thing. For Walker, it is her mother's gift to her as a writer—the knowledge and example that she could create something new and beautiful by building on traditions.[40]

If one extends the analysis of autobiographies to oral narratives that have become the basis of books, the number of African American agrarians rapidly increases. Alabamian Ned Cobb, the great storyteller whose narrative Theodore Rosengarten edited into the book *All God's Dangers,* talked less about the interdependent community and more about individual agricultural skills. He took great pride in knowing about mules, plows, seeds, and seasons, and lamented the passing of special wisdom learned from elders. He took pride as well in feeding his family and staying as independent as possible, saying that while he only occasionally bought food, "my main livin come out of the hog pen, come out of the cow lot."[41] Perhaps more surprising is the agrarian perspective of Onnie Lee Logan, whose oral narrative was the basis for *Motherwit: An Alabama Midwife's Story.* Continuing a tradition of multiple generations of midwives, Logan said she served her commu-

39. Chalmers Archer, Jr., *Growing Up Black in Rural Mississippi: Memories of a Family, Heritage of a Place,* 43, 147.

40. Alice Walker, "In Search of Our Mothers' Gardens," in *In Search of Our Mothers' Gardens: Womanist Prose* (San Diego: Harcourt Brace Jovanovich, 1983), 231–43.

41. Theodore Rosengarten, *All God's Dangers: The Life of Nate Shaw* (New York: Vintage Books, 1974), 245.

nity out of a sense of both pride in her own skill, respect for a tradition handed down to her, and a need she saw in the community. Part of her connection to her community and her sense of the necessity of service came from seeing her parents share food with other African Americans in their Marengo County home. Her mother did not wait for poor people to ask for help; "she would take em vegetables, she would take em meal, flour, piece of meat, whatever. They acted fine because we had— if my daddy killed a hog or a cow or somethin like that for meat, we always had enough to share. Love, care, and share, that's what we did."[42]

There are many reasons for the rise of African American pastoral writing since the civil rights era. Cities have not turned out to be a promised land. Some northern-born autobiographers have written of trips to the South or summers in the South as ways of coming to terms with their families' histories and therefore their own. Frustrations with faceless government programs intended to help poor people have fueled memories of face-to-face relationships, and the slow but clear North-to-South migration of African Americans have led many to look to rural communities, extended families, and folkways as possible sources of strength.[43]

What recent autobiographers rarely call on is the agrarianism of past autobiographers. None of the four great autobiographers from the early twentieth century, Washington, Du Bois, Wright, and Hurston, held up farm life as an ideal. People who were fleeing southern life or fighting it found it hard to idealize farming, but all four found something appealing about rural life—hard work or survival skills or folk culture. Recent autobiographers have been more explicit about placing rural life at the center of their understandings of the strength of African American life, and none would agree with Richard Wright that they had inherited "a crude and raw past" marked by "no regrets and no hope."[44]

---

42. Onnie Lee Logan, as told to Katherine Clark, *Motherwit, An Alabama Midwife's Story* (New York: Dutton, 1989), 6.

43. Bebe Moore Campbell, *Sweet Summer: Growing Up With and Without My Dad* (New York: Putnam, 1989); Anthony Walton, *Mississippi, An American Journey* (New York: Alfred A. Knopf, 1996); Carol Stack, *Call To Home: African Americans Reclaim the Rural South*; Nicholas Lemann, *The Promised Land: The Great Black Migration and How It Changed America*.

44. Wright, *Black Boy*, 40–41.

❧

"Of the Least and the Most"

The African American Rural Church

LOIS E. MYERS AND REBECCA SHARPLESS

In April 1941, Farm Security Administration photographer Jack Delano visited an African American church in Heard County, in the Cotton Belt of Georgia on the Alabama line. Delano's photographs documented a thriving congregation at planting time in that spring before the war. The church stands in a wide clearing, on a slight rise. Horizontal boards create a building of perhaps thirty feet in length, with three windows on each long side and a wood-shingled roof surmounted by a brick chimney. Inside, the wooden, uncushioned pews are full of well-groomed churchgoers, women and girls on one side of the aisle, men and boys on the other, and the deacons in a proud row beside the broad pulpit. The wooden walls are bare save for an American flag hanging in the back, and kerosene lamps dangle from the tall ceiling. A metal heater, in the center of the room, is probably not in use that April morning. In a white shirt, vest, tie, and dark suit, the young male minister preaches with upraised fist. After the sermon, every head is bowed as another, older man in a vest and suit prays. Although the structure sags slightly and some of the windows are missing their clear glass panes, the activity within the building obviously matters to those in attendance.[1]

1. The photographs taken of Sunday services by Jack Delano can be seen at http://memory.loc.gov/ammem/fsahtml/fahome.html. The photographs of Sunday worship are titled: "Negro church service, Heard County, Georgia," "Negro preacher in Heard County, Georgia," "Coming to church, Heard County, Georgia," "Negro church service in Heard County, Georgia," "A Negro church service, Heard County, Georgia," "During church service in a Negro church, Heard County, Georgia," "At a church service in a Negro church, Heard County, Georgia," "Before the church meeting at a Negro church in Heard County, Geor-

Similar scenes were repeated innumerable times across the rural South throughout the first half of the twentieth century. By most indications, the rural church, which represented the majority of African American congregations in the American South, was the foremost institution for African Americans. On a secular level, the church served as a social and community center, providing a safe gathering place and activities to people isolated on farms. On a spiritual level, the church played numerous roles: giving comfort to those pressed down by the crop-lien system, serving as an arbiter of morals, and, in some cases, providing the impetus for social and economic reform. Rural people knew well the need for God's presence; they saw evidence every day in the rains that did or did not come, the seeds that did or did not sprout, the landlord who could be kind or difficult. Alabama sharecropper Ned Cobb observed: "How can you get out there and plant any kind of a seed—cotton, corn, peas, tomatoes, vegetable seeds of any kind, of the least and the most, what's about you to make it sprout and come up? What about you? You got no power. God got the power. But God has got a part for you to do."[2] Many rural African Americans trusted God while striving to play the role that they believed God intended for them.

Rural African Americans believed in the importance of the church, and most of them formally belonged to a congregation. In Greene County, Georgia, in the 1930s, for example, more than 90 percent of the women and 75 percent of the men in the community had joined a church. They not only belonged but also went to services. Despite heavy work demands and poor transportation, more than three-quarters of the members of rural African American churches managed to attend church at least one Sunday per month.[3]

---

gia," and "The deacons and preacher at a Negro church in Heard County, Georgia." Fourteen images of a funeral service are all entitled "Funeral of nineteen year old Negro sawmill worker in Heard County, Georgia." For a commentary on Delano's photographs of Heard County, see Nicholas Natanson, *The Black Image in the New Deal: The Politics of FSA Photography* (Knoxville: University of Tennessee Press, 1992), 76, 262.

2. Rosengarten, *All God's Dangers,* 411.

3. In 1936, the U.S. Census of Religious Bodies enumerated almost twenty-five thousand rural African American churches. Across the South, an average of forty-

During the early twentieth century, more than 90 percent of rural African Americans were either Methodist or Baptist, with Baptists outnumbering Methodists two to one. The attractions of the Baptist faith to a rural, uneducated people were many. The decentralized structure of the Baptist church gave laypeople opportunities for service and self-expression relatively free from the control of white people and allowing for a wide range of beliefs and practices. The ease with which ministers could be ordained gave the unschooled chances to pastor and provided opportunities for churches to have ministers. Baptist polity, furthermore, allowed for the easy division and spread of congregations. Many small, rural Baptist churches maintained independence even from the variety of national African American Baptist denominations. Local autonomy, fiercely protected, allowed the laity to choose the pastor and control church property and finances. Baptist practice gave ordinary people the "opportunity for self-expression denied in other fields."[4]

---

six rural African American congregations existed in each county, and each church had an average membership of about 150 people. Arthur F. Raper, *Preface to Peasantry: A Tale of Two Black Belt Counties,* 364; Albert J. Raboteau, *Canaan Land: A Religious History of African Americans,* 101; Benjamin Elijah Mays and Joseph William Nicholson, *The Negro's Church* (New York: Negro Universities Press, 1933), 231–32; Ralph A. Felton, *These My Brethren: A Study of 570 Negro Churches and 1542 Negro Homes in the Rural South* (Madison, N.J.: Department of the Rural Church, Drew Theological Seminary, 1950), 37; Harry V. Richardson, *Dark Glory: A Picture of the Church among Negroes in the Rural South* (New York: Friendship Press for the Home Missions Council of North American and Phelps-Stokes Fund, 1947), 147.

4. According to the 1926 U.S. Census of Religious Bodies, 19,045, or 53.8 percent, of 35,367 African American churches in twelve southern states were "Negro Baptist." Methodists, from four different groups, were second, followed by the Christian and Missionary Alliance, the Christian Church, the Church of Holiness, the Church of God, Evangelical Lutherans, Episcopalians, Congregationalists, and Disciples of Christ. In rural areas, even less variety existed. A 1930 survey of 185 rural churches in Peach County, Georgia, Orangeburg County, South Carolina, Montgomery County, Alabama, and Fort Bend County, Texas, found that Baptists accounted for 67.6 percent of the members, followed by 13 percent Methodist Episcopal, 8.1 percent African Methodist Episcopal Zion, and 11.3 percent African Methodist Episcopal and Colored Methodist Episcopal. And in 1936, 24,775 rural African American churches had 2,701,988 members, of which more than 66 percent were Baptist and 24.9 percent were Methodist. Those numbers continued

The Baptist faith was intensely personal, with no intermediary needed between a person and God. Black Baptist beliefs were basically Cal-
vinist, accepting the fallen state of humanity and the belief in Jesus Christ
as the savior of humanity. They also believed that "humanity maintained some freedom to accept or reject the salvation available through
Christ." One could attain justification and regeneration through acceptance of Jesus by faith, but "full sanctification and glorification were
not attainable in life." Baptists believed in the permanence of salvation:
once saved, always saved.[5] An emphasis on faith rather than acts well
suited a people whose actions could be so tightly constrained by economics and racism.

In the South, African American Methodist churches enjoyed more
success in town than in the country. Divided by the turn of the twentieth century among African Methodist Episcopal, Colored Methodist
Episcopal, African Methodist Episcopal Zion, and all-black congregations within the predominantly white Methodist Episcopal church,
they competed among themselves for the same families and the same
support. Denominational conferences assigned pastors and owned
church property, thereby constraining the power of the laity. Methodists emphasized education among their clergy, limiting access to the

---

steady; a 1949 study of seventeen rural southern counties discovered 76.9 percent
of church members were Baptist, 6.1 percent AME Zion, 6.0 percent AME, 4.8
percent CME, and 1.4 percent Methodists. The remaining 4.8 percent was com-
posed of Congregational Christian, Holiness, Protestant Episcopal, Church of
God in Christ (Holiness), Primitive Baptist, Church of Christ, Free Will Baptist,
Church of God, Congregational Christian, Presbyterian, and Roman Catholic.
These statistics are from Carter Godwin Woodson, *The Rural Negro* (Washington,
D.C.: Association for the Study of Negro Life and History, Inc., 1930), 153–54, and
Richardson, *Dark Glory*, 15–16. See Mays and Nicholson, *The Negro's Church*, 234,
and Felton, *These My Brethren*, 36, 44–45, for comparable statistics from their re-
spective studies.

See also William E. Montgomery, *Under Their Own Vine and Fig Tree: The
African-American Church in the South, 1865–1900*, 106–8; Carter G. Woodson, *The
History of the Negro Church*, 2d ed. (Washington, D.C.: Associated Publishers,
1945), 292–93; and Hans A. Baer and Merrill Singer, *African-American Religion in
the Twentieth Century: Varieties of Protest and Accommodation*, 30.

5. Edward L. Wheeler, *Uplifting the Race: The Black Minister in the New South,
1865–1902* (Lanham, Md.: University Press of America, 1986), 9.

ministry among the devout who lived in rural areas with meager access to schooling, and they screened ministerial candidates before accepting them. A minister could not function in a Methodist church, furthermore, unless he were admitted to a conference, "and both the AME Zion and the AME Church turned down applicants who did not meet minimal moral and educational standards." Methodist ministers enjoyed more job security than their Baptist counterparts, however; once they were admitted to a conference they were "virtually assured of a place of service." Encouraged by their denomination to spread educational opportunity among their people, African American Methodist preachers often doubled as teachers in the country schools.[6]

The beliefs of the African Methodist Episcopal Church resembled those of the white Methodist Episcopal church: "Arminian in their understanding of the human will," they "affirmed the ability of the sinner to either accept or reject the salvation offered in Jesus." AME members believed that people could lose their salvation by faithlessness. Their goals tended to have fruition in the earthly life: "African Methodists were encouraged to cultivate a desire and longing for complete sanctification in this life. The AME Church believed that perfection was attainable in this life, and that 'glorification' occurred after death." In this belief they may have felt the continuing influence of Richard Allen, founder of the AME denomination and a tireless abolitionist.[7]

Despite the differences in structure and polity, African American churches shared much in common. A southern Mississippi church leader observed in 1950, "You can't tell the Methodists from the Baptists."[8] From the late eighteenth century forward, African Americans embraced an "experiential, revivalistic, and biblically oriented" brand of Christianity, with strong emphasis on an inward conversion experi-

6. Felton, *These My Brethren*, 44; Wheeler, *Uplifting the Race*, 9, 11, 13; Richardson, *Dark Glory*, 213–14. For a detailed discussion of the differences among the Methodist groups, see Wheeler, 10–15.

7. Wheeler, *Uplifting the Race*, 12; Gayraud S. Wilmore, *Black Religion and Black Radicalism: An Interpretation of the Religious History of African Americans*, 3d ed. (Maryknoll, N.Y.: Orbis Books, 1998), 105–9.

8. Merton D. Oyler, "Community and Institutional Factors in Tenure," in Harold Hoffsommer, ed., *The Social and Economic Significance of Land Tenure in the Southwestern States* (Chapel Hill: University of North Carolina Press, 1950), 381.

ence for Christian salvation. This belief institutionalized the revival as a means of "converting sinners, extending church membership, and reforming society." It also "read the Bible literally and interpreted the destiny of America accordingly." African Americans initially developed a "distinctive evangelical tradition" that sought to answer the difficulties of lives circumscribed by slavery.[9]

The congregations were not monolithic, however. Theologian Gayraud S. Wilmore identified three types of African American church traditions, beginning in the late eighteenth century. The survival tradition enabled church members "to engage in an unceasing interior struggle to preserve physical existence and psychological sanity—in short, to survive." A second tradition stressed "the idea of self-improvement, uplift, the *advancement* of colored people,' or elevation." And the third tradition was that of liberation, literally the seeking of freedom for African American people. Most rural congregations were of the type described by Wilmore as "survivalist," helping their members just to get through the daily travail of the crop-lien system and abounding racism. Ministers preached patience with the system at hand, believing that a brighter day was to come in the life beyond.[10]

African American church members unabashedly articulated the belief that God would ultimately deliver salvation. In the late 1940s, a "hard-working tenant farmer" observed, "God is going to help us one of these days. I don't know how! He will help us though, and we are just waiting for Him." And former slave Benny Dillard sang for the interviewer who came to visit him: "Jesus will fix it for you, Just let Him have His way; He knows just how to do, Jesus will fix it for you."[11]

9. Albert J. Raboteau, "The Black Experience in American Evangelicalism: The Meaning of Slavery," in Timothy E. Fulop and Albert J. Raboteau, eds., *African-American Religion: Interpretive Essays in History and Culture* (New York: Routledge, 1997), 91–92. For a concise discussion of African elements in evangelical Christianity, see Montgomery, *Under Their Own Vine and Fig Tree*, 4–27. Walter F. Pitts, *Old Ship of Zion: The Afro-Baptist Ritual in the African Diaspora* traces the similarities between Afro-Baptist and African rites.

10. Wilmore, *Black Religion*, 255–61, 262, 267.

11. Woodson, *The Rural Negro*, 151–52; Felton, *These My Brethren*, 95; Benny Dillard, "Born in Slavery: Slave Narratives from the Federal Writers' Project, 1936–1938," Georgia Narratives, volume 4, pt. 1, p. 286 (http://memory.loc.gov/ammem/snhtml/snhome.html).

Religious beliefs of this type brought vehement criticism from would-be reformers, who accused the country folk of being passive and timid and observed that religion could be merely "an opiate and an escape from life." Benjamin Mays complained: "Believing this about God, the Negro, in many instances, has stood and suffered much without bitterness, without striking back, and without trying aggressively to realize to the full his needs in this world. . . . The idea has made Negroes feel good; it has made life endurable for them; and it has caused them to go to church on Sunday and shout and sing and pray." The net effect of this compensation, according to Mays, kept African Americans "submissive, humble, and obedient. It enabled them to keep on keeping on. And it is still effective in 1937."[12] Mays and others were disappointed that rural African Americans survived but made little progress.

Reformers grew impatient, too, with the rural church's perceived lack of resistance to white landowners and to the crop-lien system. Landowners sometimes gave land and building materials for churches, believing that the existence of a church would make tenants more satisfied and that hearing sermons against vice would keep them more honest and less rebellious. Workers who accepted the status quo would probably work for fewer wages and accept poorer housing conditions. Whites were more likely, Carter Woodson noted, to give aid to African American religious work than to any other cause, "although what they do give is inadequate." The tacit approval of white landowners, creating an apparent collusion between the church and the landowner, made the church itself suspect to a number of critics. White people, Woodson observed, considered the African American minister "a moral police force to compel obedience" and to help tenants and sharecroppers forget their oppression on earth. Some observers thought ministers to be shills for white landowners, who could be "relied upon to convey to their Negro congregations the advice of the leading whites of the community."[13]

12. Mays and Nicholson, *The Negro's Church*, 249; Mays, *The Negro's God*, 26.

13. Mays and Nicholson, *The Negro's Church*, 7; Woodson, *The Rural Negro*, 149, 176. The suspicion of white interference was particularly strong for the Colored Methodist Episcopal Church, which received financial assistance from white churches; Wheeler, *Uplifting the Race*, 15. For a scornful account of an African American minister, see Maya Angelou, *I Know Why the Caged Bird Sings*, 27, 28.

According to Evelyn Brooks Higginbotham, such critics, however, missed the importance of religion to the average rural African American. Within a framework of severe poverty, Higginbotham observed, African American churches became the site of a quiet, outwardly unassuming challenge to the humiliations of the crop-lien system: even everyday activities had "a politically subversive character within southern society," which enabled African Americans to "'work the system,' as Eric Hobsbawm terms it, 'to their minimum disadvantage.'"[14]

Most rural African Americans, of course, owned no land, and membership in a church might be the closest they came to having access to property. Being a part of a congregation with a physical presence could bring a sense of security to everyday life. Carter Woodson observed in 1930 that rural African Americans had invested more money "in church property than any other institution." While the majority of rural church congregations in the South were established before 1900, it was not until after the turn of the twentieth century that most could afford to build meetinghouses. Many congregations first worshiped in a brush arbor, with a crude roof constructed from materials at hand, ranging from tree limbs to lumber scraps. Others gathered in a nearby schoolhouse or lodge hall. Once a congregation could afford materials for a permanent house of worship, its members relied upon volunteer labor to build the structure, and most were able to construct their buildings without going into debt. About a third of the churches had adjacent cemeteries, reinforcing connections to their ancestors.[15]

The churches were modest and often in need of repair. Despite the meagerness of their appearance, however, church members sought a communion with a greater good in their spaces; Harry Richardson reported, "In one of the rudest churches seen—unpainted, unsealed, its steps falling down, large cracks in the floor, the seats broken or patched with rough wood—in this church someone with a sense of beauty had placed two large jars of beautiful artificial flowers at each end of the

14. Evelyn Brooks Higginbotham, *Righteous Discontent: The Black Women's Movement in the Black Baptist Church, 1880–1920*, 17–18.

15. Woodson, *The Rural Negro*, 174; Ted Ownby, "Struggling to Be Old-Fashioned: Evangelical Religion in the Modern Rural South," 129; Richardson, *Dark Glory*, 45; Felton, *These My Brethren*, 78, 80; Mays and Nicholson, *The Negro's Church*, 263.

uncertain rostrum, and had hung pretty flowered curtains at windows that frequently lacked panes."[16]

Rural religion reinforced church members' sense of self-worth through the sermons that they heard and through the action of inter-cessory prayer. Sermons often appealed "for a higher life and greater godliness in this world." Benjamin Mays praised the messages from rural ministers: "The Negro, crushed and humiliated everyday in the week and made to feel that he was a 'nobody,' was greatly helped by 'ig-norant' Negro preachers who said to their bewildered and discouraged congregations on Sundays, 'you are God's children.' This idea was more than an opiate; it did more than help the Negro to bear the burdens of the day. It gave him more faith in himself and a firmer belief in his in-trinsic worth. It was perhaps this slowly developing but transforming idea that has enabled the Negro to accept himself as much as he does."[17]

16. Charles Evers, "From *Evers,*" in Dorothy Abbott, ed., *Mississippi Writers: Re-flections of Childhood and Youth* (Jackson: University Press of Mississippi, 1986), 204; Raper, *Preface to Peasantry,* 361, 362; Woodson, *The Rural Negro,* 174–75; Edward de S. Brunner, *Church Life in the Rural South: A Study of the Opportunity of Protes-tantism Based upon Data from Seventy Counties* (New York: George H. Doran Com-pany, 1923), 83; Mays and Nicholson, *The Negro's Church,* 257, 263; Felton, *These My Brethren,* 78, 85; Richardson, *Dark Glory,* 37, 42, 44, 45, 46–47. In addition to Jack Delano, other FSA photographers recorded rural churches. The following photographs may be searched for at http://memory.loc.gov/ammem/fsahtml/fahome.html: "Negro Baptist Church, Bushy Fork, North Carolina," taken July 1939 by Dorothea Lange; "Negro Church near Manning, South Carolina," taken June 1939 by Marion Post Wolcott; "Negro Church near Paradis, Louisiana," tak-en September 1938 by Russell Lee; "Negro Church near Krotz Springs, Louisiana," taken October 1938 by Russell Lee; "Interior of Negro church of the Mississippi Delta," taken June 1937 by Dorothea Lange; "Negro church near Greensboro, Al-abama," taken July 1941 by Jack Delano; "Negro church on the banks of the Mis-sissippi near Vicksburg," taken July 1936 by Dorothea Lange; "Negro church, southern Arkansas," taken September 1938 by Russell Lee; "Negro church, South Carolina," taken March 1936 by Walker Evans; "Negro church near Cruger, Mis-sissippi," taken September 1938 by Russell Lee; "Tower on old Negro church near Cruger, Mississippi," taken September 1938 by Russell Lee; and "Church for Ne-groes, Ellis County, Texas," taken June 1937 by Dorothea Lange.

17. Richardson, *Dark Glory,* 92; Raper, *Preface to Peasantry,* 368; Mays, *The Ne-gro's God,* 188.

Intercessory prayer also gave rural African Americans a sense of power and efficacy. A 1956 survey of African American Methodists around Orangeburg, South Carolina, revealed that, regardless of their tenure status, every person asked believed fervently in the existence of God and in the effectiveness of prayer. Mississippi civil rights activist Charles Evers recalled the supplications of his mother on Sunday morning and at bedtime: "In the prayers, Momma would say certain things out loud. She was talking to God, telling Him to help her take care of her children and help her sons to grow up to be men that the world would be proud of and not to be lazy rogues, haters or alcoholics. She'd just talk to Him, and we'd listen. . . . [Momma] wasn't the kind who just believed in praying and sitting down. She taught us: 'You pray—then you get up and go after it.' She believed in prayer."[18] Prayer combined with action, according to Jessie Evers, could change the world.

The church reinforced community among rural blacks despite class differences. Carter Woodson commented that the poor thought themselves "just as much entitled to salvation as the rich. They insist that salvation is free. They contend, moreover, that 'if religion were anything which money could buy, the rich would live and the poor would die.'" When Chester Huben preached at Bolton Creek Baptist Church in Travis County, Texas, in 1934, he told his congregation that some people didn't attend church because they didn't believe their clothes to be nice enough. Huben noted that Satan was the origin of that lie and that dress wouldn't matter in heaven where the Lord would give his children new robes that would never wear out. Huben urged his listeners to spread that message among any folks who felt that their clothes weren't good enough for church.[19]

Disparity between landowners and tenants was less pronounced

18. Ruby Funchess Johnston, *The Religion of Negro Protestants: Changing Religious Attitudes and Practices*, xxv, 85; Richardson, *Dark Glory*, 175; Charles Evers, "From *Evers*," 204, 207.

19. Mays, *The Negro's God*, 188; Woodson, *The Rural Negro*, 174; John Henry Faulk, "Ten Negro Sermons" (master's thesis, University of Texas, 1940), 22–27. William H. Pipes, *Say Amen, Brother! Old-Time Negro Preaching: A Study in American Frustration* (Detroit: Wayne University Press, 1951) presents transcriptions of seven sermons recorded in rural Macon County, Georgia, during World War II.

among African Americans than among their Anglo counterparts, as both owners and tenants wrestled with low incomes. Most rural church members were tenant farmers or sharecroppers, and even families who owned land often struggled to pay debts and taxes. In rural churches, however, socioeconomic differences could be seen within the church leadership. Landowning families enjoyed a security unavailable for tenants and sharecroppers, who moved from farm to farm every few years. Communities with high rates of tenancy often had smaller, less stable churches than did those with a high percentage of landowners, and landowners attended in higher percentages than did tenants.[20] Although the crop-lien system was mitigated somewhat by common religious beliefs and church membership, its effects did not disappear completely.

Because they lacked funds to support full-time ministers, most African American rural churches held services only one or two Sundays a month, almost always in the morning. Through the phenomenon known as half-time churches, Baptists and Methodists in particular shared church buildings wherein congregations would worship in the same place on alternating Sundays. In some cases, the congregations might share Sunday school or other church-related events, then separate for worship services. They also often held joint revival meetings. The cooperation among denominations contributed to a sense of community, smoothing class lines and any theological discrepancies.[21]

20. Baer and Singer, *African-American Religion in the Twentieth Century*, 37; Oyler, "Community and Institutional Factors in Tenure," 371; Richardson, *Dark Glory*, 49; Felton, *These My Brethren*, 36.

21. Of twenty-seven churches in nine rural communities of Alabama in the early 1930s, nine held preaching services once a month, fifteen held services twice monthly, and three had more than two services a month. On Sundays when the preacher came, some churches also held night services. In the Mississippi Delta, some congregations referred to the Sundays when they had a minister as "pastoral Sundays." See Brunner, *Church Life in the Rural South*, 87; Mays and Nicholson, *The Negro's Church*, 252–53; Richardson, *Dark Glory*, 87; Felton, *These My Brethren*, 47; Benson Y. Landis and George Edmund Haynes, *Cotton-Growing Communities* (New York: Department of Race Relations, Federal Council of Churches of Christ in America, 1934), 18; Alfred Adolphus Pinkston, "Lined Hymns, Spirituals, and the Associated Lifestyle of Rural Black People in the United States" (Ph.D. diss., Uni-

For rural people, the churches were the largest arena in which they could have leadership, autonomy, and self-determination. The pastor, although a highly significant figure in the life of the congregation, often was present only half of the time or less, and he was also likely to leave after a brief tenure. Rural churches, therefore, developed mechanisms to lead themselves, both in terms of governance and of worship. Methodists could hold positions of authority as trustees, stewards, stewardesses, or deaconesses. For Baptists, leadership came through the board of deacons, which were exclusively male.[22] In the Baptist church, in which individual congregations were responsible for calling and keeping pastors, there might be no pastoral leadership on any given Sunday. Lay members, therefore, often preached in place of the minister. Methodist churches, controlled by a central conference, had more regular preaching. They seldom used lay preachers but frequently made use of members to read Scripture during the course of the service. Lay groups within the church such as missionary societies or the usher board or outside groups such as lodges or schools or burial societies conducted devotional services.[23] These lay activities kept the church's activities going despite the absence of the clergy, and they provided opportunities for service and leadership for people who had few such opportunities in the secular world.

Despite the ability of the rural people to provide for themselves, they nonetheless wanted pastors to serve their churches, and they sacrificed financially to do so. Much of a given church's income—sometimes as much as 60 percent—went to pay the pastor's salary. Fortunate congregations with acreage around their building might cooperatively cultivate a cotton crop or rent the land for a cash infusion into the budget.[24]

Like pastors everywhere, the men whom the churches chose or had sent to them varied dramatically. Many were people of strong commitment and devotion, while others were greedy charlatans, roundly

---

versity of Miami, 1975), 65; Oyler, "Community and Institutional Factors in Tenure," 371–72, 381; Baer and Singer, *African-American Religion in the Twentieth Century*, 30, 31.

22. Felton, *These My Brethren*, 38, 39; Richardson, *Dark Glory*, 102.

23. Felton, *These My Brethren*, 75; Richardson, *Dark Glory*, 47.

24. Richardson, *Dark Glory*, 77, 79; Felton, *These My Brethren*, 78, 84; Mays and Nicholson, *The Negro's Church*, 250.

criticized by rural reformers.[25] Being a rural pastor meant, for many, traveling long distances and receiving little pay, preaching at multiple congregations where they had little opportunity to know their members. The majority of them had employment outside the ministry, and their pastoral duties had to take place after long days and weeks of work. Most of them worked as farmers or day laborers themselves, and this provided a commonality with the people whom they were serving. Farmers, however, were unlikely to have received any formal theological training, and their sermons were often unsophisticated to outsiders' ears. During the first third of the twentieth century, more than half had only an elementary-school education.[26]

25. Although the majority of rural African American church members were women, females apparently almost never held the position of pastor. They might serve as visiting preachers or evangelists, following nineteenth-century practices, and they were acknowledged as powerful preachers, particularly in the Methodist church. Eddie Stimpson, for example, was baptized by a "Sister Riddle" in Collin County, Texas, in 1936. But the pastorate itself was reserved solely for men; women were acceptable only "as long as they remained in subordinate positions." See Mays and Nicholson, *The Negro's Church*, 238–39; Felton, *These My Brethren*, 58, 67; Raboteau, *Canaan Land*, 129–30; Sylvia R. Frey and Betty Wood, *Come Shouting to Zion*, 127; Eddie Stimpson, *I Remembers: A Black Sharecropper's Recollections of the Depression*, 120; Bettye Collier-Thomas, *Daughters of Thunder: Black Women Preachers and Their Sermons, 1850–1979*, 278. Faulk, "Ten Negro Sermons," 76–83, transcribes the sermon of Sister Estelle Parsons given in the summer of 1939 on the outskirts of San Antonio, Texas. Parsons was a traveling evangelist who preached on the topic "Quickened by de Spurut." Collier-Thomas, *Daughters of Thunder*, 215–20, transcribes the 1948 sermon, "What Woman Is," by CME evangelist Mrs. F. E. Redwine, delivered in Flint, Texas.

26. A 1943–1946 survey of African American pastors in Virginia revealed that ninety pastors served 212 rural churches, an average of 2.4 churches per pastor. These rural pastors ministered to an average of 422 persons between their several congregations. The pastors often commuted at least fifteen miles to one of their charges, and, as roads improved after World War II, the distances became much greater, sometimes as far as eighty or one hundred miles. With lengthier commutes, members lost the opportunity to get to know their pastors more intimately. Living away from their members, spreading their time among several churches, rural ministers often found pastoral duties difficult if not impossible. Reformers scornfully remarked that the rural ministers were "preachers and not pastors." Other than Sunday, for funerals, or annual revivals, the average minister spent only two days a month among his church people; Richardson, *Dark Glory,*

Although outside observers questioned the motives of rural ministers, the ministers commanded great respect among their church members. Ann Odene Smith described her pastor as "a very stern man. . . .
He was a proud, independent, black man made in the image of the Cre-
ator God. He was not a loud mouthed braggart. He was mild-mannered
and modest, a God-fearing man." Her pastor lived among the members
of his congregation, farming alongside them. Carter Woodson observed that in most congregations the pastor was "still the outstanding
man in the group. . . . regarded as the most honest, the most sincere,
and the most devoted of those who toil among the lowly." Rural African
Americans had difficulty developing any other professional class, and
the clergy commanded their highest respect. Church members welcomed the influence of a person of status among them, seeking the
minister's advice on financial and educational affairs.[27]

In their sermons, pastors provided the centerpiece of worship services. Folklorist John Henry Faulk documented ten sermons in rural
central Texas African American churches in the 1930s. Faulk noted
the interplay between preacher and congregation as well as the ministers' rhythmic delivery, known in some circles as "chanting."[28] African
American churchgoers often responded to sermons by expressing overt
emotion. In so doing, they were continuing an element of Christian re-
vivalism dating to the First Great Awakening, in which both black and
white worshipers evidenced intense feeling. Shouting, as it was called,
was "apparently deriv[ed from] African forms" and became institutionalized and ritualized. The minister and the congregation responded to one another. Shouting was "very much a 'popular' ritual," one
that people learned from one another, and ministers learned from the
people. People wept and cried out during worship services, sometimes
fainting from the intensity of their feelings. While city-bred observers

---

39, 46, 65, 77–78, 96–97, 100; Mays and Nicholson, *The Negro's Church*, 238–40,
242–43, 244, 251; Felton, *These My Brethren*, 67, 71, 72, 73; Brunner, *Church Life in
the Rural South*, 89; Harry W. Roberts, "The Rural Negro Minister: His Work and
Salary," *Rural Sociology* 12 (March 1947): 286–87. Ministers' education had improved significantly by the late 1940s. See Richardson, *Dark Glory*, 124, 127.
    27. Ann Odene Smith, "God's Step Chilluns," in Dorothy Abbott, ed., *Missis-
sippi Writers: Reflections of Childhood and Youth*, 549; Woodson, *The Rural Negro*, 149.
    28. Faulk, "Ten Negro Sermons," 3, 20, 28, 31; Raboteau, *Canaan Land*, 46.

might disparage shouting, there was no substitute for those who preferred the old-time religion. Eighty-eight-year-old Ellen Payne, living near Marshall, Texas, in the 1930s, remarked to her WPA interviewer, "I still shouts at meetin's. I don't have nothin' to do with it. It hits me jes' like a streak of lightning, and there ain't no holdin' it. I goes now to camp meetin's clost to Karnack and tries to 'have, but when I gits the spirit, I jest can't hold that shoutin' back. The young folks makes fun of me, but I don't mind. Style am crowded all the grace out of 'ligion, today."[29]

Music played an integral role in worship services. The origins of the African American style of music are debated among scholars, but by the twentieth century, the music had evolved into a distinctive style. The music followed a tradition from both white and black cultures: the white Protestant tradition of lining-out songs and antiphonal structure, and call and response from West African music. Sociologist Howard Odum described the music at a service in the 1920s: "A leader opening song, swaying body, closed eyes, head backward, face heavenward, rhythmic swing of arms, slow pat of feet, rich vibrato voice, now swelling in ascendancy, now softening to appeal.

> Steal away, steal way to Jesus,
> I ain't got long to stay here.

The repertoire of spirituals and gospel songs was huge. At one revival meeting in western Tennessee, in the course of one evening the group sang at least six songs, including "Amazing Grace," "Lord, I Want to Be a Christian," and "We Are Our Heavenly Father's Children and We Know He Loves Us One and All."[30]

29. Johnston, *The Religion of Negro Protestants*, 111; Katharine L. Dvorak, *An African-American Exodus: The Segregation of the Southern Churches*, 8; Frey and Wood, *Come Shouting to Zion*, 121, 123, 124; Christine Leigh Heyrman, *Southern Cross: The Beginnings of the Bible Belt*, 49; Smith, "God's Step Chilluns," 551; Ellen Payne, "Born in Slavery: Slave Narratives from the Federal Writers' Project, 1936–1938," Texas Narratives, vol. 16, pt. 3, p. 179 (http://memory.loc.gov/ammem/snhtml/snhome.html). Felton, *These My Brethren*, 50–51, gives a detailed but disparaging account of a worship service, as does Charles S. Johnson, *Growing Up in the Black Belt: Negro Youth in the Rural South* (Washington, D.C.: American Council on Education, 1941), 137–45.

30. Frey and Wood, *Come Shouting to Zion*, 143; Howard W. Odum, *An Ameri-*

About half of rural congregations had pianos, while a handful had simple pump organs. Guitars might accompany a quartet for a special program, but rural Christians generally frowned upon instruments played in blues bars and dance halls. Clapping hands and stomping feet provided sufficient background accompaniment for many rural churches. Much of the singing was, therefore, a cappella. Singers emphasized harmony, dissonance, and "breaks in melody and key." Zora Neale Hurston observed, "Each singing of the piece is a new creation. The congregation is bound by no rules. No two times singing is alike, so that we must consider the rendition of a song not as a final thing, but as a mood. It won't be the same thing next Sunday." Likewise, feelings, not pitch, mattered to the singer. "The first notes just burst out," Hurston explained, "and the rest of the church join in—fired by the same inner urge. Every man trying to express himself through song. Every man for himself. Hence the harmony and disharmony, the shifting keys and broken time that make up the spiritual."[31]

While most congregations promised riches in heaven, a second type of rural Christian church practiced what Gayraud Wilmore termed "elevation," urging its congregants to strive for higher lives on earth. The members of these groups preached moral uplift as well as increased economic opportunity. As W. E. B. Du Bois pointed out in 1903, the church served as "a real conserver of morals, a strengthener of family life, and the final authority on what is Good and Right." To that end, congregations expected members to live moral and upright lives. John Henry Faulk described the sins that rural ministers preached against: back-biting, running with the wrong crowd, chasing around in cars, being stingy with the church, loafing, and going to saloons. Given that one study found that the social institution geographically nearest most

_____

can Epoch: Southern Portraiture in the National Picture (New York: Henry Holt and Company, 1930), 195; Felton, These My Brethren, 60. The literature on spirituals is vast. For a recent discussion of the postmodern meaning of spirituals, see Donald H. Matthews, Honoring the Ancestors: An African Cultural Interpretation of Black Religion and Literature (New York: Oxford University Press, 1998), 47–70.

31. Pinkston, "Lined Hymns," 85–86; Felton, These My Brethren, 80; Matthews, Honoring the Ancestors, 57; Zora Neale Hurston, The Sanctified Church (New York: Marlowe and Company, 1981), 80–81.

churches was the juke joint (followed in order by the lodge hall, base-ball diamond, grocery store, and dry goods store), they may have had a tall order.[32]

One of the primary manifestations of moral uplift was the revival service. While an African American family might not be able to make it to worship every Sunday, almost everyone in a community would make the effort to attend annual revival services. With its belief on in-dividual redemption, the rural African American church placed signifi-cant emphasis on a conversion experience, in which a person turned away from former ways and embraced a new and holy life as a church member. For most rural Christians, both black and white, this conver-sion experience occurred as the result of a revival meeting. In cotton country, the revivals were usually held in late summer, when the cot-ton had been laid by in preparation for harvest. Revivals were extremely popular, sometimes boasting attendance of four or five hundred peo-ple or more.[33]

Revivals combined singing and vigorous preaching to bring sinners into the fold. Children of school age sat on the so-called mourner's bench under the prayerful watch of deacons, choir members, and mothers and in the direct line of the preacher's exhortation to repen-tance. Carter Woodson observed that the ministers preached "three times a day on temperance, righteousness, and judgment to come." The attendees prayed hourly for those "out of the 'ark of safety,'" and even the most worldly sinner could not withstand such "fervent ap-peal." Woodson commented, "Even the young ladies seeking beaux will refuse to socialize with sinners. 'Before you talk love with me,' one would say, 'you must get your soul right with God.'" Sinners might hold

32. Du Bois, *The Souls of Black Folk*, reprinted in *Three Negro Classics* (New York: Avon Books, 1965), 340; Faulk, "Ten Negro Sermons," 3, 20, 28, 31; Felton, *These My Brethren*, 87; Woodson, *The Rural Negro*, 154–55.

33. Raboteau, "The Black Experience in American Evangelicalism," 91–92; Brunner, *Church Life in the Rural South*, 86; Mays and Nicholson, *The Negro's Church*, 253–54; Richardson, *Dark Glory*, 53; Myrlie Evers, "From *For Us, the Living*," in Dorothy Abbott, ed., *Mississippi Writers: Reflections on Childhood and Youth*, 225–26. Felton, *These My Brethren*, 59–60, 69, again presents a detailed but disparaging description of revivals.

out for the first two days until "some notorious person" had joined the church. Then others would follow suit and join.[34]

One of the centerpieces of the revival meeting was the preaching, conducted either by the church's pastor or by a visiting minister, sometimes from a distant city. Sermons might last as long as two hours, with many amens and shouts of assent. The sermons tended to be emotional pleas, and critics often charged that people were terrorized into joining the church. Carter Woodson reported that rural African Americans believed that Jesus Christ gave His life to "save evildoers, who must die in their sins and be brought to life in Jesus, if they hope to escape the fire and brimstone of hell; and even after being thus born again they must be careful, for the devil is always busily planning to swerve the faithful from the way to glory." The church, according to Woodson, was built on fear: God is "Jehovah, Lord of Hosts, working the destruction of those who do not heed His commands." Churches worked to "fire the communicants' emotion from time to time and to keep people sufficiently scared of evil by referring frequently to the horrors of the damned and the blessings of the 'beautiful island of by and by.'" Church members believed in the terrors to come for the unrepentant. Former slave Nicey Kinney declared that she, for one, acknowledged the existence of hell: "Yes, Honey, de Lord done put it on record dat dere is sho a burnin' place for torment."[35]

Critics notwithstanding, many people found their conversion experiences meaningful. C. L. Franklin recalled his conversion to Christianity at St. Peter's Rock Baptist Church in Cleveland, Mississippi, about 1925, when he was nine or ten years old. He attended a revival meeting for six or seven hundred people. He recalled sitting on the mourner's bench at the front of the church, where other people prayed for him before the sermon. At the conclusion of each service, the min-

34. Ernestine Garrett Anderson, tape-recorded interview by Lois E. Myers, March 30, 1999, in Riesel, Texas (Baylor University Institute for Oral History, 1998, transcript); Woodson, *The Rural Negro*, 162–63, 174.

35. Mays and Nicholson, *The Negro's Church*, 254; Felton, *These My Brethren*, 50, 59, 69; Woodson, *The Rural Negro*, 154; Nicey Kinney, "Born in Slavery: Slave Narratives from the Federal Writers' Project," Georgia Narratives, vol. 4, pt. 3, p. 33 (http://memory.loc.gov/ammem/snhtml/snhome.html).

ister extended an invitation, or "opened the doors" to join the church, and a number of people, including Franklin, responded to the invitation. Franklin had thought about it and decided that the time had come to become a full-fledged member of the congregation.[36]

At the conclusion of the revival, recent converts were baptized, usually by immersion in a nearby stream, pond, or river. C. L. Franklin was baptized in the Sunflower River, eight or ten miles from the church. Franklin recalled: "The members of the church were lined up on the riverbank, singing. The minister talked on the subject of baptism, the validity of baptism, the necessity of baptism, the tradition of baptism, and so forth. The deacons and pastor were out in the water, receiving the candidates as they marched out. And the pastor baptized us one by one." For both adults and children, baptism was an emotionally charged event. Sterling Plumpp was eleven when he entered the waters of Lake Kickapoo for his baptism, wearing a gown made of a cornmeal sack. He remembered, "The entire evening after my baptism, I felt relieved, cleaned, chosen. I was very conscious of my words, walks, and ways." And Ned Cobb, immersed as an adult, recalled, "When the preacher pulled me up out of the water, the deacons was there to catch my hands and lead me up. I felt, when I hit the air—and it was early winter when I stepped up out of that water—I felt just like somebody done poured a kettle of warm water over me. I weren't cold a bit. And I commenced a shakin hands all around and laughin and goin mad for joy."[37]

Because of the intensely personal nature of evangelical religion, an experience with God was supposed to engender changes in behavior. Benny Dillard recalled that his church in Georgia examined potential members to ensure that their change of heart was genuine: "When somebody wanted to jine our church us 'zamined 'em and if us didn't think dey was done ready to be tuk in de church, dey was told to wait and pray 'til dey had done seed de light." All new converts were expected to adhere to a certain moral code, in particular eschewing vices.

---

36. C. L. Franklin, *Give Me This Mountain: Life History and Selected Sermons,* edited by Jeff Tood Titon (Urbana: University of Illinois Press, 1989), 7–8; Richardson, *Dark Glory,* 53.

37. Franklin, *Give Me This Mountain,* 7–8; Sterling D. Plumpp, "From *Black Rituals,*" in Dorothy Abbott, ed., *Mississippi Writers: Reflections of Childhood and Youth,* 515; Rosengarten, *All God's Dangers,* 411.

After Ned Cobb was converted in Alabama in the 1940s, he told the examining members of the Pottstown Baptist Church: "The Bible says you must lay off your mortal ways and put on immortality—accept of God in your soul and live it. I won't tell a lie on God—He freed me from my sins. He put the finishin touch on me. I am a true born child by the blood of the Lord and Savior Jesus Christ. I aint goin to let you catch me drinkin; I aint goin to let you catch me gamblin; I ain't goin to let you catch me walkin the road and tellin lies, running after women worse than a hog'll run at a pot of slops."[38]

Revival meetings also had social sides to them. For people who had been largely absorbed in the growing crops, the meetings gave them a break before harvest season began. Myrlie Evers observed that so-called tractor meetings that she attended in Mississippi "represented the only large social gathering of the year, and there was a special sadness in going home when they were over." With daylong preaching, families had to bring enough food for two meals a day. Even those not interested in salvation could "feast and socialize with friends." Feeding the body as well as the soul, women brought cakes, pies, fried chicken, and other delicacies to keep up people's strength between the services.[39]

On occasion, after World War II, revivals provided rare meetings for members of different races. African American ministers preached at white churches, white ministers preached at black churches, and in at least one instance black and white churches conducted a joint revival. White people attended African American revival meetings. Revivals also brought further cooperation between African American Baptists and Methodists. Churches in a given area staggered their revivals so they would not compete with one another, and members of one congregation often attended the services of the other.[40]

Central to the mission of elevation in the church were organizations and auxiliaries. While they did so in much smaller numbers than their urban counterparts, rural African Americans did participate in affiliat-

38. Dillard, "Born in Slavery," 295; Rosengarten, *All God's Dangers,* 410; Franklin, *Give Me This Mountain,* 5.

39. Myrlie Evers, "From *For Us, the Living,*" 226; Felton, *These My Brethren,* 59, 60, 69.

40. Woodson, *The Rural Negro,* 160; Oyler, "Community and Institutional Factors in Tenure," 381.

ed groups. A few of the larger churches had special organizations for young people, branches of the societies common in their denomination. The largest church organization was the burial society, wherein members cared for each other in death. Burial societies collected small monthly dues, provided burial expenses, and provided recreation "from time to time."[41]

A second common activity was membership on the usher board, a small but powerful organization in most rural churches. Ostensibly to provide members to serve as ushers, the boards rapidly took on "the nature of church or community clubs." They were composed of male and female, young and old. In the late 1940s, Harry Richardson observed, "The boards conduct weekly 'sings' to which groups from other churches are invited; they present programs in the churches on Sundays in which other boards join; they promote activities to raise money for the church and for charities among their members; many of them give social or recreational affairs that are quite popular in many communities." Ushers were organized into "usher boards" with elected officers. These usher boards had district, state, and national meetings and carried on "many church enterprises." In some communities, they were "responsible organizations with officers and a treasury and regular business meetings." Theirs was a coveted position. In many communities they "attract more young people than any other church organization."[42]

Rural churches also maintained close ties with lodges, societies, and clubs, such as the Knights of Pythias and its female auxiliary, the Courts of Calanthe, and the Prince Hall Masons and its female auxiliary, the Heroines of Jericho. These organizations provided death claims and sick benefits, while affording "the elders the opportunity of selective membership, secret rites, and organized participation in the ambition or mission of their lodge." They also engaged in rituals and pageantry. Lodge halls frequently were built adjacent to rural churches. The church and the lodge, observed Ralph Felton, were "about the only organizations where the Negroes in the South can hold office."[43]

41. Woodson, *The Rural Negro*, 171; Richardson, *Dark Glory*, 119; Felton, *These My Brethren*, 52, 90.

42. Felton, *These My Brethren*, 38, 39, 52, 53, 57, 60; Richardson, *Dark Glory*, 104.

43. Felton, *These My Brethren*, 38, 39, 68, 89, 97; Raper, *Preface to Peasantry*, 373–74.

Rural African Americans were, of course, almost all poor. Yet they gave generously to their churches. The idea of such poor people giving away their meager incomes struck some observers as ridiculous. Yet church people gave of their pitiful incomes as a way of participating in a communal good, becoming a part of something bigger than themselves. They also broadened their horizons by sending part of their church's income for missionary work. Many were interested in foreign missions and gave money directly to foreign missionaries. The concern for foreign missionaries gave rural people an awareness of others outside of their neighborhood.[44]

Of a more immediate nature was the local missionary society. These societies, composed of the women in the congregation, met the needs of the sick and suffering. The missionary society members existed to be "present at the birth of each baby, care for the sick, help the widows and take cheer to the aged." Lacking access to the formal position of pastor, women ministered in informal, communal ways, and in so doing provided important temporal care.[45]

Another typical arena for women was in the Sunday school, frequently shared by Baptists and Methodists. Almost every church offered Sunday school, giving instruction from the cradle to the grave. Most churches broke their Sunday schools into at least two "grades," the minimum being for children and adults, or for "beginners and advanced." The adult classes were usually well attended and afforded an opportunity to train lay leaders. In a typical church, there were two female Sunday school teachers for every man, providing a crucial role for women in the life of the church.[46]

44. Charles Evers, "From *Evers*," 207; Raper, *Preface to Peasantry*, 369; Felton, *These My Brethren*, 52–53. Richardson, *Dark Glory*, 70, found that the annual per capita contribution of rural African Americans in 1947 was $5.12, greater than the national average for "the Negro church as a whole." We were unable to find any evidence of the practice common in the white church of paying the ministers with chickens, pigs, vegetables, and other farm produce. Felton, *These My Brethren*, 52, 53, 57; Brunner, *Church Life in the Rural South*, 88.
    45. Felton, *These My Brethren*, 57.
    46. Brunner, *Church Life in the Rural South*, 87; Felton, *These My Brethren*, 38, 44, 49; Richardson, *Dark Glory*, 89, 107, 109, 111; Woodson, *The Rural Negro*, 166; Mays and Nicholson, *The Negro's Church*, 256.

The African American rural church served as the center for much community and social life. The information that people gathered might be informal. A minister observed of a church in Thomas County, Georgia: "Here he [the rural African American] learns the price of cotton or the date of the next circus; here is given the latest fashion plates or the announcement for candidates for justice of the peace."[47] Along with the schoolhouse, it was usually the only public space available to African Americans. Churches hosted emancipation celebrations, ice cream socials, and barbecues. They were the site of rural improvement work, hosting 4-H clubs and home demonstration clubs. Leadership skills practiced before World War II became important in following years as rural churches shared in work for the improvement of race relations, working with chapters of the National Association for the Advancement of Colored People. In the postwar period, a rural minister was more likely to belong to the NAACP than to any other community organization.[48] By fostering organizations both sacred and secular, the churches placed themselves squarely in the urban tradition of congregations interested in uplift and improvement.

Along with moral, spiritual, and social betterment, the rural church sometimes also encouraged economic improvement for its members. Such was the case in Central Texas in the mid 1940s, when S. A. Keesee, pastor of the Springhill Methodist Episcopal Church, preached the message, "God wants the best for you, and God equipped you with the knowledge of things that you can do for yourself. He will help you, but he's not going to do it for you. You have to have the initiative. And he did not mean for you to stay in bondage." Keesee told the congregation that he was going to purchase one hundred acres of sandy land across the road from the church and resell it in parcels to church members willing to forgo their dependency on sharecropping. Five families contracted with the pastor to buy portions of the land. The soil was too poor and the acreage too small for productive cotton farming, so off-farm employment made Keesee's dream a possibility. To pay for the

47. W. H. Holloway, "A Black Belt County, Georgia," in W. E. B. Du Bois, *The Negro Church* (Atlanta: Atlanta University Publications, no. 8, 1903), 57–64, quoted in Milton C. Sernett, *Bound for the Promised Land: African American Religion and the Great Migration* (Durham, N.C.: Duke University Press, 1997), 28.

48. Felton, *These My Brethren*, 168.

land and the materials to build a house, the men of the households took jobs as laborers in cotton gins and oil presses, and the women worked as housekeepers and cooks in nearby Waco. Landownership enhanced self-esteem among the church members and also assisted Springhill Church to survive rural depopulation. Attachment to the land and the church that helped make the land their home inspired Springhill families to maintain an active congregation into the twenty-first century.[49]

Social and economic uplift helped build confidence among rural congregations. Before World War II, however, poverty and lack of opportunity limited many southern African American churches from open resistance to racial and economic oppression. Yet in the radical movements of the 1930s one finds significant participation on the part of rural churches, foreshadowing the active roles of congregations in the Civil Rights movement. These activities might be described as liberation, the third strain in African American churches identified by Gayraud Wilmore.

Despite the rarity of open rebellion among rural African American Christians, it would be a mistake to overlook the role that the rural church played in the agricultural protests of the 1930s and 1940s. A writer for the *Daily Worker*, traveling in Alabama in 1944, came upon a sharecropper in Chambers County, Alabama, whom he described as "an elder in the Zion [A.] M.E. Church who 'trusts God but keeps his powder dry'; reads his Bible every night, can quote from the Book of Daniel and the Book of Job . . . and he's been studying the Stalin book on the nation question."[50] During these turbulent years, the God of Nat Turner and Denmark Vesey came to the fore for a number of rural African Americans, part of the radical and prophetic tradition in the Christian church.

Organizers for groups such as the Southern Tenant Farmers' Union recognized that they would profit from using existing social institutions, particularly the churches, and they found it easy to draw parallels between rural Christianity and the protest movement. Historian Donald Grubbs observed, "Identification of the planter with Pharaoh was

49. Anderson, interview.

50. Wilmore, *Black Religion*, 169; Joseph North, *No Men Are Strangers* (New York: International Publishers, 1958), 227, quoted in Robin D. G. Kelley, *Hammer and Hoe: Alabama Communists during the Great Depression* (Chapel Hill: University of North Carolina Press, 1990), xi.

traditional with Southern black men; Scripture could be used to support organizing speeches as well as sermons; and churches were commonly the only buildings available for meetings of any kind." Union organizers found song to be a particularly effective motivation, modifying familiar hymns for more secular purposes. By far the most successful was "We Shall Not Be Moved," an alteration of an old camp-meeting song, "Jesus Is My Captain." The churches provided leadership, too, for the movement. E. B. McKinney, the pastor of an African American church in Marked Tree, Arkansas, was "the leader of Marked Tree's Negroes," and he proved a highly effective organizer for the STFU.[51]

Throughout the 1930s, African American Communists met in rural churches across Alabama, and they patterned their meetings after rural church services, including call and response. Like the STFU, the Communists revised spirituals into political songs.[52] Although both of these movements, like radical movements across the South, faded away, they nonetheless demonstrated that rural African Americans could become part of the liberation movement within the church.

Changes over time brought instability to rural African American congregations. The mobility of the South's sharecropper and tenant farmer population had long kept the church population on the move. As transportation improved, with better roads and increased access to automobiles, African Americans could choose to attend the church nearest them, or to attend another, more distant, that was more to their liking. At the end of World War II, most African American churches were "on or near" improved roadways—roads that were more than dirt or mud. As the population shifted, some churches simply picked up and changed their physical locations. By 1949, almost a third of the churches surveyed had changed locations; when a large number of the members moved, they simply moved the building nearer to the people. Other rural churches merged memberships to remain open.[53]

51. Donald H. Grubbs, *Cry from the Cotton: The Southern Tenant Farmers' Union and the New Deal* (Chapel Hill: University of North Carolina Press, 1971), 65, 66–67; Kelley, *Hammer and Hoe*, 105–6.

52. Kelley, *Hammer and Hoe*, 105, 107, 135.

53. Mays and Nicholson, *The Negro's Church*, 274, 276; Felton, *These My Brethren*, 41; Baer and Singer, *African-American Religion in the Twentieth Century*, 30.

Rural churches lost membership as their followers migrated to the nearby cities or to the distant North. In Green County, Georgia, for example, the African American population dropped from 11,636 in 1910 to 6,628 in 1930. Predictably, church membership dropped as well: from 3,290 members in 1920 to 1,404 in 1928. The rural church became increasingly isolated, as communities declined and members found themselves having to go many miles for entertainment and groceries. Finding fewer and fewer people in church pews on Sundays, some African American ministers followed their members into town and opened up churches there.[54]

Yet many of the churches persisted, at least in the short run. As African Americans moved to the nearby market centers and cities, some continued to attend the rural churches of their childhoods. Of 483 churches surveyed in 1949, almost half had decreased in size during the previous decade. Despite the perceived heavy loss in membership through migration, however, a similar study found that only three churches had closed. The researcher observed, "The general tendency is for the members remaining to carry on the church program, even though the number may not be enough to justify it, and the financial burden of maintaining the church falls very heavily on the few." One extreme example in Calhoun County, South Carolina, showed a community stripped of its population. Fifteen years prior, the church had 250 members; by 1947, it had 12, "all middle-aged or old people." The church building was falling down, and the parsonage had been uninhabited for years. But there was room for hope, Harry Richardson found: "Yet in this atmosphere of rot and desertion, the twelve members meet regularly once a month for service. They meet in the church when the weather is good, and in a home when it is not. An aged pastor serves them, and funds are raised to meet the church expenses. Whatever else may be said of this, it is an expression of firm loyalty to a cause."[55]

Such loyalty persists into the twenty-first century. In McLennan

---

54. Raper, *Preface to Peasantry*, 184, 363; Woodson, *The Rural Negro*, 178; Mays and Nicholson, *The Negro's Church*, 235–37; Felton, *These My Brethren*, 43, 87; Sernett, *Bound for the Promised Land*, 76, 79.

55. Felton, *These My Brethren*, 46; Richardson, *Dark Glory*, 65–66.

County, Texas, the steeple of Mount Moriah Baptist Church still thrusts its many-pointed star toward heaven. Three miles away, Goshen Cumberland Presbyterian Church in America opens its double doors to worshipers just as it has for the last century. Nearer the Brazos River, at Springhill United Methodist, families that have been members since the 1870s appear on the Sundays when the pastor drives out from Waco, fifteen miles away. Just on the other side of the river, the people of Downsville divide themselves into Mount Olive and Mount Pleasant Baptist Churches, following the practices of their great-great-grandparents. Members of these congregations have survived the crop-lien system and legal segregation, and they continue to work for a better life here on earth even as they lay up rewards in heaven. They honor the faith of their ancestors.

꧁꧂

Shifting Boundaries

Race Relations in the Rural Jim Crow South

MELISSA WALKER

In the late 1930s, American anthropologist Hortense Powdermaker spent one year conducting a field study of race relations in a rural Mississippi county. Predictably, she noted the workings of a segregated society. "The separation and the contrast [between the races] persist," she explained. She hastened to add, "The arresting feature, however, is less the basic fact of segregation than the completeness and complexity of the interaction that takes place above it."[1] Oral histories and other first-person accounts of life in the American South in the first half of the twentieth century lend insight into the complex nature of the interactions Powdermaker observed. Again and again, rural southerners described a highly articulated racial etiquette that differed from place to place and from person to person. Yet in spite of the fact that most African Americans lived in the countryside, many historians studying southern race relations have focused primarily on the urban South. Scholars who have studied rural race relations have not fully explored the ways conditions of rural life gave unique shape to race relations in the countryside.[2]

1. Hortense Powdermaker, *After Freedom: A Cultural Study in the Deep South* (New York: Viking Press, 1939), 14.
2. Most studies of both the Jim Crow South and the Civil Rights movement focus on cities and towns. Although many studies of agriculture or labor in the Jim Crow South touch on race relations, few studies have focused exclusively on rural race relations or examined them in depth. For good examples, see Jack Temple Kirby, "Black and White in the Rural South, 1915–1954," *Agricultural History* 58 (July 1984): 411–22, and *Rural Worlds Lost: The American South, 1920–1960;* Neil R. McMillen, *Dark Journey: Black Mississippians in the Age of Jim Crow;* and Kelley, *Hammer and Hoe;* Orville Vernon Burton, "Race Relations in the Rural South since 1945." Contemporary studies of race relations by sociologists, journalists, and an-

Perhaps some of the neglect grows out of the difficulty in demarcating the rural and the urban. In the rural states of the pre–World War II South, lines between country and town were never sharply drawn. The cultures of many county seat towns and trading villages were more rural than urban. Moreover, rural people, particularly African Americans, moved back and forth between town and farm. In the off-season, rural blacks often flowed to town for jobs or to send their children to better schools. At harvest time, domestics from town might go to the farms to assist with cotton picking or vegetable harvesting. Because of these fluid boundaries, no study of race relations in the rural South can exclude examination of the interaction between blacks and whites in the dozens of crossroads villages and commercial and county seat towns that dotted the countryside. Nonetheless, most of the interactions between rural whites and blacks took place in the country. Therefore, our understanding of race relations in the Jim Crow South must center on the countryside.[3]

Yet the very conditions of rural life molded race relations along different lines than urban life. Because most rural black southerners were farmers, usually sharecroppers or tenants, many interactions between rural whites and African Americans took place in the context of the landlord-tenant relationship. In rural areas, racial and class hierarchies were intertwined. Segregation and economic oppression and exploitation were mutually reinforcing to a greater degree than in cities, and the struggle for economic self-determination was inextricable from the struggle against the Jim Crow system. Historian Nan Elizabeth Woodruff has shown how, for African Americans in the Arkansas and Mississippi Delta, citizenship went beyond voting rights to include "the right to eat, to work, and to have a home." As she put it, "By removing African Americans from the realm of citizenship through segregation and disfranchisement, employers could intervene in areas of their workers' lives that in liberal democracies are the preserve of civil society. Planters extended their authority into workers' private or cultural space, into

---

thropologists are often the most revealing sources on rural racial interactions. See Powdermaker, *After Freedom;* Johnson, *Growing Up in the Black Belt;* Baker, *Following the Color Line.*

3. McMillen, *Dark Journey,* 154–55; Powdermaker, *After Freedom,* 7–8.

their families, homes, churches, and lodges. . . . The weak separation between state and civil society set limits on the success of African American challenges to their oppression." As a result, in rural areas the segregated system could operate in flexible and locally peculiar ways even as it rigidly circumscribed the economic opportunities available to African Americans. A look at first-person accounts from blacks and whites who lived in the countryside sheds light on the obvious and subtle ways rural race relations operated to oppress African Americans.[4]

The lines between the races were as fluid as the lines between town and country, far more fluid than racial boundaries in the South's big cities. Although segregation in public accommodations had been enshrined in law by the end of the nineteenth century, the rural South possessed few public facilities to segregate. There were no streetcars and few buses, hotels, or restaurants where the races might mingle. Southern blacks and whites had always attended separate schools, a practice formalized by segregation laws in most states around the turn of the century. Blacks and whites rode separate railroad cars, but they met on roads, streets, and sidewalks, in retail establishments, on farms, and in white homes. The organization of racial interaction in these settings was highly localized. For example, although African Americans generally enjoyed limited access to most small-town retail establishments, in many small towns, some businesses were off-limits. Texan Grover Williams recalled in 1991 that he had never been in Heine's barber shop in Burton, Texas, because the establishment had been reserved for whites. Though it is doubtful that Burton's whites were still enforcing that prohibition in 1991, the ancient cultural restriction remained very much alive to Williams.[5]

In the countryside, some towns might be predominantly black, such as Mississippi's Mound Bayou, while others might be out of bounds to

4. Nan Elizabeth Woodruff, "African-American Struggles for Citizenship in the Arkansas and Mississippi Deltas in the Age of Jim Crow," *Radical History Review* 55 (winter 1993): 33–51.

5. McMillen, *Dark Journey*, chap. 6; Grover L. Williams, Sr., interviewed by Dan K. Utley, on five occasions between November 25, 1991, and June 12, 1992, Burton, Texas, Institute for Oral History, Baylor University, Waco (hereafter IOH, Baylor University).

African Americans. The exclusion of blacks from particular towns was not based in law but rather in practice. Domestic worker Sara Brooks, recalling her childhood in rural Alabama, remembered a train stop in Foxfield where a sign warned passengers, "'Niggers, read and run.' The letters was in red up there on a board. 'Niggers, read and run.' I guess a lotta poor white people were livin there and they didn't want no colored people around in that place where they were livin, see what I mean? My father knew about it, but he didn't say nothin. And at that time we was just so glad to get on the train. We didn't say nothin and we didn't question anything. Nope. We just went. But when we start thinkin, gettin older, then we'd ask each other, say, 'Wonder why?'" Oliver Anderson reported that in his hometown of Iredell, Texas, "There wasn't any niggers out there. Used to, when these niggers from South Texas would come through Iredell going to West Texas to pick cotton, if they had a flat there in town, they wouldn't stop and fix it. They'd run on the flat till they got out of town. . . . [N]o nigger would stop in Iredell." When asked why blacks avoided the town, he explained that they knew blacks weren't welcome in Iredell even to buy "gasoline or anything else." Apparently this information had been shared among African Americans far and wide since even South Texas blacks knew they should avoid Iredell. Anderson added that the wealthiest man in town was reputed to have a black cook, "but nobody'd even see her."[6]

For every space where lines between the races stood out in bold relief, in dozens of other spaces, boundaries were less clearly drawn and were certainly not buttressed by the force of law. Country stores, rural roads, and cotton gins were generally not segregated. Young single men of both races might drink or gamble together at saloons, cockfights, and card games. At mutual aid events such as threshing parties, white landowners and black hired hands often worked side by side while white farm wives and their black domestics prepared the workers' meal.[7]

6. Thordis Simonsen, ed., *You May Plow Here: The Narrative of Sara Brooks* (New York: W. W. Norton and Company, 1986), 63; Oliver Anderson, interviewed by Sharon Siske, June 28, 1992, Meridian, Texas, IOH, Baylor University.

7. McMillen, *Dark Journey*, chap. 6; Jeannie M. Whayne, *A New Plantation South: Land, Labor, and Federal Favor in Twentieth Century Arkansas*, 2; Johnson, *Growing Up in the Black Belt*, 280.

Where the races mingled, a highly articulated racial etiquette governed personal interactions. Historian Neil McMillen argues that "the black Mississippians' 'place,' as whites defined it, was always more behavioral than spatial in nature." Largely informal, the Jim Crow system was based on unwritten and flexible rules that varied from place to place. In locations where the two races came together, McMillen says, "the forces of social habit and white opinion were in themselves usually sufficient to ensure that the races knew their places and occupied them with neither a statute nor a 'white' or 'colored' sign to direct the way." McMillen goes on to explain that "Precisely because so much was left to custom, particularity seemed to be the only universal rule. Much as they agreed that the black place was a separate and subordinate place, whites . . . were not precisely of one mind about how to address the 'negro question.'" In fact, argues historian Grace Elizabeth Hale, because southern black inferiority could not be assumed, southern whites created a social order in which black inferiority would be constantly "performed."[8]

One way in which whites performed this script of racial inferiority was by withholding everyday courtesies from blacks, a practice well-documented by historians and often noted in personal accounts. In his landmark 1941 study of rural black youth in the South, sociologist Charles S. Johnson addressed the ways rituals of daily contact reinforced black inferiority. For example, blacks were always expected to address whites with the courtesy titles "Mr." and "Mrs." Sometimes African Americans were allowed to call white children by their first names, but by the time children reached adolescence, blacks called them "Mr." or "Miss." White Texan Cora Jones related her own experience with the black hired hand who drove her to school every day: "One day Andy said, Miss Cora. I looked at him and said, Don't call me Miss Cora. That's what everybody calls Aunt Cora. . . . And he said,

8. McMillen, *Dark Journey,* 10, 11, 23; Grace Elizabeth Hale, *Making Whiteness: The Culture of Segregation in the South, 1890–1940,* 284. For more on the informal and changing nature of most of the Jim Crow system, see Kirby, *Rural Worlds Lost,* 236; Frenise A. Logan, *The Negro in North Carolina, 1876–1894* (Chapel Hill: University of North Carolina Press, 1964), 174–75; Lisa Lindquist Dorr, "Black-on-White Rape and Retribution in Twentieth-Century Virginia: 'Men, Even Negroes, Must Have Some Protection,'" 746.

'Well, Miss Cora, you getting grown and I think I better say Miss Cora.' And I said, 'Andy I don't say Mr. Andy, and if you start calling me that, I'll have to call you Mr. Andy.' He said, 'No ma'am.' And so you see there that situation."[9]

As Andy's response suggested, whites rarely addressed blacks with any sort of courtesy titles because the use of such titles would have implied social equality. Hortense Powdermaker noted, "Just what the white person withholds in avoiding the use of these titles is suggested by those he is willing to employ." Even white children addressed blacks by their first names. Sometimes women were called "Aunty" and men "Uncle," forms of address that white people regarded as respectful. When whites were being less kind, they referred to black men as "boy." Whites sometimes addressed black professionals as "Doctor" or "Professor." Powdermaker observed, "The prohibition against courtesy titles extends to the telephone. If a Negro puts in a long-distance call for 'Mr. Smith' in a town fifty miles away, the operator, who can tell where the call comes from, will ask: 'Is he colored?' On being told that he is, she replies: 'Don't you say 'Mister' to me. He ain't 'Mister' to me.'"[10]

Not only did whites articulate black inferiority through naming rituals, but they also withheld other ordinary courtesies from rural blacks. Still the great variation in practice from place to place and person to person demonstrates the complexity of the practice. Southern men took great pride in their chivalrous behavior toward white women, but chivalry did not extend to black women. Powdermaker noted that white men thought nothing of sitting while black women stood, though they would have quickly offered their seats to white women. Sometimes blacks were required to yield town sidewalks to whites or to doff their hats to whites in public spaces, but this courtesy was rarely

9. McMillen, *Dark Journey*, 24–25; Johnson, *Growing Up in the Black Belt*, 277–80; Cora Lee McCall Jones, interviewed by Doni Van Ryswyk, on nine occasions from January 25, 1988, to May 4, 1988, Waco, Texas, Texas Collection, Baylor University, Waco (hereafter TC, Baylor University).

10. McMillen, *Dark Journey*, 24–25; Ruth Rhodes Culpepper, interviewed by Caroline Baum and Kitty Wiggins, June 24, 1980, Waynesboro Oral Histories, Accession 35470, Personal Papers Collection, Library of Virginia, Richmond (hereafter LOV, Richmond); Johnson, *Growing Up in the Black Belt*, 277–80; Powdermaker, *After Freedom*, 44–46.

returned. In general whites did not shake hands with blacks, but sociologist Charles Johnson found exceptions to this rule in some southern communities. In stores and other public places, blacks usually had to wait for white customers to be served first, even if the whites arrived after the blacks. Texan Grover Williams described this process: "You had to wait until they got through. Then he'd [the clerk] say, 'Now what else do you want, Grover?' Then you'd tell him, and if he was waiting on you, then somebody else come, he might stop then, in midways of that process, and wait on them." Often white clerks kept blacks waiting even when there were no whites waiting for service. One upper-class black person complained to Powdermaker that whites never responded politely to a black person's "thank you." Instead whites would make no reply at all or would grunt "all right."[11]

Whites did not receive blacks as guests in their homes. For example, Texan Fred Tucker noted, "In this area, when you worked for the white folk, you'd have to go out, sit in the yard, wait until they came out. . . . You're not good [enough to go in their homes]—at that time." Blacks often bitterly recalled being forced to go to the back doors of white homes, but like most other aspects of racial etiquette, this practice was flexible. Alabama sharecropper Ned Cobb noted, "It's been the custom and the habit in this country for niggers to go around to the back door of white folks' houses. Some colored folks would go in, where they was workmens for the whites, workin there all the time, they'd go in the front door. But not just *any* Negro." While Cobb attributed flexibility to familiarity between particular whites and blacks, Powdermaker associated it with whites' security with their own class status. She gave an example of two middle-class women, one descended from the "best people" in town and another who had only recently attained middle-class status. Powdermaker said:

> The son of the second woman happened to see the first woman's cook leave the house by the front door. "Do you allow your cook to go out that way?" he asked in surprise. His hostess replied that it didn't make any difference to her which door her cook used. The boy exclaimed that his mother would never allow anything like that; one day when their

11. Powdermaker, *After Freedom*, 49–50, 346; Johnson, *Growing Up in the Black Belt*, 277–80; Williams, Sr., interview.

cook did try to go out the wrong way, his mother picked up a piece of wood from the fireplace and threw it at her.[12]

Blacks and whites rarely mingled socially. Like extending ordinary courtesies, visiting and social interaction would have implied equality. White Texan Cora Jones insisted that there was no social contact between the races. White Alabaman Sarah Cazalas concurred. When an interviewer asked if blacks and whites attended the same churches, she exclaimed, "Oh no! Well . . . it seemed like I might have seen one or two [blacks] in the country churches. They'd go and sit on the back row." Other whites described occasional visits to black churches to attend revival meetings. Texan Martha Emmons noted that her family occasionally went to church with one of their black domestics, and she described an incident in which white boys from the community disrupted the service for fun.[13]

In general, blacks and whites also did not eat together, but here, too, there was some flexibility in daily practice. Children of both races played together when young and often ate together. White Tennessean Lucille Thornburgh recalled that during her girlhood, "If we happened to be in a black family's home at lunch time, we ate with them. And if the black kids were over playing with us, they ate with us." Black Texan Maggie Washington recalled, "When I lived out in the country, the people that we leased from would come by on holidays and sit down and eat with us." Powdermaker noted exceptions to the prohibition against adults of both races eating together. For example, "if a white man and a colored man went fishing, they might grill their fish over an open fire and eat together, in the open." Nonetheless, black and white adults socializing over meals appears to have been rare, particularly if white women were present.[14]

---

12. McMillen, *Dark Journey,* 24; Johnson, *Growing Up in the Black Belt,* 277–80; Fred Douglas Tucker, interviewed by Jay M. Butler, August 26, 1993, Waco, Texas, IOH, Baylor University; Rosengarten, *All God's Dangers;* Powdermaker, *After Freedom,* 48.

13. Cora Jones interview; Sarah Louise Reynolds Cazalas, interviewed by Glenn R. Adwell, February 25, 1984, Birmingham, Ala., American Folklore and Oral History Collection, Auburn University (hereafter AFOHC, Auburn); Martha Emmons, interviewed by Rebecca S. Jimenez, on three occasions from August 29 to September 19, 1985, Waco, Texas, TC, Baylor University.

14. McMillen, *Dark Journey,* 24; Lucille Thornburgh, interviewed by June

Even the practice of sharing water jugs in the fields varied from place to place. Historian Jeannie Whayne noted that on Arkansas Delta cotton plantations, separate drinking buckets or cups were provided for black and white workers. White Texan Avery Downing vividly recalled "picking cotton by the side of this black man," a tenant on his father's farm. Downing explained that "At the end of the row, there would be a jug of water and he'd drink first and I'd drink second right out of that jug of water, you know, and that—that was not a problem at all. But if we had gone to town, and in a public situation, I wouldn't have—I wouldn't be allowed to sit next to him or drink with him or eat under any circumstances." As Downing's experience suggests, in the countryside, racial boundaries were more flexible in "private" settings such as farms than in "public situations" where a white person's status might have been compromised or where his commitment to the Jim Crow system might have been called into question if he tolerated excessive familiarity between the races.[15]

Rural whites thought of blacks as, in the words of a white Texas woman, "a serving race"; as a result, they thought nothing of demanding that blacks they did not know perform menial tasks for them. For example, black Texan Grover Williams told an interviewer how white men handled flat tires. He explained, "You didn't go up to the filling station and say, 'Oh, I got a flat down here and I'd like for your man to—' You saw me standing on the corner. You say, 'Come here boy. Look in that trunk there and fix that tire.' Well, that's the way it was. You jacked it up, took the tire off and put it [on]—you're thinking he might give you a quarter, he might give you a dime." As a child, Williams was often ordered by the owner of a local café to burn trash while the mother of a white playmate frequently demanded that he pick up her son's

---

Rostan, April 30, 1978, *Twentieth Century Trade Union Women: Vehicle for Social Change* Oral History Project, Institute of Labor and Industrial Relations, Michigan State University and Wayne State University; Maggie Lanham Washington, interviewed by Doni Von Ryswyk on three occasions from March 10, 1988, to May 19, 1988, Waco, Texas, TC, Baylor University; Powdermaker, *After Freedom,* 47.

15. Whayne, *A New Plantation South,* 196; Avery R. Downing, interviewed by James M. Sorelle and Thomas L. Charlton, August 23, 25, 1983, Waco, Texas, TC, Baylor University.

toys. Williams's childhood experiences socialized him to do the bidding of whites whether or not he knew them or worked for them.[16]

White Texan Etta Carroll described this expectation of black help from the white point of view. She described her family's expectations for their sharecroppers: "If you got a good colored family, that's what we always called them, and could depend on them, a lot of times, they'd go help you do things and they wouldn't charge you for them. A lot of times we'd give them milk or we'd give them butter because they were good to us." Thus southern whites often rationalized their expectations of black subservience as part of a larger paternalistic system of reciprocal obligations. White South Carolinian Carrie Jerome Anderson confirmed Powdermaker's analysis. She told an interviewer that her family's black servants often hid firewood, food, or other property under the Jerome family's laundry when delivering it to the laundress. She said, "They didn't consider that [stealing]. They was just dividing things up a little bit." Anderson's statement indicates that whites were well aware of theft by their domestic help, but her words are revealing of something else. In rural parlance, "dividing things up" referred to sharing goods equitably. Thus, Anderson seems to be admitting the inequities in the racial and economic hierarchy of her family's household.[17]

In fact, in the years after the end of Reconstruction, southern whites developed an elaborate ideology of paternalism to justify the development of a segregated society. In general, paternalism held that whites, as the superior race, had an obligation to teach inferior and incompetent blacks how to get along in the world and be good citizens. In return, blacks had an obligation to work hard, to obey whites, and to show them appropriate deference and loyalty. In the eyes of most whites, the Jim Crow system actually protected the best interests of blacks.[18]

16. Martha Emmons, interview; Grover Williams, interview.

17. Donnie Lee and Etta Lillian Hardy Carroll, interviewed by Rebecca Sharpless, on seven occasions from September 21, 1990, to July 11, 1991, Waxahachie, Texas, IOH, Baylor University; Carrie Jerome Anderson, interviewed by Mary Long, June 9, 1977, Rock Hill, S.C., Extension Homemakers Oral History Project, Dacus Archives, Winthrop University, Rock Hill, S.C.

18. Guion Griffis Johnson, "Southern Paternalism toward Negroes after Eman-

Still, genuine mutual aid between blacks and whites did exist. Historian Jack Temple Kirby noted that "Blacks' recollections of integrated rural life in the South are mixed with memories of helpful friendship and bitterness at the limits imposed by the region's racial rules." He quotes a Florida woman who recalled her father and their white neighbor. "They farmed together and was right around together for fifteen or more years. . . . Papa would help him, he would help Papa. Course you couldn't go in they home and sit down, but then some [whites] were better than others." Tennessean Edna Spencer recalled that just as black women often nursed sick whites in the neighborhood, sometimes white women nursed sick black women. "Outsiders would have some difficulty with this. It's best understood when you realize that there were some good people in that Valley, and they came in more than one color." Nonetheless, it would be a mistake to accept these examples of mutual aid as egalitarian sentiment on the part of whites. As the Florida woman's statement suggests, cordial mutual exchanges were based on blacks' remembering their inferior position, on their not attempting to "go in they home and sit down." For whites, engaging in mutual aid with blacks was both a way of cementing loyalty from particular blacks and a means of acting out a magnanimous and superior paternalism.[19]

The notion that some whites were "better than others" was widely shared among rural African Americans. For many blacks, "better" whites were those of higher socioeconomic status. Sociologist Charles S. Johnson lamented that

> although the Negro sharecropper and domestic are employed and often exploited by well-to-do whites, personal relations tend to obscure this fact in the thinking of the Negro group. White employers are frequently generous and kindly in dispensing small personal favors. This generosity does not often extend to the point of adequate wages because it is believed this would upset both the wage scale and the Negro scale of living. The Negro worker senses vaguely that he is being victimized but he does not direct his resentment against the "good white folks."

---

cipation," in Charles E. Wynes, ed., *The Negro in the South since 1865: Selected Essays in American Negro History* (University: University of Alabama Press, 1965), 103–34.

19. Kirby, *Rural Worlds Lost*, 244; Edna P. Spencer, "What Color Is the Wind?" (master's thesis, Clark University, 1985); Edna Spencer, interview with author, January 26, 1995.

Johnson is too quick to dismiss the ability of rural blacks to clearly see their exploitation. Indeed, blacks understood their exploitation at the hands of white elites, and they often resented it. Still, they understood the consequences of open rebellion against the system, and they preferred kind exploitation to the harsh treatment they sometimes received at the hands of poor whites. One man from Mississippi told Johnson, "Now the poor white folks is them that ain't got nothing, but thinks they is somebody. They like to pick on Negroes. They cheat them, 'buse them and meddle with them. An aristocratic white person is more decent about it. 'Course they cheat Negroes too, but they's nice about the way they do it."[20]

As these examples suggest, even "good" whites liked to ensure that blacks stayed in their "place." Whites resented few things so much as signs of material success among blacks, the ultimate symbol that African Americans aspired to attaining white status. Blacks who wore dress clothes on weekdays might be subject to harsh comments or even violence. Ned Cobb recalled a verbal confrontation with a white man who implied that because Cobb had purchased a late-model Chevrolet he would not be able to pay his bills. On another occasion, some whites visited Cobb's farm just after the family had killed three hogs. The meat was spread around the barnyard, waiting to be preserved. Cobb said, "They looked hard, didn't stop lookin. After a while they crept on out of there, still stretchin their eyes at that meat. They didn't like to see a nigger with too much; they didn't like it one bit and it caused them to throw a slang word about a 'nigger' havin all this, that and the other. I didn't make no noise about it. I didn't like that word, but then that word didn't hurt me; it was some action had to be taken to hurt me. I just rested quiet and went on preparin that meat."[21]

Blacks understood very well that these daily indignities were designed to reinforce a racial hierarchy. A Macon County, Alabama, man told Johnson, "White folks are all right long as a man stays in his place. Down here in the South a Negro ain't much better off than he was in slavery time. We work all the time but we don't get nothin' for it 'cept

20. Johnson, *Growing Up in the Black Belt*, 283.
21. McMillen, *Dark Journey*, 24; Rosengarten, *All God's Dangers*, 192, 287.

a place to live and plenty to eat. I ain't got nothin' 'gainst white people, but they won't give Negroes a chance. We all equal and ought to have an equal chance, but we can't get it here." The man's daughter added, "I don't like white people. I don't know why. There ain't no reason 'cept they think they are better than colored and try to keep the colored people down. Maybe all white people ain't alike, but I don't like none of them."[22]

Blacks also understood that whites often played a game of "divide and conquer" to undermine black solidarity and collective efforts at resistance. Ned Cobb put it this way: "If they could get niggers scattered and apart, they'd enjoy the results of that. Let niggers keep up a uproar between em and then, if one of em was a good nigger, obedient and do what the white man wanted done, they'd help him out or stand up for him. Oh, it was a mess. White man rejoicin if he could get the niggers tied up against one another. And old fools, they'd do it, too."[23]

Even the blacks that Johnson called "upper class" found themselves restricted by the Jim Crow system. One black youth from a family of considerable status in the African American community put it this way: "Here it is not like it is up North where you just say 'yes' and 'no.' You talk to white people up there just like you do to colored. . . . If you don't just play ignorant and humble to white people [here] they want to string you up for the buzzards."[24]

The racial hierarchy was designed as much to maintain the economic dominance of white landowners as to buttress white supremacy, a fact that was not lost on rural African Americans. Sara Brooks recalled the relationships between sharecroppers, landlords, and furnishing merchants: "At the end of the year when you harvest your crop, they [landlords and merchants] get theirs first, and if there's any money left, you get it, and if there isn't, you just bill it up for the next year where you done took things up at the store. I'll tell you, at that time, the black people, they didn't have nothin, and they couldn't get much, and if they got a little somethin, sometime it was taken from you." Texan Eugene Webster echoed Brooks's analysis: "Sharecrop—that was

22. Johnson, *Growing Up on the Black Belt*, 314.
23. Rosengarten, *All God's Dangers*, 469.
24. Johnson, *Growing Up on the Black Belt*, 84–85.

the white man furnish everything and you get—you do the work and get half the crop. That's the way they said it was done, but they were taking half of it. . . . They were taking it all away. Black man didn't have a chance." Ned Cobb recalled that "The white folks in this country were goin in that direction anyways—nigger couldn't have any of their money. . . . Afraid a nigger might do somethin if he got the money in his own hands, do as he please; might hold on to it if he wanted to hold it, might spend it accordin to his pleasure. The white people was afraid—I'll say this: they was afraid the money would make the nigger act too much like his own man." Historian Jack Temple Kirby has said that most blacks felt bitter about the "order of economic relationships which demonstrate their recognition of race and class as one." He quotes an Arkansas sharecropper who told a white Federal Writer's Project interviewer: "De landlord is landlord [i.e., white], de politicians is landlord, de judge is landlord, de shurf [sheriff] is landlord, ever' body is landlord, and we ain't got nothin'."[25]

White oppression was also designed to control access to a cheap and plentiful labor supply. Lonnie Graves described how, in the late 1920s, a new principal at the black school in Satin, Texas, was able to extend the school term at the black school from six to seven months in spite of some opposition from local whites. (The white school term was nine months.) The next year, however, the principal's contract was not renewed, and the school term reverted to six months. Graves explained, "There was a reason for this, and I thought—because at the time . . . the farm owners wanted the kids to stay out and harvest crops. . . . They wanted to get [us] out of school and go to the field and chop cotton and corn and all this kind of stuff. And this [extending the school year] prolonged the school and it kept the kids out of—off the farm, and they wanted them working. . . . So they [whites] were not just bubbling over about the situation."[26]

In fact, blacks resented economic oppression far more than formal segregation. Neil McMillen noted that many blacks preferred segrega-

25. Simonsen, ed., *You May Plow Here,* 105; Eugene Webster, interviewed by Jay M. Tucker, July 8, 1993, Downsville, Texas, IOH, Baylor University; Rosengarten, *All God's Dangers,* 265; Kirby, *Rural Worlds Lost,* 239.

26. Lonnie Graves, interviewed by Anne Radford Phillips, October 10, 1991, Satin, Texas, IOH, Baylor University.

tion of schools and their own social and religious organizations as "a matter of pride and preference." Controlling their own institutional life provided blacks with more autonomy. Their complaints about segregation generally centered on the inferiority of facilities reserved for blacks rather than the separateness of those facilities.[27]

Blacks learned how to cope with a system that varied from place to place and was based on unwritten and flexible rules. Local blacks taught newcomers how to behave in a given community. Young people learned from their parents, from keen observation, and from personal experience how to behave around whites. A Johnston County, North Carolina, black schoolgirl explained to Johnson, "Papa told me how to get along with white people. He say 'Don't raise your voice but talk quiet like. Don't talk too much. Let them talk. Let them have their way.' If I wanted to do my way they might get angry and start trouble. I don't be around any of them any more than I can help. None except this family up here [white neighbors]. They acts just like colored folks, you can't tell the difference." Ned Cobb also learned about getting along with whites from his father:

> I . . . learnt to obey the white man. I aint quit that yet in some ways. My daddy told me, many a time, to obey the white man, do what he tell you to do and avoid trouble; and also, even my daddy's ways and actions told me that. My daddy stood back off of white folks considerably. . . . But it was just a matter he thought he had to go thataway; he was born and raised in slavery habits. He shunned white people, never did give a white man no trouble, not in my history. He'd make out like sometimes he told em this, that, and the other and he done this, that, and the other, but I never did see him do it.

A young man in Madison County, Alabama, told Charles Johnson: "Ain't nobody tell me how to act around them [white people]. I just knowed how to tend to my business and let them tend to theirs. I knowed if I didn't, there'd be trouble. I was scared of white folks when I was small. I thought they had the rule. . . . I can't remember nobody telling me that."[28]

27. McMillen, *Dark Journey*, 290; Johnson, *Growing Up in the Black Belt*, 14.
28. McMillen, *Dark Journey*, 11–12; Johnson, *Growing Up in the Black Belt*, 311, 319, 320; Rosengarten, *All God's Dangers*, 48.

Blacks who challenged the racial system might be subject to violence, and the threat of racial violence deterred open resistance. Neil McMillen has called violence "the instrument in reserve," and Johnson noted that lynching in particular had profound psychological consequences for young blacks. As white Texan Martha Emmons put it, "I don't remember an out-and-out lynching any time in Mansfield, but oh, they all always had that idea that it could be done all right." Guy Miller of Shelby County, Tennessee, told Johnson, "I like white folks all right, but I just don't want to have no trouble with them. Oh, if I did get in trouble with 'em I wouldn't do nothing. I couldn't do nothing. They'd kill me. White folks don't play with no colored folks. You have to do what they want or else your life ain't worth nothing."[29]

Whites occasionally recalled incidents of racial violence and injustice in the rural Jim Crow South. Texan Cora Jones recalled that when her grandfather was sheriff of Robertson County, he presided over the execution of a black man convicted of raping a white woman. Jones admitted that the black man "didn't have a Chinaman's chance to start with, but it may have been true. It [the rape] did happen." Texan Wilson Rutherford remembered seeing blacks bodily thrown from trains when he was a child. Incidents like these reminded African Americans of the consequences of challenging the Jim Crow system.[30]

Blacks may have acknowledged the constant threat of racial violence, but those who came of age early in the century rarely admitted witnessing such violence. In many cases, their parents sheltered them from the worst instances. Often they described incidents they heard about rather than confrontations they had seen. Alice Caulfield recalled hearing adults in her family discuss the lynching of Jesse Washington in Texas. Fred Tucker recalled hearing about an incident in which a white landowner near Waco, Texas, chased a black man through a churchyard and "they beat him up. I think they ran him over and broke his leg, or something like that." Grover Williams witnessed the beating of a young black man by some white boys after a confrontation in town one day.[31]

29. McMillen, *Dark Journey*, 30; Whayne, *A New Plantation South*, 56–57; Johnson, *Growing Up in the Black Belt*, 299, 317–18; Martha Emmons, interview.

30. Cora Jones, interview.

31. Alice Owens Caulfield, interviewed by Rebecca Sharpless on eight occa-

Rural African Americans coped with the oppressive racial climate in a variety of ways. Most often blacks complied with white rules, at least on the surface, and some seemed to accept the system. When asked if there was much tension between blacks and whites in Satin, Texas, Lonnie Graves replied, "Not really. I might say this and . . . trying to be honest—there might could have been, but at that time the black people accepted their situation. They were not satisfied. But they were not antagonistic about it. . . . They were, shall I say, scrupulous." Charles Johnson described this as a form of outer conformity that masked inner discontent. As Johnson put it, "What constitutes the race problem is not the fixed character of the relations, but their dynamic character. There would be no race problem if the Negro group uniformly accepted the status assumed for it."[32]

Instead of open resistance, most blacks turned to time-tested strategies of individual and subtle resistance. They might work slowly, commit vandalism or arson, play dumb, steal, and dissemble. Hortense Powdermaker described this form of resistance and noted that it reinforced patriarchal notions about race relations:

Whites simply assume that their yard boys will lie and their cooks take food home with them, and that neither is cause for discharging a servant. Instead, the mistress will talk indulgently or regretfully about how they always steal and never tell the truth. Such evidence is regarded as proof that the Negro is unstable, incompetent to fend for himself, and actually better off under white domination. The constant opportunity to be indulgent reaffirms the belief that the white person is not only right, but also kind and good. Such assurance is valuable in the circumstances, and is added to the satisfaction derived from the feeling of moral and social superiority.

All this helps to make the White feel that whatever he grants to the Negro is a gift rather than a right.[33]

sions between January 20 and April 21, 1993, Waco, Texas, IOH, Baylor University; Tucker, interview; Williams, Sr., interview.

32. McMillen, *Dark Journey*, 137; Graves, interview; Johnson, *Growing Up in the Black Belt*, 276, 296.

33. Robin D. G. Kelley, *Race Rebels: Culture, Politics, and the Black Working Class* (New York: Free Press, 1994), 37; McMillen, *Dark Journey*, 137–38; Johnson, *Growing Up in the Black Belt*, 297; Powdermaker, *After Freedom*, 39.

Other blacks resisted the system by working as hard as they could, hoping to succeed on white terms in a white world. Ned Cobb said, "Well, I was a Negro of this type: regardless to what people said, regardless to how much I knowed that they was a enemy to me, I just pulled myself along anyhow to the best of my abilities and knowledge. Didn't hold myself back like they wanted me to." Harvey Goodson, a black farm owner of Greene County, Georgia, explained a similar philosophy to Johnson: "Go on getting what you can slow and be quiet about it." Texas African American Lonnie Graves said:

> There was prejudice in the community on both sides. . . . We were second class citizens in many ways. But as I said, there were black people— there were a group of black people in this community, and as I'm sure in other communities as well, who had a lot of pride, who worked hard, who earned their living, who made their land pay off. And they could spend their money for what they wanted. . . . They bought new cars, just like the white people did. . . . Sent the kids off to finish school in Marlin and Waco or Austin or wherever they could send them to stay with relatives and finish high school and go on to college. And they did this in spite of, you know, the hard things, the disadvantages that they had to live with. . . . Some of these people made great people out of themselves and out of the community.[34]

Hard work and striving for success could not protect blacks from white hostility. For this, some blacks sought out the protection and patronage of powerful whites to survive the Jim Crow world. Whites as well as blacks acknowledged this fact. For example, when asked about race relations in the village of Hammond, white Texan Cora Jones said, "The blacks have always had their protectors. Always there's been one or two [whites] that would speak up, and I think that kept it pretty well on an even keel." Blacks, too, recalled that powerful whites had intervened on behalf of blacks who had conflicts with whites in the community. African American Joe C. Trotter, when asked about the presence of racial tensions in Satin, Texas, explained that "there was a bunch of young white boys, . . . and they'd meddle with the colored boys right smart. But they finally, this one man . . . he got on the colored side and told those white boys they going to keep a messing with these black

34. Rosengarten, *All God's Dangers*, 193; Johnson, *Growing Up in the Black Belt*, 91; Graves, interview.

boys until they got hurt." Lonnie Graves concurred. He explained that "things that didn't go just right, they [black people] had a way of going to certain people, you know, white people in the community, and say, 'Look, this is not right, and this happened and that happened, and we feel like that it would be in all of our interest if this could be corrected.' And for that cause we were able to avoid any high tension."[35]

Sometimes whites provided other types of help to blacks they liked. Lonnie Graves described how a white landowner named Mr. Duty helped Graves's father buy a one-hundred-acre farm shortly after emancipation, and his comments reflect Edna Spencer's statement about white women who nursed sick blacks in her childhood community. Graves noted, "People have to understand that there's always been good white people. . . . It's not so that all black people are alike and it's not true that all white people are alike." Mr. Duty apparently fit into the category of good white people.[36]

Not all African Americans trusted whites enough to seek benefactors. Instead, some blacks tried to avoid whites. One black youth told Johnson, "Yes, them white folks is mighty nice, but I stays as far away from 'em as I can. I treats 'em nice when I comes in contact with 'em, but I don't have much to say. I don't never forget they's white. . . . I don't like 'em [whites] and I don't hate 'em. I just stays out of their way."[37]

Many blacks made decisions about what type of treatment they would accept from whites even as they tried to hide their resentment. Powdermaker related several stories of resistance on these terms. For example, "A woman of high position among the Negroes says that everyone calls her Rose and she doesn't mind that, or at least she's used to it. But when a saleswoman called her 'girl,' she turned around and walked out of the store." Another woman shopped for silk stockings in a store where Negroes were usually well treated. "The clerk, who was new, asked, 'Anything else, Aunty?'" Powdermaker recounted. "'No,' answered the customer, 'and I don't want those stockings either.' On her way out, she was stopped by a floorwalker who happened to know

---

35. Jones, interview. See also Joe C. Trotter, interviewed by Jay M. Butler, June 30, 1993, Satin, Texas, IOH, Baylor University; Graves, interview.

36. Graves, interview.

37. Johnson, *Growing Up in the Black Belt*, 295.

her and came up to ask what was wrong. When she explained, he apologized for the clerk, who was 'green' and didn't know any better." Similarly, black Texan Alice Caulfield noted she did not patronize white businesses that did not serve blacks equally: "I never was going to accept anything from the back door. . . . We were taught you didn't do that. If you can't be served at the front, don't be served."[38]

Hortense Powdermaker noted that blacks valued the use of courtesy titles and insisted on using them among themselves:

> A colored woman of the upper class, after a successful performance which she had arranged was called upon to introduce some Negro singers to an audience that was largely white. She found herself in a serious dilemma. Knowing the white attitude all too well, she nevertheless felt that she could not betray her own people, and therefore used the titles Mrs., Mr., Miss, in introducing them. Nothing was said, but the warm enthusiasm evoked by the entertainment immediately gave way to a perceptible chill. Very few Whites came up afterwards to say how good it was.[39]

As this story indicates, blacks developed a strong sense of intraracial solidarity. Ned Cobb noted that whites often pumped him for information about other blacks. Sometimes a "white man come up to me and ask me, 'What about So-and-so over yonder? What did he do? What did he say? What did he come over here for?' And all like that. I learnt years ago to keep my tongue still." A youth told Charles Johnson, "If colored folks do good or if they do bad, I'm always with 'em 'cause they's my race."[40]

Whites found organized resistance to the Jim Crow system and community efforts to gain greater autonomy suspicious. As Neil McMillen put it, "The specter of unified black action, particularly that of field hands, aroused the most intense white anxieties, evoking ancient fantasies of Negro 'risings,' threatening white social and economic control, provoking unreasoning white violence." Nonetheless, blacks worked together to resist racial oppression. For example, black teachers and school principals tirelessly worked to improve education

38. Powdermaker, *After Freedom*, 344; Caulfield, interview.
39. Powdermaker, *After Freedom*, 343.
40. Rosengarten, *All God's Dangers*, 48.

and often enlisted the help of the black community as well as white officials. Texan Lonnie Graves related several memories about collective efforts to improve black schools. In the 1920s, when the black school in Satin became overcrowded and in need of expansion and upgrading, "The black community got together and said, 'Well, we'll just raise enough money to build a room on the school.' And this they did. . . . They raised the money and hired a carpenter and built the third room on the school. . . . Those children who had come back to school again were able to go to a nice room with a lot of windows—had a lot of sunlight and so forth. . . . It was done by the black citizens." A later school principal, Mrs. Heard, tried to get the whites to build a new black school during the depression. The school board insisted that it did not have the money. So Mrs. Heard appealed to the Rosenwald Fund for funds. Rosenwald Fund workers cooperated with local Works Progress Administration officials to begin construction of a new school. Graves noted:

> In 1939, the building got started, but for whatever reason, it turned out that the white people got the new school. . . . And the black people . . . took three rooms in what were the existing white school and moved them over there in the black settlement of town. So they gave us three rooms and they built a real nice roomy school [for whites]—restrooms, dining room, kitchen, nice classrooms, principal's office, and all these things, and put in gas and all that. . . . A large playground, swings and things like that. The school they gave us—they put it on one lot. . . .
> It was a great improvement over what we had. But it wasn't what we wanted. And by that time, old Mrs. Heard . . . had succeeded in getting a tenth grade year. . . . When all this came about, they did not renew her contract.[41]

During the Great Depression, black and white sharecroppers made some abortive attempts at interracial unionization. Jack Temple Kirby has noted that these unions undermined the old racial system, building fragile, but real, cross-racial alliances and promoting "a culture of assertiveness among the poor." The Share Croppers' Union (SCU) had limited success in Alabama, and the Southern Tenant Farmers' Union made some strides in Arkansas and Mississippi, but their efforts col-

---

41. McMillen, *Dark Journey,* 134; Graves, interview.

lapsed in the face of white opposition and violence. Blacks who joined these groups often faced harsh repression. Ned Cobb, for example, was involved in a shoot-out with the local sheriff's department when the SCU tried to stop foreclosure on a black man's farm, and he served many years in prison for the offense.[42]

When all other coping mechanisms failed, many blacks simply left the countryside for southern cities or even for the North. Black out-migration was small prior to World War I, but it was one of the only effective avenues of protest available to blacks, and many took it. Before the First World War, many black migrants remained in the state, but moved to cities where job opportunities were better and the ability to insulate oneself from contact with whites was greater. Texan Louie Mayberry recalled an incident in his community in which a white boy initiated an argument with a black boy who knocked him to the ground in retaliation. Later the Mayberrys saw the white boy and his father pass by on the road with the black boy with them. "I never did see them strike him, but they was taking him in [to jail]. And Mama was looking out the window, and she . . . said, 'They'll never do this child [Louie] like that.' And she made up her mind at that time she was leaving there." The family picked cotton that season to raise their train fare and then moved to San Antonio. Apparently, many black families used the Mayberrys' strategy. Between 1890 and 1910, for example, Mississippi's urban black population tripled, and it nearly doubled again between 1920 and 1940. After World War I, greater job opportunities, better information about northern life, and improved transportation made it easier for blacks to leave the South entirely. Between 1910 and 1960, 938,000 blacks left Mississippi alone.[43]

Many rural African American youth believed the North would be a more hospitable oasis from racial oppression than southern cities. One young black man in Mississippi told sociologist Charles S. Johnson

---

42. McMillen, *Dark Journey*, 135; Kirby, *Rural Worlds Lost*, 259–71.

43. McMillen, *Dark Journey*, 261–70; Johnson, *Growing Up in the Black Belt*, 299; Kelley, *Race Rebels*, 37; Louie Edward Mayberry, interviewed by Rebecca Sharpless, March 19, 1987, Goliad, Texas, IOH, Baylor University. Nan Elizabeth Woodruff points out that migration was a political movement in which African Americans claimed both political and economic rights. See Woodruff, "African-American Struggles," 33–51.

that he'd like to go to Detroit. He had heard relatives describe it as a place where "You wouldn't have to work like you do here, and you have more freedom there. You don't have to be cowed like you do here." Johnson lamented that "migration to other areas brings only a partial solution."[44]

Other blacks preferred to remain on the land. Ned Cobb, for instance, was a farmer at heart and did not want to leave the land. He explained that in the 1920s

> A heap of families . . . was leavin goin north. Some of my neighbors even picked up and left. The boll weevil was sendin a lot of em out, no doubt. . . . They was dissatisfied with the way of life here in the south. . . . But my family was prosperin right here, I didn't pay no attention to leavin. I wanted to stay and work for better conditions. . . . I thought somehow, some way, I'd overcome it. I was a farmin man at that time and I knowed more about this country than I knowed about the northern states. I've always been man enough to stick up for my family, and love them, and try to support em, and I just thought definitely I could keep it up. In other words, I was determined to try.[45]

Southern race relations were not static. Jack Temple Kirby traces the collapse of the racial system in the South to the middle decades of the twentieth century. Massive out-migration by blacks, the leveling tendencies of the automobile, the depression and New Deal programs, and the formation of radical (albeit not very successful) interracial farm worker unions all undermined the old hierarchies. As a result, race relations often grew worse before they grew better. He noted that "as the region—along with the ranks of the poorest farmers—grew whiter, traditionally 'black' status was assumed by whites, rendering the last two decades or so of the old tenure system fraught with tension and confusion."[46]

Ned Cobb summarized rural Southern race relations this way:

> I didn't like conditions but what could I do? I had no voice, had no political pull whatever. . . . I had business with many a white man and I come out of the little end of the horn with too many of em. . . . I've gotten along in this world by studyin the races and knowin that I was one of the

44. Johnson, *Growing Up in the Black Belt*, 53, 299.
45. Rosengarten, *All God's Dangers*, 295–96.
46. Kirby, *Rural Worlds Lost*, 237–59.

underdogs. I was under many rulins, just like the other Negro, that I knowed was injurious to man and displeasin to God and still I had to fall back. I got tired of it but no help did I know; weren't nobody to back me up. I've taken every kind of insult and went on. In my years past, I'd accommodate anybody; but I didn't believe in this way of bowin to my knees and doin what *any* white man said do. Still, I always knowed to give the white man his time of day or else he's ready to knock me in the head. I just aint goin to go nobody's way against my own self. First thing of all—I care for myself and respect myself. . . . I've played dumb—maybe a heap of time I knowed just how come they done such-and-such a trick, but I wouldn't say. And I could go to em a heap of times for a favor and get it. . . . They'd have dealins with you, furnish you whatever you needed to make a crop, but you had to come under their rules. They'd give you a good name if you was obedient to em, acted nice when you met em and didn't question em bout what they said they had against you. You begin to cry about your rights and the mistreatin of you and they'd murder you. When I jumped up and fought the laws, that ruint me with the white people in this country.[47]

For historians, a number of questions regarding rural race relations remain. The first relates to the issue of class. As most of these stories suggest, class distinctions among whites played a powerful role in shaping individual whites' approaches to racial interaction, but no clear, consistent pattern emerges. Did economic competition create more tensions between poor whites and blacks, tensions that translated into a more oppressive racial climate when people at the bottom rung of the economic level came into contact? Certainly, Kirby's suggestions that race relations worsened as poor whites lost status would seem to indicate that poor whites had much at stake in maintaining the racial caste system. Many of these personal accounts seem to support this interpretation, indicating that blacks were more likely to have congenial relations with whites of a higher socioeconomic standing. For wealthier whites, the lines were always clear, while poor whites may have felt more need to perform their racial superiority. Nonetheless, congenial relations are often still exploitative relations, and other accounts suggest that at least some poor whites recognized the similarities between their own economic position and that of blacks. These stories stress re-

47. Rosengarten, *All God's Dangers*, 543, 544, 545.

lations based on mutual aid. By the time of the Great Depression, many rural blacks and whites acted collectively on their economic exploitation by forming those interracial unions. We will not achieve a clear understanding of rural race relations until we have a better picture of the way class dynamics shaped those interactions.

Another important question is how race relations in the countryside differed from those in the cities. Johnson found the most rigid racial boundaries in plantation counties where whites were economic competitors of blacks. In nonplantation areas, especially areas without a long tradition of racial hostilities and limited contact between blacks and whites, racial boundaries seemed to be less rigid. He noted that in his studies of urban areas, black youth expressed less hostility to whites than did those in rural areas. Johnson concludes that "rural plantation life is associated with unfavorable attitudes toward whites." He believed that this was due to two factors: the economic operation of the plantation, which left blacks feeling they had been treated unfairly, and the social distance between blacks and whites in the plantation areas. In other words, according to Johnson, rural blacks resented the economic oppression and social inferiority imposed on them in the rural areas more than blacks resented conditions in the cities. On the other hand, Johnson wrote, "Village youth have more personal contact with white people as playmates and as employers. Some of these contacts are pleasant and some are unpleasant. They serve, however, to disturb stereotyped concepts. To them some white people seem to be 'all right.'" He found more race consciousness and "race pride" among urban black youth than among rural black youth.

Oral accounts from rural blacks challenge Johnson's analysis, however. Some African Americans did feel more vulnerable to racial violence in the countryside, while others felt that their economic outlook would be brighter in the city, as evidenced by their departure from the land. Nonetheless, many rural blacks who later moved to the city found urban race relations were more oppressive. Black Alabaman Flossie Wood told an interviewer, "Here out in the country, people has always been nice to us. But back in town, you know, . . . they didn't want to live beside the blacks. . . . And our children, you know, growing up. . . . *All* [emphasis hers] the children played together . . . out here in the country." Her husband explained that this difference was because rural blacks lived and worked on whites' farms and had individual personal relationships. Texan Maggie Washington concurred, recalling that she had not felt much racial oppression until her family left their farm and moved into Waco. "So it was only after we moved to Waco, you know, that we knew—understood—except for train rides. Yes, when we lived in the country we had no real contact—we children did not." These accounts suggest that in the countryside, young people saw visible reminders of racial oppression, such as "colored" and "white" signs and rigidly segregated public facilities, less often. Instead, just as Johnson found in towns, rural blacks formed personal relationships with whites, some pleasant and some unpleasant. African Americans knew the hierarchy existed, and indeed their accounts testify that all were aware of the potential for racial violence, but perhaps the day-to-day reminders of black inferiority were less oppressive than in cities. Clearly, the differences between rural and urban race relations needs more study.[48]

Another unanswered question concerns the extent to which the disintegration of the old plantation system actually fueled the Civil Rights movement. In the early twentieth century, race and class were intertwined systems, but agricultural mechanization, federal agricultural policies, and better opportunities off the land reshaped southern agriculture and the southern labor market after the outbreak of World War II. If Jack Temple Kirby is right and race relations actually deteriorated as the countryside became whiter and poor whites lost status, did the resulting increase in racial tensions make rural blacks more willing to challenge the Jim Crow system? Scholars have noted the importance of young people in the Civil Rights movement. If Charles S. Johnson is right that race relations were worse in the countryside, were the young people involved in the movement rural people moved to town or children of rural people moved to town?[49]

48. Johnson, *Growing Up in the Black Belt*, 305, 307–9, 252; Flossie and Monroe Wood, interviewed by Pamela Grundy, May 28, 1987, Delta, Ala., Pamela Grundy Oral Histories, Auburn University; Washington, interview.

49. Although he does not analyze rural-urban dynamics, historian John Dittmer's account of the Civil Rights movement in Mississippi examines the way the movement unfolded differently in the countryside. He also discusses the role of youth in transforming and revitalizing the movement in the late 1950s. See *Local People: The Struggle for Civil Rights in Mississippi*.

The personal accounts of rural blacks also provide evidence of a generational difference in blacks' responses to the Jim Crow system that would have influenced both the timing and shape of the Civil Rights movement. For example, the father and daughter whom Johnson interviewed demonstrate this difference. The father noted that some whites were "all right" while his daughter asserted "I don't like none of them." Several accounts suggest that people who came of age in the 1930s were less accepting of white oppression than their parents and grandparents. We need to know more about the racial attitudes of rural African Americans who grew up during the depression in order to more completely understand the motivations of southern civil rights activists.

World War II, of course, was the watershed that changed everything in the South. Nonetheless, subtle changes in race relations had been underway throughout the 1920s and 1930s, and most of these changes occurred in the countryside where the majority of blacks and whites lived. We will achieve a fuller understanding of the dynamics of black resistance to segregation when we better understand early-twentieth-century rural race relations.

The author thanks Baylor University's Institute for Oral History for providing funding to make much of the research for this article possible. Special thanks belong to Rebecca Sharpless, Lois E. Myers, and Becky Shulda at the Institute for Oral History and to Ellen Brown at the Texas Collection at Baylor for all their assistance. She is particularly grateful to Converse colleague Corrie Norman who read an earlier version of this manuscript. Thanks are also due to Converse undergraduate intern Rebecca Crandall for tracking down citations and other information for this article.

African American Rural Culture, 1900–1950

VALERIE GRIM

Between 1900 and 1950, the social, political, and economic conditions of African Americans living in rural communities throughout the United States were atrocious. Housing, for the majority, was poor, wages were low, and educational opportunities were limited for rural black children. Many felt oppressed, exploited, and in serious need of relief. Opportunities for self-identity and expression of beliefs and values evolved, however, within rural enclaves throughout the South. African American rural culture was quite diverse and represented interactions across institutional, religious, social, racial, class, recreational, and gender lines. Culture, as defined here, includes any act, behavior, idea, value system, or activity that illustrates how blacks lived and celebrated life at work, school, church, home, and throughout the community. Landowners, tenants, renters, sharecroppers, day laborers, and simple rural nonfarming residents composed this rural population. Business people, teachers, and preachers provided leadership.[1]

The literature concerning the culture of rural African Americans is replete with negative interpretations. Much has been written about the life of poor black sharecroppers, or peasants, as they were commonly called. Studies such as *Preface to Peasantry* and *Shadow of the Plantation* examined the activities of blacks in twentieth-century plantation communities. Within these analyses, rural blacks were included as a sec-

---

1. Raper, *Preface to Peasantry,* 35–47. See also William Terry Couch, ed., *Culture in the South* (Chapel Hill: University of North Carolina Press, 1934), 711; Gilbert C. Fite, *Cotton Fields No More: Southern Agriculture 1865–1980;* Pete Daniel, *Breaking the Land: The Transformation of Cotton, Tobacco, and Rice Cultures since 1880;* Gilbert C. Fite, *American Farmers: The New Minority* (Bloomington: Indiana University, 1981); Powdermaker, *After Freedom;* Simonsen, ed., *You May Plow Here.*

ondary topic within the larger framework of southern history. This approach, however, has allowed many generalizations to prevail about the cultural and survival practices of this oppressed group.[2]

Carter G. Woodson stands out as the father of rural black history. He has published the only seminal work concerning this population, even though the text repeated many of the commonly held racial and cultural stereotypes of rural blacks held by whites. In *The Rural Negro* (1930), Woodson attempted to record this experience from a social, political, cultural, religious, and economic perspective. While his provocative work provided new insights, it failed in interpreting the viewpoints of rural African Americans regarding their cultural experiences.[3]

The Rural Negro, however, conceptualized a historical framework useful in understanding why this rural culture has been maligned. Woodson wrote that this "low culture" evolved from the conditions in which blacks lived: "These people have such difficulty in making a living and must spend so much of their time in this important effort at self-preservation that little or no time is left for organized or directed recreation. . . . Worn out by the end of the day, only the most robust have sufficient energy to spend a few hours of the night in seeking pleasure. . . . The time allotted for amusements among Negroes in the rural district to date does not differ much from what it was during the days of slavery. Work, then, is for the Negro peasants while pleasure is reserved for their employers."[4]

2. Glenn Clark, *The Man Who Talks with Flowers: The Intimate Life Story of Dr. George Washington Carver* (St. Paul: Macalester Park Publishing Group, 1939), 1–63. See also Wilma Dykeman and James Stokely, *Seeds of Southern Change: The Life of Will Alexander* (New York: W. W. Norton, 1976), 23–34; John Dollard, *Caste and Class in a Southern Town* (New York: Anchor Books, 1957); William Alexander Percy, *Lanterns on the Levee: Recollections of a Planter's Son.*

3. William Edward Garnett and John Malcus Ellison, "Negro Life in Rural Virginia, 1865–1934," Virginian Agricultural Experiment Station *Bulletin* no. 295 (June 1934): 59. See also Clarence Paul Edward Knuth, "Early Immigration and Current Residential Patterns of Negroes in Southwestern Michigan" (Ph.D. diss., University of Michigan, 1969), 181; W. E. B. Du Bois, *Darkwater: Voices from Within the Veil* (New York: Schocker Books, 1969).

4. Woodson, *The Rural Negro*, 82–83; Lance George E. Jones, *The Jeanes Teacher in the U.S., 1908–1933: An Account of Twenty-five Years Experience in the Supervision*

Scholars such as Gunnar Myrdal and T. J. Woofter supported Woodson's thesis. Their research documented the view that pleasure was not
meant for black peasants, and that wealthy white planters and landlords
supported black cultural inferiority to maintain control over their workers. Woodson, Woofter, and Myrdal claimed that early African American rural culture was a manifestation of what planters and the law permitted and also of what planters believed were the true and only ideas
blacks had. This was evident in the way the white rural elite described
blacks' behavior, values, and socialization when separated from whites
and any institution organized and managed by whites. Using the words
of white southerners, Woodson, Woofter, and others characterized
African American rural culture as vulgar and unexpressive. White
newspapers attacked blacks for taking time off from work to celebrate
holidays and indulge in pleasure, as though such activities were only for
the ruling class.[5]

These primarily southern newspapers were filled daily with exag-
gerated accounts of blacks' cultural and recreational activities. They described blacks as licentious, their behavior largely restricted to drinking
and sexual indulgence. According to the majority of pre-1970 rural accounts, especially by white writers, sexual indulgence was a popular
recreation, especially between blacks and whites. According to one
scholar, "The pleasure-seeking peasant finds such gratification under
the cover of the night, rejoices over the conquest, and returns in an exhausted condition to work on a few days longer until there comes the
impulse for another such thrill." This alleged behavior caused the cultural critics of that day to consider rural blacks immoral.[6]

Nearly all studies on southern rural life portrayed African Americans

of *Negro Rural Schools* (Chapel Hill: University of North Carolina Press, 1937),
125–46. See also A. B. Kennerly, "Prairie View: A Leader in Negro Education,"
Texas Agricultural Progress 7 (September/October 1961): 15–18 and Ira Laster, "A
Historical Study of the Negro Farm and Home Organization of Chatman County, April 1944–1964" (Ph.D. diss., University of North Carolina, 1969), 187.

5. Clare Booth Luce, "The Saintly Scientist: George Washington Carver," *Vital
Speeches* 13 (February 1, 1947): 241–45. See also Myrdal, *An American Dilemma*.

6. David Manber, *Wizard of Tuskegee: The Life of George Washington Carver* (New
York: Crowell Collier Press, 1957), 168. See also Ruth A. Morton, *Men of the Soil:
The Story of Black Rural Life School* (New York: AMA, 1945), 16.

as unsophisticated and uncouth; only occasionally did anyone suggest a cultural dimension existed. Wholesome activities in which rural blacks actually engaged included husking bees, barn raisings, quilting parties, singing schools, spelling competitions, hunting, fishing, and picnicking. They amused themselves at the sugar stew or taffy pulling, pound parties, marriage feasts, and harvest festivals. Interest in dancing for recreation and socialization developed. Dance halls sprang up so that people from surrounding hamlets came to town to join in the fellowship. In the summer, outdoor recreation for the young folks consisted of playing with marbles and tops. Baseball was very popular, and most rural communities had a team. Berry picking and nut gathering served a nutritional purpose as well as providing opportunities for the children to frolic outdoors.

In numerous studies of southern society that have appeared between 1930 and 1970, the African American rural experience has been examined. Anthropologists, political scientists, geographers, sociologists, economists, agriculturists, and historians are now presenting data that show rural existence in a more diverse and positive light. Efforts have been made to view the rural poor from their own perspective. Novels and oral history projects have contributed greatly to a more positive interpretation of African American rural existence.[7]

Stereotypical images of rural black communities, however, were aided by African American scholars such as Booker T. Washington, W. E. B. Du Bois, Ida B. Wells, and George Washington Carver, who espoused cultural values and beliefs similar to the majority society. Yet, each of these leaders preached the need for exemplary moral living to rural blacks through the ownership of property—houses, land, and businesses. They emphasized that the home was where the culture of African American rural people had to be conceived and practiced.[8]

7. Percy, *Lanterns on the Levee.* See also David Cohn, *God Shakes Creation* (New York: Harper and Brothers, 1935); Melissa Walker, *All We Knew Was to Farm: Rural Women in the Upcountry South, 1919–1941; The Negro Farmer,* April 1, 1940, and June 27, 1965. See also William Lynwood Montell, *The Saga of Coe Ridge: A Study in Oral History* (Knoxville: University of Tennessee Press, 1970); William L. Gibbs, ed., *Indiana's African American Heritage* (Indianapolis: Indiana Historical Society, 1993); and Janet Sharp Hermann, *The Pursuit of a Dream* (New York: Vintage Books, 1983).

8. Richard Wright, *Uncle Tom's Children* (New York: Harper and Row, 1937). See

Home was where children learned and parents practiced their faith and the teachings of the rural church. Families believed in the Ten Commandments. Parents advocated the cultural values of love, sharing, cooperation, and hard work. Children were taught to be pious and submissive to God and those in positions of authority. Domesticity was encouraged. Rural African Americans believed that cleanliness was next to godliness. Profanity, vulgarity, and drunkenness were strongly discouraged. The majority viewed themselves as moral equals of whites. They believed their lifestyle debunked many, if not all, of the stereotypical images whites and some urban blacks had about them.[9]

Rural blacks celebrated certain cultural events in their homes. For example, activities surrounding the birth and naming of a child were common. Before the birth, the women quilted, sewed, had slumber parties, and developed a sisterhood group around the expectant mother. They met at her house and prepared it for the new arrival. Once the baby was born, they danced, sang, toasted the new mother with iced tea, and reminisced about old times, especially the last birth before this one. Much time was spent thinking of a name for the child and celebrating its meaning, which more often than not reflected family ancestors and traditions.[10]

Naming celebrations had their own peculiarities and functions. People came from all over to find out for whom the child was named. The name was often announced throughout neighborhoods, in churches,

---

also Du Bois, *The Souls of Black Folk* (Atlanta: Atlanta University, 1903); Washington, *Up from Slavery* (London: Grant Richards, 1902); Linda O. McMurry, *To Keep the Waters Troubled: The Life of Ida B. Wells* (New York: Oxford University Press, 1998); Linda O. McMurry, *George Washington Carver: Scientist and Symbol* (New York: Oxford University Press, 1981).

9. William Saunders Scarborough, "Negro Farmers' Progress in Virginia," *Current History Magazine* 25 (December 1926): 384–87. See also V. Schottelmayer, *White Gold: The Way of Life in the Cotton Kingdom* (Evanston, Ill.: Row Peters, 1941), 64; George A. Sewell, "A Hundred Years of History," *Negro History Bulletin* 34 (April 1971): 78–79; Kenneth Marvin Hamilton, *Black Towns and Profit: Promotion and Development in the Trans-Appalachian West, 1877–1915* (Urbana: University of Illinois Press, 1991); James D. Anderson, *The Education of Blacks in the South: 1860–1935* (Chapel Hill: University of North Carolina Press, 1988).

10. Montell, *The Saga at Coe Ridge.* See also Elizabeth Bethel Rauh, *Promised Land* (Philadelphia: Temple University Press, 1981).

and at the local schools. Relatives and friends visited to see if the name suited the child's physical, intellectual, and emotional characteristics. The naming ceremony had dancing and singing. Community members brought food, and the new parents and older siblings had the opportunity to tell well-wishers how excited they were about the new baby and how his or her name continued family traditions.[11]

Foods not raised on the farm were hunted and gathered, such as berries and nuts. When combined with wild herbs and mushrooms, they often made interesting meals for many families. Roots were dug to supplement the diet and for medicinal purposes. During gatherings, children played games as their parents sang work songs, told jokes, smoked tobacco, and drank alcoholic beverages and their favorite "brought along" drinks.

The woodland was home to rabbits, squirrels, raccoons, opossums, turkeys, boars, bears, and deer. During the winter, men hunted and brought home meat for stew. Hunting parties usually included drinking, telling jokes, and playing practical jokes on each other. Sometimes after warming themselves by the fire, the men chatted about their children, wives, and church life. Men and women often went fishing to celebrate achievements or as a reward for finishing the fieldwork. Fish were plentiful in creeks, springs, and rivers—especially catfish and perch. Often families fished in groups, and these gatherings were times for discussing politics, the Bible, and money. During fishing expeditions, single men and women sometimes began a courtship as they ate their packed lunches while boating down the river. Hunting and fishing could bring blacks and whites together. Jewish, Italian, German, Chinese, and English Americans were the guests of African American and white landowners. Such activities were one way that recreation and nutritional needs crossed racial lines in America's rural communities.[12]

11. Donald Crichton Alexander, *The Arkansas Plantation 1920–42* (New Haven, Conn.: Yale University Press, 1943), 118.

12. "Agriculture and Hampton," *Southern Workman* 57 (June 1928): 206–8. See also Christian H. Banks, "Balancing a Community with Agriculture," *Southern Workman* 57 (February 1928): 72–79; Jeannie Whayne and Williard B Gatewood, *The Arkansas Delta: Land of Paradox;* N. C. Bruce et al., "Report of Committee on Farm Labor and Rural Life Conditions of Missouri Negro People" in *Second Re-*

In addition, the preservation of vegetables and fruit products as well as the killing, butchering, and smoking of meat created a spirit of community celebration. Women had canning parties where, in addition to putting by jams and jellies, they exchanged stories, sang, swapped recipes, and drank brandy (for medical purposes no doubt). During the fall and winter, families' meat supplies for the year needed replenishing. The killings were carried out communally. Families usually gathered at the homes of black landowners, where at least one cow and a half dozen hogs were butchered. On killing day, some whites stopped by to offer their help and to look over the cuts of meat to be sold. Outside over an open fire, some women roasted a ham or pork shoulder, while inside the house others prepared vegetables and fruit to keep those involved in the butchering well fed. Periodically, musicians stopped by with harmonicas, bucket drums, and homemade guitars to play and sing as the work continued. At the end of the day, meat was salted down and smoked. Workers, mostly sharecroppers who had helped, were given fresh meat to take home. Still more white families stopped by to purchase fresh meat, canned vegetables, eggs, and dairy products.[13]

Outside the home, African American families participated in events sponsored by the rural church and school that promoted cultural literacy for children and adults. Such events included road improvement drives, mail delivery campaigns, youth programs, dramas, and forums. In the Mississippi Delta, for example, the church and school combined to play a vital role in establishing literacy. Rural churches held educational fund-raisers and book drives. Families attended these events where poetry, Scripture, and stories by black writers were read, then made donations and pledges. They listened to gospel and instrumental music. In the Yazoo between 1920 and 1940, preachers and teachers taught reading, writing, and arithmetic at Merry Grove. East Mount Olive, Brooks Chapel, and Palestine Church of God in Christ also served

port of the Missouri Negro Educational and Industrial Commission, compilation by Robert S. Cobb (Jefferson City, Mo.: Hugh Stephens Co., 1921), 17–21.

13. Banks, "Balancing a Community," 72–79. See also E. C. Branson, "Farm Tenancy in the South," Journal of Social Forces 1 (March 1923): 213–21 and 1 (May 1923): 450–57; Charles S. Johnson, The Shadow of the Plantation (Chicago: University of Chicago Press, 1934); Raper, Preface to Peasantry; Hurston, Mules and Men.

as schools during the 1930s. Reverend Robinson, pastor at the Palestine Church, taught the children history and Latin three days each week. Henry James provided instruction in English and writing at the same church on Tuesdays and Thursdays. At Brooks Chapel, Elizabeth Farmer taught literature, while Deacon A. L. Gordon and Missionary Mary Harris taught drawing and painting alternately at the East Mount Olive Baptist Church. Parents were invited into the church schools to teach music, play instruments, and read poetry.[14]

Many African American rural churches organized competitions. The community-wide beautification contest, sponsored by the church, encouraged families to fix up their homes and yards. Many trees, flowers, and shrubs were planted and arranged in circles, squares, crosses, and animal designs. "People laughed and fussed over the best lookin' yard, flowers, trees, house, porch, screened doors and windows, and home-made but painted furniture as well as who had the best gardens and livestock, and who was goin' to win the contest and have they name announce in all the churches," Steve Hearon explained. Prizes of fifteen, ten, and five dollars were awarded to first-, second-, and third-place winners.[15]

More important, the church's beautification contest gave leaders an opportunity to survey the amount of goods and material wealth each member possessed. Preachers, deacons, and missionaries used this contest to determine which families needed assistance. They gave the names of families in need to those who had a surplus of food, clothes, bedcovers, and other items and who could afford to share. This contest was critical because "it helped black people look after each other."[16]

14. Zora Neale Hurston, *Their Eyes Were Watching God* (Philadelphia: J. B. Lippincott, 1937). See also Hurston, *Dust Tracks on a Road;* Jodie Hearon, interview by author, Memphis, Tennessee, July 3, 1989; Steve Hearon, interview by author, Ruleville, Mississippi, June 16, 1989; Edward Scott, interview by author, Ruleville, Mississippi, July 7, 1989; Freddie Wiley, interview by author, Ruleville, Mississippi, June 10, 1989; Conference on Negro Extension Work, *Proceedings,* Orangeburg, South Carolina, 1927 (Washington, D.C.: U.S. Extension Service, Office of Cooperative Extension Working, 1927).

15. Thomas L. Dabney, "Colored Rural Life Conference of Central Virginia," *Southern Workman* 55 (May 1926): 224–27.

16. C. M. Arthur, "N.F.A. Achievements," *School Life* 23 (November 1937): 79. See also Z. T. Hubert, "Log Cabin Community Center and Country Life," *Southern Workman* 63 (August 1934): 249- 52.

Church-related festivals encouraged rural African Americans' energy and talents in different ways. Emphasis was on meeting spiritual needs through baptismal ceremonies, weddings, funerals, church anniversaries, reunions, and carnival associations. While many of these events might be perceived as religious or social, the ways in which rural blacks expressed themselves were cultural. For example, before 1950, the majority of baptisms took place at the nearest river during summer and fall. Dressed in white, preachers, deacons, and those to be baptized took this opportunity to showcase the conversion of new believers. After submersion, new Christians came up shouting how much they believed and how happy they were to know Jesus as lord and savior. The activity included dancing and singing. River baptisms often concluded with prayer and feasting, indicating that the soul and body had to be fed to live a godly life.[17]

Weddings were small, just family, friends, neighbors, and rarely out-of-towners. The bride usually wore a white dress made by a local seamstress; the groom wore his best suit. Music and tears of joy flowed as the church, decorated with homegrown and wild flowers, filled with men, women, and children decked out in their Sunday best. Pews were festooned with ribbons, and rice was thrown. After the ceremony, the bride and groom joined in a toast to their good fortune with their guests over a large meal prepared by family and friends. A dance, in honor of the newlyweds, followed later in the evening at the home of the bride's parents.[18]

Funerals expressed what rural African Americans believed about life after death. Many of the best musicians of the countryside paid tribute to friends. The choir sang traditional gospel songs, and from time to time, members of the congregation stood and proclaimed how good the deceased was. Testimonials and pleas for assistance to the bereaved family were made. Like weddings, rural funerals were decorative, with everyone wearing their best dress-up clothes. Singing was loud and preaching was spirited. The service was filled with high energy, much

---

17. Charles Spurgeon Johnson, *Shadow of the Plantation* (Chicago: University of Chicago Press, 1934), 214.

18. Cornelius King, "The Colored Farmer Must Help Himself," *Opportunity* 17 (October 1939): 296–98.

moaning and groaning, and a call for unbelievers to return to God. Believing that life continued after death, some rural churchgoers sent the deceased "home" with books, clothes, jewelry, and other valued personal possessions. Bodies were laid to rest in rural cemeteries behind the churches, and family members decorated burial plots with flowers.

Church revivals were coordinated with anniversary celebrations. They were homecoming reunions in a cultural sense. Friends and families who had moved away returned to give back to the community and to inform fellow believers about their success. Returnees dressed in the latest fashion, spoke a more "proper English," and gave lengthy testimonials about their new life in the city. Church members applauded and heaped kindness and compliments upon them to show they were always welcome.[19]

Announcements, read at church in loud tones and with much energy and good humor, informed those living throughout the community of such significant events as the church association, weddings, and funerals. The church association took on a carnival atmosphere. While the primary objective was for church leaders to meet at one of the local churches to discuss the spiritual development of African American rural communities and families, much energy was expended attending the association dinners, picnics, rallies, bake sales, musicals, and plays. Surrounding churches in what was considered the "district" sent representatives who enjoyed the spirit of fellowship, celebration, and worship.[20]

African American rural communities developed as residents gained access to more knowledge and placed more emphasis on literacy. The production of plays and dramas drawn from the work of black writers became increasingly popular. On Easter, Thanksgiving, and Christmas, the rural school became an auditorium where children and parents put on plays dealing with slavery, fieldwork, turkey dinners, and the crucifixion. The local schoolteacher frequently served as script writer and producer.[21]

19. Benson Young Lands and George Edmund Haynes, *Cotton Growing Communities: Case Studies of Rural Communities and 30 Plantations in Alabama* (New York: Department of Race Relations, Federal Council of Churches of Christ in America, 1934), 42.

20. Montell, *Saga at Coe Ridge*.

21. John Howard Griffin, *Black Like Me* (New York: Signet, 1960). See also

Other literary endeavors flourished. The number of African American novels increased; musical compositions written by black musicians began to appear; magazines discussing the needs and conditions of rural African Americans were published. Scholars at black land-grant institutions began to conduct research that explained and contextualized how rural African Americans responded to degradation, destitution, exploitation, and oppression through cultural means. Much of the emphasis placed on literacy was evident not only in artistic expression but also in the increasing number of people writing letters.[22]

Rural mail delivery aided this development. Before the 1940s, letter carriers delivered mail to a common location in the community—the country store, the church, or the office at the school. Mail was delivered once a week, usually on Saturdays. After the work had ended for the week, families cleaned up and went in search of their mail on Saturday afternoons. Churchyards, school grounds, and the porches of stores were filled with people anxiously awaiting word from far-flung family members. When a letter came from the North, it was greeted with much enthusiasm because usually it contained money and critical information about a job. Laughter and joyous conversation ensued, while singing and dancing followed any great news received. Mail produced a contagious interactive spirit that kept people around the mail hubs for hours. Some even brought along snacks to start off the weekend celebration, which produced a comradely spirit that lasted into Sunday morning worship.[23]

Taulbert, *Once Upon A Time When We Were Colored;* Nell Irvin Painter, *Exodusters: Black Migration to Kansas After Reconstruction* (New York: W. W. Norton, 1970).

22. Benson Young Lands and George Edmund Haynes, *Cotton Growing Communities: Case Studies of 10 Rural Communities and 10 Plantations in Arkansas* (New York: Department of Race Relations, Federal Council of Churches of Christ in America, 1935), 47. See also Ernest J. Gaines, *The Autobiography of Miss Jane Pittman* (New York: Bantam Books, 1971).

23. O. E. Leonard and C. P. Loomis, "A Study of Mobility and Levels of Living among Negro Sharecroppers and Wage Laborer Families of the Arkansas River Valleys," *Bureau of Agricultural Economic Farm Populations and Rural Life Activities* 3 (April 15, 1939): 1–11; also cited in Arkansas Agricultural Experiment Station's *Rural Service Report,* no. 13, 1939. See also Jay David, *Growing Up Black* (New York: Pocket Books, 1969); Alice Walker, *The Color Purple* (New York: Pocket Books, 1982); Jacqueline Jones, *Labor of Love, Labor of Sorrow: Black Women, Work, and the Family from Slavery to the Present* (New York: Basic Books, 1985).

Many of the rural traditions and the heritage of blacks in the fields and living off the land appeared in their art and language. Paintings illustrated the struggles of blacks on the land and in their homes and churches. Sculptures were of common people and animals as well as trains and farm equipment. African American speech patterns dominated the way rural black experiences were chronicled in literature and music. The contents of novels and the lyrics of spirituals, work songs, and blues were often presented and performed in black dialect. Word endings such as g's and s's were dropped. Many scholars associate the language of rural blacks with African languages and the legacy of slavery. Yet they credit southern blacks with the creation of a unique dialect.[24]

The country store was a cultural hub where African American language was spoken and heard. White and black men sat on the porch discussing the latest developments. Conversations focused on farm production, the price of land, marketing of crops, problems with labor, and family needs. When black men had the opportunity to sit awhile, they talked about how hard they were working, their need for money, and the many things they were asked to do. When both races sat together, white men initiated and dominated the conversation. Most white planters were interested primarily in being praised and thanked for how good and caring they were. The store's porch was where societal norms often reminded black people of their place.[25]

The porch was not a place for women, especially young, married black women. Porch conversations could be vulgar and filled with sexual and racial jokes. A woman was likely to have passes made at her and insults meted out if men's propositions were refused, especially white ones. In the absence of white men, however, black women met on the store porch and generally conversed about their families, their husbands' work, and their children. Sometimes they commented on their own work, what they were growing in the garden, canning for the winter season, or doing for the church. Such conversations prevented, for the most part, public pursuit of men's wives and their young daughters.

24. Lee McCrae, "Salvaging Little Black Souls," *Missionary Review of the World* 53 (July 1930): 518–20. See also Pete Daniel, *Lost Revolutions: The South in the 1950s;* Pete Daniel, *The Shadow of Slavery: Peonage in the South, 1901–1969.*

25. B. L. Moss, "The Truth about the Sharecropper," *American Mercury* 43 (March 1931): 289–96.

But for single adult black women, the store porch served as a meeting place; many unmarried black women went to the store to see who they could meet and to engage in conversations about possible relationships with men who could offer gifts and money. These women were approached, asked for sexual favors, and were popular among black and white men within the porch culture.[26]

The country store was an institution where whites and blacks worked together. Whites, of course, were the only ones permitted to operate the cash register or to handle the money. If a store employed Jewish help, they stocked the shelves and kept the inventory. Blacks, on the other hand, assisted families in locating items they needed to buy. Blacks also carried goods to people's wagons and made deliveries throughout the community. Merchants from different ethnic backgrounds introduced rural blacks to foreign products. Chinese and Jewish merchants often bartered or sold decorated fabrics, silver and tableware, statues, musical instruments, furniture, and toys. These exchanges were generally positive. Many rural African Americans were able to establish credit with the peddlers for items that the country store did not regularly carry. Friendships often developed from these negotiations.[27]

Entertainment of a quieter variety, when young couples desired privacy for courting, happened at other locations. Lacking opportunities to go to movies, parks, local hotels, or other segregated public recreational facilities, the majority of rural African American young adults met on riverbanks, at turn roads, and at the end of fields to escape their parents and siblings. Some of these areas became known as lovers' lanes if they evolved into places where the consummation of relationships took place.[28]

26. Hurston, *Their Eyes Were Watching God*. See also Zora Neale Hurston, *Tell My Horse* (Philadelphia: J. B. Lippincott, 1938); Herman Clarence Nixon, *Forty Acres and Steel Mules* (Chapel Hill: University of North Carolina Press, 1939), 98; Peter Nelson and Earl T. Etter, "A Study of Negro Farming in the Boley Area of Oklahoma," *Oklahoma Current Farm Economics* 12 (October–December 1939): 136–40.

27. Reinhold Niebuhr, "Meditations from Mississippi," *Christian Century* 54 (February 10, 1937): 183–84. See also Du Bois, *Dusk of Dawn* (New York: Harcourt, Brace, and World, 1970); Raper, *Preface to Peasantry*.

28. John Popham, "South Acts to Aid Negro Farmer," *New York Times*, June 21, 1950.

Improvement in roads was significant for widening cultural horizons. The addition of gravel made traveling to events and celebrations easier. "Good roads made it possible for folks to go back and forth to town if they need to and out to evenin' church service, and they made it easy for folk to visit," Mae Liza Williams explained. "Even with horse and buggy," Minnie Brown recalled, "people visit more when we got some gravel." "I can remember folks comin' from surroundin' plantations on Saturday and Sunday evenin' to visit and to go to church," Margaret Ball remembered, "'cause it didn't take so long to push through all that mud and dirt, and even when it rained, folk on the other plantation didn't mind comin' out."[29]

With improved roads, rural African Americans felt comfortable purchasing automobiles. In the 1940s, the automobile removed confinement. The car also exposed the younger generation to a different world. As families spent more time visiting neighboring communities and states, "the children could see how other folk behave, 'specially in the larger cities and towns where music, dancin', ball games, and other things was going on." "This goin' out of the community and havin' a car made the older children want to drive, so that they could go out of town and find different fun." But more important, Mason Cooper added, "the car and better roads made it easier for us to go back and forth to town, church meetin' and club functions."[30]

Club meetings provided additional opportunities for recreation and entertainment. Rural blacks belonged to national and local organizations. Fraternal clubs were initially formed to provide burial insurance but evolved into social groups. Throughout African American communities, the Masonic Lodge was the largest fraternal order. Rural blacks joined other national organizations such as the "colored" Pythians, Elks and Woodmen, the Brothers and Sisters of Love and Charity, the Sacred

29. Minnie Brown, interview by author, Drew, Mississippi, June 3, 1989; Morton Rubin, *Plantation County (Field Studies in the Modern Culture)* (Chapel Hill: University of North Carolina Press, 1951); Margaret Ball, interview by author, Drew, Mississippi, May 29, 1989.

30. Morton Rubin, "Social and Cultural Change in the Plantation Area," *Journal of Social Issues* 10 (January 1954): 28–35; Rubin, *Plantation County;* James Fountain, interview by author, St. Louis, Missouri, July 6, 1988; Alexander Scott, Jr., interview by author, Drew, Mississippi, August 15, 1991.

Order of Perfection, Fishermen of the Red Cross Relief, Lone Star Race Pride, Black Sons and Daughters, Sir Knights and Daughters, Order of the Eastern Star, and the Knights and Daughters of Tabor. These affiliations provided opportunities for pleasure and leadership.[31]

Local organizations met specific needs, maintained community solidarity, and were important for individuals who wanted to belong but did not have the money or time to participate in national organizations. Homemaker Clubs existed for women, while men participated in the Farmers Club. Women's clubs discussed ways of improving housing conditions, health, food and nutrition, medical care, sewing, and general improvements in household responsibilities. Men discussed "the business of farming, what to grow, what not to grow, when it was best to plant, and where to take the crops to sell 'em." They "talk 'bout ways we could help each other farm and make things better in the community for our wife and children." Both men and women became members of home demonstration clubs through the Agricultural Extension Service and also joined farmers institutes and farm societies.[32]

Many rural children participated in club activities. The 4-H clubs, organized by the Agricultural Extension Service, were common in southern states. In these clubs, boys and girls learned how to raise and care for animals, while girls also learned how to manage a home. Many African American rural communities organized fairs where youngsters could exhibit their animals and produce. Girls could also display sewing and quilting projects as well as baked goods.[33]

The establishment of the Parent Teacher Association (PTA) in rural communities represented cultural and intellectual development. At the

31. Julian E. Bagby, "Negro Boys' Club Work in Virginia," *Southern Workman* 50 (July 1921): 318–20. See also McMillen, *Dark Journey;* Tony Dunbar, *Our Land Too* (New York: Pantheon Books, 1969).

32. Hearon, interview. See also Margaret A. Ambrose, "Handbook for Members of Negro Girls' Home Demonstration Clubs in Tennessee," Tennessee Agricultural Extension Service, *Publication* no. 194, May 1936, 18; Walker, *All We Knew Was to Farm;* David Cohen, *Where I was Born and Raised* (Boston: Houghton Mifflin Co., 1935); Rebecca Sharpless, *Fertile Ground, Narrow Choices: Women on Texas Cotton Farms, 1900–1940.*

33. Neil Foley, *The White Scourge: Mexicans, Blacks, and Poor Whites in Texas Cotton Culture.* See also Hurston, *Dust Tracks on a Road.*

Penn School in South Carolina, for example, parents and teachers met to focus on the needs of children and the community as a whole. They discussed the literacy needs of adults as well as reading, writing, and mathematical skills of children. Attention to issues such as health and medical care, sanitation, nutrition, and housing helped to improve rural students' performance. PTA meetings were well attended throughout the school year.[34]

About the same time, juke joints evolved as places for adults to congregate and establish a support system. For the most part, juke joints were little shacks or attached rooms behind someone's house, or old barns turned into nightclubs. "You see, there was somethin' that folk could do at these fun houses," Estella Thomas explained, "that they couldn't do nowhere else, 'specially not at the school and church functions." "They could be loud and talk 'bout all kinds of things and still be consider a Christian and a decent person."[35]

Inhibitions could be overcome at juke joints. Gambling, excessive drinking, dancing, and love affairs took place. Many juke joints were open Thursday through Sunday nights. They were often associated with noise and danger since fighting occurred frequently. Despite the unsavory image of juke joints, rural African Americans who frequented them argue that they were essential. In addition to entertainment, they provided a social outlet for men and women who wanted to get away from their children and interact with other adults. People who spent long days at work used the juke joints as places for relaxing with friends. Indeed, the spirit of the juke joint permeated African American rural culture.[36]

34. Fred T. Mitchell, "Superior Teacher of Vocational Agriculture," *Southern Workman* 59 (July 1930): 313–17. See also *New Farmers of America Guide for New Farmers of America: The National Organization for Negro Students Studying Vocational Agriculture* (Baltimore: New Farmers of America, 1938–1944).

35. Estella Thomas, interview by author, Drew, Mississippi, April 30, 1989; *1939 Proceedings of the Fifth National Convention of the New Farmers of America and Results of National Contests for Negro Students of Vocational Agriculture.* U.S. Office of Education–Vocational Division, *Miscellaneous Publication* no. 2289, November 1939, 66.

36. Jeannie M. Whayne, ed., *Shadows over Sunnyside: An Arkansas Plantation in Transition, 1831–1945.* See also Louise Gordon, *Caste and Class: The Black Experience in Arkansas, 1880–1920.*

Any cause to celebrate ignited great enthusiasm. Festivals in honor of the blues, rice, wheat, and the harvest in general appeared to have been the occasions most widely observed, primarily in the summer. In southern states, such as Louisiana, Mississippi, Tennessee, Arkansas, and Missouri, rural African Americans displayed their talents. People from all over the Mississippi Delta region also celebrated the Fourth of July by coming together with their guitars, harmonicas, drums, buckets, and other homemade instruments. During the Fourth of July and fall harvest festivals, children found ways to amuse themselves. The barn served as a basketball court. The children also shot marbles, and played card games and checkers there. Youngsters swam in the swimming hole. Sometimes they went into town to see a movie at a segregated theater.[37]

Many blacks who had moved away returned in the fall for harvest celebrations. When cotton, rice, tobacco, sugar, and wheat crops had been harvested, African American rural communities organized festivals to celebrate. Anticipating profits to be made, families organized pasture picnics. They placed tables underneath trees in the pastures and roped off areas for cookouts and picnics. Lots of eating and dancing took place, along with giving thanks to God through prayers and praising. Children ran around the pasture, anticipating the new clothes and toys they would get after the crops were sold. They turned the gleaned fields into playgrounds and baseball, kickball, and football fields. Throughout the day, friends and neighbors visited each other's farms to see the bales of cotton and trailers of corn and rice. Later they accompanied each other to the gin and grain elevators to see how much the harvest would earn. Sometimes the men stopped along the way to talk, sing old songs, and take a drink of the best bootlegged whiskey distilled in the community.[38]

37. Lauris B. Whitman and Anne O. Lively, *A Study of Low Income Farm Families in Two Southern Rural Communities,* National Council of Churches of Christ in America, Department of Town and Country, 1958, 65; James Cobb, *The Most Southern Place on Earth: The Mississippi Delta and the Roots of Regional Identity.* See also Benjamin C. Wilson, *The Rural Black Heritage between Chicago and Detroit: 1850–1929* (Kalamazoo, Mich.: New Issues Press, 1985).

38. Wisconsin Governor's Commission on Human Rights, *Negro Families in Rural Wisconsin: A Study of Their Community Life* (Madison: Governor's Commis-

The adoption of communication technology provided a greater opportunity for rural African Americans to express themselves culturally and socially. Between 1900 and 1950 some of them purchased telephones and radios to keep informed of local, state, and national developments. These purchases also indicated that rural blacks had become interested in learning about other cultures. Through the minstrel shows, they already knew how whites presented blacks. Southern blacks in general especially wanted to hear and see if whites would show the same disrespect for their own culture and heritage that they had shown for that of rural blacks.

Fannie Turner remembered the importance of the radio: "It was somethin' else to have somethin' like a radio in the house. To hear a voice in the house other than you own or your folks' was different. That was really somethin' special. We had not seen anything like it before. To sit there listenin' to the news, ball games, and all kinds of other things was so unusual. Everybody was excited 'bout being able to buy one of them little things 'cause you knowed what was goin' on. The news and the rest of the programs made us yearn for more, back then, when that was really the only way you could find out 'bout things without leavin' home or the community."[39]

Acquisition of a radio produced great excitement. According to Edward Scott, "The radio was a fantastic thing 'cause we could, then, hear different things from 'round the whole state and Delta." It also meant listening to ball games, music, drama, and comedy. The radio broadcasts of Joe Louis's boxing matches and Jackie Robinson's baseball games became important events for rural blacks. Across the rural South, African Americans who owned radios celebrated the dominance of black athletes. Radio broadcasts of Jesse Owens's 1936 Olympic performance in Berlin resulted in many celebrations in rural African American communities. Rural blacks organized picnics, musicals, and parties

---

sion on Human Rights, 1959), 72. See also George K. Hesslink, *Black Neighbors: Negroes in a Northern Rural Community* (Indianapolis: Bobbs-Merrill Company, 1974); Whayne, *A New Plantation South*.

39. Fannie Turner, interview by author, Drew, Mississippi, July 5, 1989. See also Lillian Smith, *Killers of the Dream* (New York: W. W. Norton and Company, 1949).

to celebrate the positive image of blackness presented by African American athletes, many of whom came from rural areas.[40]

Ella Hearon remembered, "Everybody was talkin' 'bout the radio and how it was helpin' people feel better and how the folk who didn't have one was gonna get it as soon as they got some extra money." For individuals who could not immediately afford a radio, "they was welcome to come to our house or go to some of the other folks' house who had one to listen to." African Americans "would sometimes on a Saturday evenin' get together to listen to the radio and talk 'bout what they heard and pass on the information." The radio came to symbolize hope. "If we could ever find out what was goin' on or what everybody else was doin', we would know what to do." With the radio, rural African Americans felt less isolated; they had plugged into the rest of the world.[41]

The radio influenced styles and standards of living among rural African Americans. Women learned important information about health, medical care, and eating habits. Some of the public service announcements offered tips "like what to do when children got sick or where a person could go for medical help or supplies when the home remedies was not workin'." "From listenin' to . . . the . . . radio, we learn more 'bout washin' and the best kind of soap or washin' detergent to use." Women believed this technology added greatly to the material culture "'cause we learn so much 'bout every area of life and our friends could come over and listen. This was our recreation, and we learned something at the same time."[42]

40. Allison Davis, Burleigh B. Gardner, and Mary R. Gardner, *Deep South: A Social Anthropological Study of Caste and Class* (Chicago: University of Chicago Press, 1941). See also Rosengarten, *All God's Dangers;* Margaret Just Butcher, *The Negro in American Culture* (New York: Alfred A. Knopf, 1957).

41. Ella Hearon, interview by author, Memphis, Tennessee, July 3, 1989. See also Kelley, *Hammer and Hoe;* Lillian Smith, *The Journey* (New York: W. W. Norton and Company, 1954); Mary Sargent, interview by author, Memphis, Tennessee, July 3, 1989; Josephine Griffin, interview by author, Des Moines, Iowa, April 15, 1989; Kirby, *Rural Worlds Lost;* Mandle, *The Roots of Black Poverty.*

42. Pearline Cosby, interview by author, Charleston, Mississippi, June 12, 1990; Ball, interview; Mae Liza Williams, interview by author, Drew, Mississippi, April 29, 1989; Irene Scott, interview by author, Drew, Mississippi, April 28, 1989; Birdell Vassell, interview by author, Drew, Mississippi, April 28, 1989.

Farmers also benefited from the electronic media. "You could always hear 'bout the weather," explained Mason Cooper, "and the forecast help we men know what to do from day to day." "It help us know mo' 'bout when to plant, plow, fertilize, run water furrow, disk, and when to start gatherin' the crop." "When we hear mo' 'bout the sun and rain and all the other kind of weather, that just help us." "Not only did the . . . radio give out weather report," Edward Scott explained, "they also help us know 'bout farm sale, grains, fertilizer and where to go in the Delta to do business."[43]

When telephones came on the scene, they fulfilled rural blacks' goal of improving communication. The telephone was a welcome addition to the community "'cause if you need to know somethin' or if you miss out on the news or even somethin' goin' on in the community, you could get on the phone and call someone to find out what was goin' on." One contemporary remembered, "The one nice thing 'bout the phone was that it help out on runnin' errand, and with it one could now call and see if a store had what you need befo' you made a blank trip out there." More important, "if you need to know somethin' or get a word to somebody," Golden Walker explained, "you just get on the phone and call to the closest place where a phone was and ask that person to take a message to who you was wantin' to speak to and that began a celebration of some sort, 'cause the call usually brought joy and laughter to a family."[44]

While families purchased these communication technologies for practical purposes, African American rural people celebrated their adoption in cultural ways. When a telephone or radio was introduced into a community, the owners invited neighbors and friends over to toast their good fortune. Some families had a cookout, others had a party to showcase the new phone—having someone telephone them to initiate the celebration. At times, firecrackers were set off and bonfires

43. Mason Cooper, interview by author, Drew, Mississippi, July 5, 1989; Willie Ester McWilliams, interview by author, Drew, Mississippi, June 5, 1989; Earnest McWilliams, interview by author, Drew, Mississippi, June 5, 1989; Scott, interview. See also Daniel, *The Shadow of Slavery.*

44. Leroy Vassel, interview by author, Minter City, Mississippi, April 30, 1989; Hearon, interview; Golden Walker, interview by author, Drew, Mississippi, May 17, 1988. See also Daniel, *The Shadow of Slavery.*

built. While music and news issued from the new radio, wieners would be roasted and games played. Some sat around drinking coffee and whiskey as they listened to their first radio program, while others took turns calling on the new phone and singing and laughing about the wonders of this new technology.[45]

The cultural significance of each communication technology concerned the church and caused tension between preachers and their congregations. These purchases were the first time that parishioners had fought to have more control over their private lives. Rural African Americans believed that these developments encouraged more interactions as well as cultural and recreational programs to which they could identify. The local preachers were less enthused. Church leaders believed that uncensored public information would make their parishioners too secular. They believed music and ball games on the radio were ungodly entertainment. Even though most radio programs were quite tame, church leaders believed parishioners spent less time praying and praising God and more time listening to "sinful behavior."[46]

Preachers suggested productive ways families could use the telephone: They were a valuable resource for tracking agricultural markets, conducting business, keeping abreast of transient family members or of shut-ins, and counseling individuals during times of bereavement and disappointment. Both the telephone and the automobile bridged the physical space between family members and brought them closer during a time when American communities were highly segregated and hostile to African Americans, even in the large cities.

Between 1900 and 1950, African American rural culture was energetic and diverse and included many social, spiritual, and educational activities. Through their ideas and the ways they interacted and behaved, rural African Americans created an identity that embraced their expressions and empowered their sense of blackness.

45. Whayne and Gatewood, *The Arkansas Delta*. See also Roger Whitlow, *Black American Literature: A Critical History* (Chicago: Nelson Hall, 1976).
46. Lemann, *The Promised Land*. See also Dittmer, *Local People*.

Benign Public Policies, Malignant Consequences, and the Demise of African American Agriculture

WILLIAM P. BROWNE

African Americans "are big city oriented," concluded two of the foremost late-twentieth-century observers of racial politics.[1] The truth in that comment reflects bitter irony. African Americans, freed from slavery, came from the South to the North, for generations. Their hope was to find industrial jobs, which were city based. The irony was that these were largely agricultural workers, when they worked at all, and their life experiences were largely rural. In consequence, a rural people became an urban people, primarily by reacting to changes resulting in large part from federal farm policy.

Even after 1960, when large numbers of African Americans moved from the North back to the South, their destinations were urban centers of the Sunbelt, where industrial and service jobs had recently been created. Agriculture never came calling with even limited opportunities, even as African Americans became ensconced in—and identified with—an urbanized "national ghetto system."[2]

This analysis is about that irony, in which rural people lost their ties to agricultural jobs. The major concern of this work is the politics and trends of the 1920s and into 1950. In another irony, it was the radically unique and so often idealized agricultural policies of the Great Depression's New Deal that finally destroyed African American agriculture. This happened even as President Franklin D. Roosevelt became an

1. Lucius J. Barker and Jesse J. McCorry, Jr., *Black Americans and the Political System*, 2d ed. (Cambridge, Mass.: Winthrop Publishers, 1980), 5.

2. Ibid., 6–7; Harold Rose, *The Black Ghetto: A Spatial Behavioral Perspective* (New York: McGraw Hill, 1971), 15.

icon for American blacks, permanently cementing their ties to the Democratic party.[3]

Although this analysis focuses on the 1920–1950 era, the demise of African American agriculture must be understood in a broader context. Thus, earlier events and trends are discussed first. Post-1950 years are necessarily addressed last as culminating experiences to events of the depression years.

The destruction of African American agriculture was in large part the work of American governing institutions and the politics of institution building. Institutions, in a historical context, are the formal rules of government. Those rules create basic laws such as the Agricultural Adjustment Act of 1938, programs to implement policies such as the distribution of cash payments to farmers, and organizations such as the U.S. Department of Agriculture (USDA).[4] Each of these institutional types direct the benefits of governmental largess to constituent users. Even the best intended of institutions, and the most socially well accepted, have a bias in favor of some types of users and against others. Those who are biased against become at least partially disenfranchised by government, in this case from the opportunities in farming. That bias, existing as it does in the most benignly intended of U.S. public policies, is the thread that holds this story together. Therefore, let us start at the thread's origins.

Discrimination is a slippery concept. In operation, it means more than, for example, a social order that specifically assigns certain racial types of people to the back of the bus. Discrimination also takes place when that social order, through government, creates policies to keep certain types of farmers in business but ignores the types of farmers characteristic of a certain race. That was what occurred when the United States created governing institutions that went about modernizing and developing the farm sector.[5] African Americans had little interest

3. Walter Dean Burnham, *Critical Elections and the Mainsprings of American Politics* (New York: W. W. Norton, 1970), 142, 154.

4. Institutions are specific and tangible public entities. Douglass C. North, *Institutions, Institutional Change and Economic Performance* (Cambridge: Cambridge University Press, 1990), 1–10.

5. Louis Ferleger, "Arming American Agriculture for the Twentieth Century:

in playing by the rules of these new institutions. Nor did they have the chance.

What were these institutions, and what was the nature of their rules? All must be understood in context. Agricultural development and national expansion, or development again, had long been topics of American political debate by 1862. However, rivalries between North and South had stymied both forms of development. In particular, southerners saw the upgrading in capacity of the traditional American yeoman farmer as a danger to three interrelated phenomena: slavery, plantation control of the farm sector, and the admission of new slave states to the Union. For twenty years such fears blocked calls for bettering the lot of all U.S. farmers and making them more capable stewards of the western frontier. But by 1862 southern members of Congress had gone home from Washington as their states seceded, leaving northerners alone to build agricultural institutions as well as those serving western expansion.

Thus, 1862 was a very good year for agriculture and for Wall Street investors, bankers, railroaders, lumbermen, and whatever other industrial interests were to be served by frontier expansion. Four distinct acts constituted that year's presentation.[6] Each had its own sponsors. The Transcontinental Railroad Act promised to hasten farm product and farm supply movement from east to west and back, as well as to provide revenue for railroaders in an otherwise bleak financial era. New Orleans was not to be the hub to the West, as southerners had wanted. The U.S. Department of Agriculture was created as a small but broadly tasked federal agency, one to distribute goods (seeds and plants) plus services (information on how best to use them) to agrarian producers. Also institutionalized in this early USDA was a lasting scientific enterprise, one committed to empirical positivism as a means of discovery for bettering agrarian production.[7] This was farm science to farm peo-

How the USDA's Top Managers Promoted Agricultural Development," *Agricultural History* 74 (spring 2000): 211–40.

6. John Y. Simon, "The Politics of the Morrill Act," *Agricultural History* 37 (winter 1963): 103–11; William P. Browne, *The Failure of National Rural Policy: Institutions and Interests* (Washington, D.C.: Georgetown University Press, 2001), 37–49.

7. Wayne B. Rasmussen and Gladys L. Baker, *The Department of Agriculture* (New York: Praeger, 1972), 3–13; Louis Ferleger and William Lazonick, "Higher

ple, for the benefit of bringing modernization and development to the sector. And the department had the ever-flexible assignment of taking its scientific tasks as far as future budgets and expanding creativity would allow.

The final two acts ensured the USDA of ready support, both long and short term. The Morrill Land Grant Act provided tracts of public land to the states. These tracts were to be used in whatever way possible to establish higher educational institutions to teach the latest facts and findings, or the science, of agriculture and mechanics. The USDA thus had potential outlets, and perhaps even partners, for its work. Finally, there was the original Homestead Act, which legitimated squatting on designated and generally less desirable tracts of open frontier land. The plethora of both knowledgeable farmers and itinerant know-nothings who homesteaded gave the USDA and the land grant colleges able clients to serve in addition to hapless souls to save. All were moving west, farmers and institutional operations of varied sorts.

The tasks of science, service, and salvation were too formidable for the emerging institutions to handle. Federal experiment stations were added in 1887 to further agricultural modernization and development. They were set up locally, usually adjacent to the agriculture colleges, to undertake scientific solutions to the unique problems of nearby farm production.[8] Their intent was to provide ever more applied scientific research to advance the farm sector.

In 1914 a truly federal Extension Service was created as an outreach institution for taking scientifically based agricultural techniques and products directly to individual farmers. Some states and their colleges had already employed such extension workers, often since the late eighteenth century, and the states were accordingly given the lead in these federal partnerships. In the meantime, the growing USDA was elevated to full Cabinet status, giving farm advocates a presidential adviser who was at least formally equal to such cabinet members as the Secretary of War. In this midst as well, nearly thirty years behind, the 1890 Schools, or the African American Land Grants, were created in the

Education for an Innovative Economy: Land Grant Colleges and the Managerial Revolution in America," *Business and Economic History* 23 (fall 1994): 116–28.

8. Ferleger and Lazonick, "Higher Education for an Innovative Economy."

southern states. Blacks after all were not permitted in or served by segregated southern colleges, even though these were not at the time as proficient as those in the North. African American disadvantages were not only those of race, though. It became quite clear early on that many farmers, especially of the most needy and subsistence type, were reluctant to be saved by science and service interventionists.[9] That reality, which undoubtedly led to farm failures among the itinerants, cannot detract from the fact that most Republicans from all regions and walks of life considered these various institutions to be nobly intended.

By the onset of World War I a wide-ranging set of agricultural laws, programs, and organizations was in place, as rules that enhanced production and finally helped capture increased farm incomes in light of forthcoming higher wartime prices. As a set of institutions, these rules and their makers were driven in large part by scientific principles of discovery; they were consequently directed to greater and increased production by a modernizing and more technically developed farm sector. The institutional set as a whole was unplanned, yet pragmatically assembled by a variety of public policy players. This was at a time when the number of workers leaving agriculture remained consistently high even as many new entrants joined the sector. The only unifying thread between the institutions was that of applied scientific and knowledge-based intervention in farming. That intervention was to be the work of a theoretically integrated trinity: doing science, teaching science's greatest accomplishments, and actively seeking out farmers who needed or wanted applied scientific findings. The integration of institutional purpose was sufficient for one of the nation's foremost agricultural

9. Alfred C. True, *A History of Agricultural Extension Work in the United States, 1785–1923* (Washington, D.C.: U.S. Government Printing Office, 1928); Roy V. Scott, *The Reluctant Farmer: The Rise of Agricultural Extension to 1914* (Urbana: University of Illinois Press, 1970); E. Pendleton Herring, *Public Administration and the Public Interest* (New York: McGraw Hill, 1936); Barbara R. Cotton, *The Lamplighters: Black Farm and Home Demonstration Agents, 1915–1965* (Washington, D.C.: U.S. Department of Agriculture, 1982); Ralph D. Christy and Lionel Williamson, eds., *A Century of Services: Land Grant Colleges and Universities, 1890–1990* (New Brunswick, N.J.: Transaction Books, 1992); Gladys L. Baker, *The County Agent* (Chicago: University of Chicago Press, 1939).

economists, Theodore Schultz, to later describe this early public as-
semblage as the core of an "Agricultural Establishment," one that eventually could and would drive otherwise private farm production.[10]

But for whom was this Establishment tolling its carillon bells? The
answer was: Not for African Americans. With the bulk of black farmers doing business in a racially stressed South, agricultural institutions
were not organized to reach out effectively. As Jeannie Whayne points
out in a later chapter, the 1890 Schools were understaffed, underfund-
ed, and far from equal to even southern whites-only colleges.[11]

There was more to the African American agricultural problem than
inferior service by farm institutions. A major portion of the problem was
that blacks who had farm wants and needs found nothing that mattered
within the Establishment. Evidence reveals a southern agriculture divided in three parts during and just after Reconstruction.[12] Science and
better production mattered only to those of the first part, farmers who
were newly committed to reorganizing to enter a market-driven economy. These white and wealthier farmers accepted modernization and
technical development, as well as expansion based on economy and efficiency. Other white farmers, or the second part, sought to remain yeoman or subsistence producers, preferably on their own land. Winning in
the marketplace and producing for consumer demand were for them
unimportant, beyond the pale, so to speak. Keeping home and hearth
together was what mattered, as well as preserving a few traditional farming rights such as grazing their cattle on the commons of public land.

The third contingent of nineteenth-century southern farmers, African Americans, cared rarely at all for going to college, experimenting
with new farm methods, of listening to Extension agents. They seemed
willing to live with their often exhausted soils. Since they were not

10. Theodore W. Schultz, *Redirecting Farm Policy* (New York: Macmillan, 1943);
Theodore W. Schultz, *Agriculture in an Unstable Economy* (New York: McGraw-Hill,
1945).

11. The Board of Agriculture, *Colleges of Agriculture at the Land Grant Universities: Public Service and Public Policy* (Washington, D.C.: National Research Council,
1986).

12. Richard L. McCormick, *The Party Period and Public Policy: American Politics
from the Age of Jackson to the Progressive Era* (New York: Oxford University Press,
1986), 106–8.

market-oriented, and even sometimes spoke out bitterly against a market-driven economy, agricultural professionals were not of their demand. Thus, efforts to create more jobs for African American agents received little grassroots support. So even though agricultural institutions seldom served black southern farmers, no one really cared about the neglect—not even those same southern African Americans. Agricultural institutions as they developed prior to World War I appear largely irrelevant to black farmers, whether or not they were available for use. African Americans did not need science to farm when farming was mostly, for them, about being free. Values of science and freedom did not mesh. An Agricultural Establishment would only have been useful if it helped African Americans to claim land, or if it redistributed land to them. That, however, was not these institutions' purpose. They were enabled as institutions of social progress, not of social justice.

Because that purpose was not the institutional point, the numbers of African American farmers in the late nineteenth century may well have peaked by the end of Reconstruction and then decreased. That was probably true of landowners. Yet alternately, it may have been that the total number of black farmers continuously increased. After all, the demand for tenants as renters on large, white landholdings was high while a lack of other employment sources made for large numbers of African Americans ready to till the soil. No data exists to sort out this question of more or less. The federal government and its Census of Agriculture did not begin to collect information by race until 1900.[13]

As can be seen in Table 1, there were 746,715 African American farm operators in 1900. This represented just more than 13 percent of all U.S. farmers. Of these, 732,362—or 98.1 percent of blacks—were in the South. Most, as can be surmised from more discriminating data collected for 1910 and 1920, were tenants. While total numbers of black farm operators in the United States increased to 893,370 and then 925,708, only 218,972 and then 218,612 were landowners. Thus, tenants constituted 75.3 percent of the African American farm operator force in 1910 and 76.2 percent in 1920.[14] Surely the Agricultural Establish-

13. U.S. Department of Commerce, *Historical Statistics of the United States: Colonial Times to 1970*, pt. 1 (Washington, D.C.: Bureau of the Census, 1975), 451.

14. U.S. Department of Commerce, *1969 Census of Agriculture*, pt. 1 (Washing-

Table 1. **African American Farm Operators, 1900–1997**

Year*	All U.S. Farms	Black-Operated Farms	Percent of Black-Operated Farms
1900	5,739,657	746,115	13.01
1910	6,361,502	893,377	14.04
1920	6,453,991	925,710	14.34
1930	6,295,103	882,852	14.02
1940	6,102,417	681,790	11.17
1950	5,388,437	559,980	10.39
1959	3,710,503	272,541	7.35
1969	2,730,250	87,393	3.20
1978	2,257,775	37,351	1.65
1987	2,087,759	22,954	1.10
1997	1,911,859	18,816	0.97
Rate of Decline	−3,827,789 (66.66%)	−727,299	97.48%

*Variations by decade reflect changes both in time of census of agriculture and agency in charge.

Source: J. Allen, "Race Data from 1900 to 1992," National Agricultural Statistical Service Library, January 4, 1999; U.S. Department of Agriculture, *1997 Census of Agriculture,* vol. 1, pt. 51 (Washington, D.C.: National Agricultural Statistical Service, 1999), 25.

ment and the science of farming mattered little to African Americans then. Nor did the dreams of land ownership matter to the vast majority of these black farmers, who undoubtedly believed after Reconstruction that they would never see the day when land was their own.

African American farmer numbers reached their twentieth-century zenith somewhere around 1920 and went into continuous and eventually dramatic decline from that time on. From 1920 to 1950 black farm operators, as a percentage of all farmers, fell from 14.8 to 10.9 percent.

---

ton, D.C.: Bureau of the Census, 1970), 96; U.S. Department of Commerce, *1950 Census of Agriculture* (Washington, D.C.: Bureau of the Census, 1950), 964. Farm managers were also included: 1,434 in 1910 and 2,026 in 1920 to equal 100 percent.

This occurred as the total of U.S. farms dropped by 16.5 percent. Black farmers, therefore, were failing at a faster rate than their none too economically stable white counterparts.

Why were things in such disarray? Economics obviously were important, as high World War I prices dropped and agriculture entered a depression lasting throughout the 1920s and 1930s.[15] That depression broke many farmers, leading to farm losses and continued financial instability of the sector.

Yet, as can be seen in Table 1, losses from 1920 to 1940 were far smaller for African American as well as other producers than from 1940 forward. Black farmers, though, were particularly hard hit after 1940, with an astonishing loss from 681,790 operators to 18,816 by millennium's end. This was more than a 97 percent decline in six decades. Rate of decline for other, almost all white, farmers for this period was only 68.7 percent.[16] This was so far from a random drop for African Americans that it suggests, on its face value, that institutional factors as well as economic ones were largely at work after 1920. Apparently, institutions first provided help between 1920 and 1940 and then withdrew it. An additional reason for that conclusion is that the state assumed an even greater interventionist role in farm sector production after 1920.[17] This was a continuation of the Agricultural Establishment's commitment to modernizing and developing the farm sector to better serve a market economy.

But the 1920s Establishment institutions encompassed more than simply education, research, and extension. Federal farm loans were funneled to producers through cooperatives, which were themselves exempt from anti-trust laws. A credit system was established, as were market agreements; middlemen were regulated so as not to corrupt farm-to-market trade. All such efforts were of greatest use to those farmers hoping to produce more for the market—not free market—

15. H. Thomas Johnson, *Agricultural Depression in the 1920's: Economic Fact or Statistical Artifact?* (New York: Garland, 1985).

16. In 1940, there were only 41,714 nonblack minority farmers, or about 6 percent of all minorities. J. Allen, "Race Data from 1900 to 1992," National Agricultural Statistical Service Library, January 4, 1999.

17. Adam D. Sheingate, *The Rise of the Agricultural Welfare State: Institutions and Interest Group Power in the United States, France, and Japan* (Princeton: Princeton University Press, 2001), 99–149.

economy. Such institutions mattered little to poverty-ridden farm tenants, and therefore to most African American operators. Other failed initiatives, which gained great congressional attention, were of little potential assistance to black tenants either. Tariff legislation to allow two-tiered pricing and foreign dumping of low-priced commodities was defeated. A Federal Farm Board that was to drive up commodity prices by voluntarily restricting production passed but was short-lived.[18] Debt relief for black tenants, which was truly needed, never came to the legislative agenda. So, it seems, African American farmers of this era were at first simply riding out economic hard times because there was little or no place else to go.

Franklin D. Roosevelt's election brought on evolutionary change in government's orientation to agricultural policy. In the end, that change did not aid African Americans, however. It was quite the reverse. In fact it seems to explain rapid African American farm exits after 1940, along with, of course, the opening of more industrial jobs in the North during World War II. The emphasis of Roosevelt-era change moved to keeping farmers who had previously received so much government attention and support on the land. The Agricultural Adjustment Act of 1933 was one distinct effort, and it did so best for the largest and most locally influential land holders who produced most of the crops. The AAA awarded domestic production allotments for previously farmed acres and provided cash payments to farmers who voluntarily cut acreage production at designated levels. Who won and who lost? The largest landholding growers won, since AAA was about boosting prices and so necessarily focused on these producers. Smaller growers lost, especially tenants, which meant almost all African Americans. These yeomen simply produced too little to be targets for farm modernization and development. They had too little impact on price. Moreover, unlike landowners, tenants could make few decisions about land reductions in planting.

18. Murray R. Benedict, *Farm Politics of the United States, 1790–1950: A Study of Their Origins and Development* (New York: Twentieth Century Fund, 1953), 282–83, 302–15; Douglas E. Bowers, Wayne D. Rasmussen, and Gladys L. Baker, *History of Agricultural Price Support and Adjustment Programs, 1933–84* (Washington, D.C.: Economic Research Service, U.S. Department of Agriculture, December 1984), 3–10.

Another facet of farm policy was established in 1933 as a complement to AAA. Because the effects of AAA would have a one-year time lag, more immediate programs were developed for farm financial relief. Farm loans from government entered American agriculture. In essence, the government loaned money to farmers who were storing crops. Loans were set at specific rates tied to market value, with farmers entitled to forfeit stored crops if prices fell below loan value. This established a floor for prices of specific crops, under which farm receipts for debtors would not fall. The setting of loan levels and the provisions of loans became perhaps even more integral to farm policy than were price supports. Both, though, meant federal checks for farmers, in very uneven amounts depending on farm size. When AAA was reinstituted in 1938, loans were guaranteed in its provisions, if, that is, county committees agreed to individual requests. Once again, farm tenants were left out in favor of the largest landowners.

AAA and other New Deal policies were even more insidious to black farmers than at first blush. Local responsibility for signing up farmers for supports and determining their allotments was given to the Extension Service for administration, and its county agents for organizing, and ultimately to those county-by-county elected farmer committees for granting benefits. To activate and involve farmers, the American Farm Bureau Federation and its county-by-county locals worked closely with national, state, and county Extension personnel.[19] Since local Extension offices most often received county funding in their efforts to modernize and develop area farmers, county supervisors also came to be influential in seeing who served on the committees, and thus who gained sign-ups, allotments, and federal dollars. In the South, which was home to most African American farm owners, this implementation plan was a perfect one for allowing bigotry and discrimination to flourish. Moreover, the black farmer was hardly the typical neighbor in either the North or the West. Accordingly, few considerations went their way, even for black landowners.

Despite the negative consequences of AAA for the minority of black farmers who owned their own farms, other plans within the Roosevelt

---

19. William J. Block, *The Separation of the Farm Bureau and the Extension Service* (Urbana: University of Illinois Press, 1960).

administration sought to, in reverse fashion, assist tenant farmers, who still constituted at least three-quarters of all black producers. Secretary of Agriculture Henry A. Wallace was genuinely moved by the plight of the southern rural and agricultural poor. After Roosevelt's first reelection, Wallace established and chaired a Special Committee on Farm Tenancy, which lobbied through Congress the Bankhead-Jones Farm Tenant Act of 1937.[20] Bankhead-Jones authorized the government to make long-term, low-interest loans to tenant farmers for the purchase of land and equipment. Wallace created the Farm Security Administration within the USDA to implement the act, reorganizing the previously independent Resettlement Administration into the FSA. The 1935 RA had been enormously unsuccessful in its own efforts to assist tenant farmers; it had employed up to sixteen thousand civil servants in hope of relocating half a million tenants from depleted farm lands. At the time of its death by reorganization, the two-year-old RA had relocated only 4,441 families and in frustration redirected its efforts toward making small loans for tenants to keep them more comfortable on their marginal plots of rented or sharecropped land. Mules and wood stoves were common purchases, at least for those who received sufficient funds to do so.

The FSA took more aggressive action than did the RA, making $516 million in loans to tenants through 1943.[21] Tenants made payments to own farms, purchased equipment and supplies, and in large numbers bought stock in farm cooperatives. Much of the stock purchase money was directed to the generally smaller-scale-farmer member National Farmers Union, with its several cooperative marketing associations and its bitter rivalry with the more large-farm, market-economy oriented Farm Bureau.

Tenants, and thus blacks, won from this second facet of New Deal agricultural policy. But, as shown in Table 1, the drop in the number of African American farm operators still more than doubled from the 1920s to the 1930s; those numbers decreased at an even faster rate be-

---

20. John C. Culver and John Hyde, *American Dreamer: The Life and Times of Henry A. Wallace* (New York: W. W. Norton, 2000), 169–71, 227–30.

21. Theodore Saloutos, *The American Farmer and the New Deal* (Ames: Iowa State University Press, 1982), 267.

tween 1940 and 1950. During that period, the percentage of all tenants on U.S. farms was declining, from 42.4 percent in 1930 to 38.7 in 1940, and then more sharply to 26.5 in 1950.[22] Tenant agriculture remained strongest in the South, even as African Americans were losing ground. Whatever tenants in general and African Americans in particular won was awarded for but a very brief time. As Whayne's later chapter demonstrates, county agents believed that these minute victories contributed only to a few black beneficiaries.

The FSA was closed in 1946, after three years without funding. There were two reasons. First, the FSA did not meet expectations that government should serve those farmers who were the leading edge of modernization, development, and technological adoption. Second, those who held these expectations also held prominent positions within the dominant and conservative agrarian development factions within Congress and the USDA, in the Extension Service, and as allied leaders of the Farm Bureau. They waged a classic case of institutional warfare against the FSA, the allied Farmers Union, and an urban liberal faction within the USDA that favored poverty programs. FSA supporters lost that battle. As at least one scholar indicates, there was more than a hint of racism in that attack, especially from southern members of Congress. Congressional attitudes were understandable, since any sweeping tenancy reform would have struck hard at the social fabric of the South. Thus they would have put at risk their ability to be reelected. And such reforms would not have merely led blacks to rend that social fabric. White farmers with large farm holdings feared the ascendancy of lower-class white yeomen as well. And so did gentile white society. Accordingly, as so many scholars have observed, southern officeholders discriminated against white subsistence and tenant farmers as well as against blacks. Tenants in the South operated more than 55 percent of all farms in 1930 and were increasing at a rate of forty thousand per year early in that decade.[23]

22. U.S. Department of Commerce, *1950 Census of Agriculture*, 85.

23. James T. Young, "The Origins of New Deal Agricultural Policy: Interest Groups' Role in Policy Formation," *Policy Studies Journal* 21 (summer 1993): 190–209. See also Jess Gilbert, "Eastern Urban Liberals and Midwestern Agrarian Intellectuals: Two Group Portraits of Progressives in the New Deal Department of Agriculture," *Agricultural History* 74 (spring 2000): 162–80; Mary Summers, "The

By 1950 two institutional forces were therefore set in motion that made farming nearly impossible for late-twentieth-century African Americans. The first force was the omnipresent institutional legacy of AAA. National farm politics for the remainder of the century was about altering and modifying an ever-expanding array of locally administered programs, procedures, and assumptions about price support and loan policy, plus accepting some infusion of mid- to upper-class social-cause policy.[24] That social-cause policy was about nutrition, consumerism, organic foods, and the environment, or what so many modern farmers have called "rich kids politics."

It was not about the rural poor, farm tenants, or African American farmers. That void in social-cause policy interest has been the second institutional force affecting black farmers. Because of the demise of the FSA, and because there have been no subsequent replacements for its general intent, no precedent exists any longer for discussing and focusing on the interests of typical African American producers when attentions turn to contemporary U.S. agricultural policy. Black farmers, in their astonishingly low numbers, have been left, therefore, between the proverbial rock and a hard place, between the invisible stature of the FSA and the little groups of white neighbors from AAA. It is no wonder that in 1997, black operators accounted for less than 1 percent of all American farmers, whose own ranks had been depleted by 67 percent since 1900 (see Table 1). In an age of farm decline, African American farming was all but already dead.

Blaming institutional structures for trends that have been in evidence over such a long time, however, is risky at best. Such claims would be easily subject to dismissal were it not for the convincing work of emi-

New Deal Farm Programs: Looking for Reconstruction in American Agriculture," *Agricultural History* 74 (spring 2000): 241–57. The most venerable scholar who mentions discrimination against white subsistence and tenant farmers in several books is V. O. Key, Jr., *Politics, Parties, and Pressure Groups*, 5th ed. (New York: Crowell, 1964). Holley, cited in James T. Young, "The Origins of New Deal Agricultural Policy," 203.

24. William P. Browne, *Private Interests, Public Policy and American Agriculture* (Lawrence: University Press of Kansas, 1988), 130–49.

nent scholars of American statism.[25] Their lesson has been simple: the institutional policy that has been put in place lives on in its influence, particularly if superceding institutions fail to reverse or significantly shift those causal elements initially embedded in law and legal culture. From those initial and stable directions (if comprehensive enough) come the state, and its governance.

In the case of African American farmers, it is unnecessary even to prove over time the institutional linkages and directions within a conservative USDA administration, a locally based county management process that owes itself to AAA, and a near absolute neglect of tenants and small-scale farmers. The politics of the 1990s have been the proof. They have confirmed those linkages, first as black clients rebelled and second as the USDA acknowledged its own long-term guilt.

By 1990 complaints from black farmers to their own local members of Congress had reached, in one member's words, "epidemic levels." He continued, "It's clear to me that the Department of Agriculture systematically and by choice discriminates by race—USDA today is as blatant in its actions as was the Birmingham (Alabama) Chamber of Commerce in 1954."[26] As a result of constituent complaints, this member and his staff had been for more than two years taking the plight of black farmers to the congressional leadership, the Congressional Black Caucus, the USDA, and assorted federal civil rights agencies and civil rights interest groups. "And so have been colleagues in the House," he concluded.

Many of those complaints from grassroots farmers had been orchestrated by two interest groups that had formed and become prominent by the mid-1990s: the Black Farmers and Agriculturalists Association (BFAA) and the National Black Farmers Association (NBFA). Their interest-group strategies were common ones: leaders kept up continuous contact with public officials, testimony was offered at public hear-

25. Stephen Skowronek, *Building a New American State: The Expansion of National Administrative Capacities, 1877–1920* (Cambridge: Cambridge University Press, 1982); Kenneth Finegold and Theda Skopol, *State and Party in America's New Deal* (Madison: University of Wisconsin Press, 1995).

26. Anonymous personal interview, May 1992. See also William P. Browne, *Cultivating Congress: Constituents, Issues, and Interests in Agricultural Policymaking* (Lawrence: University Press of Kansas, 1995), 223–31.

ings, members were activated to meet with their own congressional representatives, media attention was cultivated, and attention-gaining protest rallies were staged.[27] This was not merely interest-group-driven policy-making strategy, however.

Some African American members of Congress from southeastern states had been encouraging the NBFA and BFAA to organize and press complaints in greater numbers.[28] They, rather than group activists, were the real policy entrepreneurs. The NBFA was not founded until 1995. The congressional advocates' initial goal was to guarantee that African Americans be specifically provided protections in the planned 1995 farm bill, or at least that a prominent hearing, which they had not received in the 1990 farm bill, be won. Only extensive publicity on behalf of black farm plight, they believed, would provide such a guarantee. To this end, Black Caucus members had earlier persuaded the House Congressional Committee on Government Operations to publicly charge the USDA with blatant discrimination in its loan practices.[29]

Both the House and Senate agriculture committees appeared still unresponsive in 1995 to congressional member complaints, interest-group lobbying, or the advice of some USDA officials to encourage a reorganization of the department's civil rights programs. NBFA and BFAA leaders—with advice from black congressional representatives, Farm Service officials, and a few national environmental interest-group leaders—abruptly switched gears. In an increasingly common strategy for interest groups that are otherwise failing to win, the NBFA and BFAA solicited members who would litigate.[30] Two class-action suits were filed in U.S. District Court, District of Columbia in 1996: *Timothy C. Pigford, et al. v. Dan Glickman, Secretary, the United States Department of*

27. Anthony J. Nownes, *Pressure and Power: Organized Interests in American Politics* (Boston: Houston Mifflin, 2001), 88–102.

28. William P. Browne addresses the importance of congressional office enterprises in agricultural policy making, see *Cultivating Congress,* 9, 18, 19, 35–36, 211.

29. U.S. House of Representatives, *The Minority Farmer: A Disappearing Resource.* H. Rept. 101–984 (Washington, D.C., Committee on Government Operations, Government Information, Justice and Agriculture Subcommittee, November 20, 1990).

30. Nownes, *Pressure and Power,* 102–4.

Agriculture (Civil Action No. 97-1978) and *Cecil Brewington, et al. v. Daniel R. Glickman* (98-1693).

The common complaint was that black farmers had been purposely driven to bankruptcy through discriminatory procedures of the Farm Service Agency and the local farmer committees that approved USDA program entry. The USDA, it was also charged, had furthered this discrimination through its failure to effectively maintain its Office of Civil Rights.[31]

The USDA promptly responded by acknowledging guilt through the Office of the Secretary. A moratorium on the foreclosure of black-owned farms was initiated in 1996. This was accompanied by dozens of reports from USDA agencies on minority issues, mostly in 1995–1997.[32] Then came a series of twelve listening sessions held by the USDA around the country. Feedback on both racial and gender discrimination was encouraged. Secretary Glickman or Deputy Secretary Richard E. Rominger attended all but one of the sessions, giving the meetings both elevated status and high visibility in order to counter previous negative publicity about USDA indifference.

Those listening sessions plus a review of USDA program delivery procedures led to what many in Congress—both pro and con—angrily saw as startling admissions by the department. *Civil Rights at the United States Department of Agriculture* was released in February of 1997. John Sparks, Glickman's assistant for civil rights, later and quite accurately described its central theme: "The department did not treat African Americans and other minorities fairly in the area of lending and program delivery and the servicing of loans. That's just a fact."[33]

Even though the legal challenges covered the years 1981 through 1996, the refrains of the report might well have been offered in 1940. The mea culpas went on and on in a litany of admissions. First were the charges that the USDA, from any perspective, was far from a progressive federal agency. Paperwork was cumbersome for loans and services.

31. Internal case documents, both suits.

32. Civil Rights Action Team, *Civil Rights at the United States Department of Agriculture* (Washington, D.C.: U.S. Department of Agriculture, February 1997), 100–108.

33. Ibid., 2–5; Charisse Jones, "Black Farmers Say They've Been Cheated," *USA Today*, January 5, 1999.

Officials exercised powers with impunity and without accountability. The Office of Inspector General was used to harass minority farmers with unsubstantiated investigations. There was a department-wide lack of commitment to diversity and equal opportunity, in employment and in loan practices. The Assistant Secretary of Administration in charge of civil rights laws, rules, and regulations lacked authority to affect either senior executive or general employee performance.

Management skills were often absent. Agencies had few resources for diversity management; most had no measurable goals for equal opportunity. Black farmers saw a conspiracy by white managers to take their land. No actions were forthcoming to allay those fears. Overall, rural development missions were directed without accountability for job performance, with no dictates for minority service. These missions lacked strong leaders to advance them. Managers considered nonfarm issues burdensome. Reorganizations were routine and mindless. Reform proposals gathered dust and many central recommendations were ignored. No accountability was built into program delivery, and employees felt no threats of oversight. Little emphasis was placed on eliminating discrepancies. Leadership changes were frequent.[34]

These conditions made it all the more probable that employees and farm committee members would simply fall back on the rhetoric and traditions of the USDA, modernizing and developing farmer expertise and technical capacity. Or, as sociologist Jess Gilbert found of New Deal agricultural policy making, the USDA has been dominated by "conservative agrarians," with little room and minimal support for close-knit intellectual groups who sought internal policy reforms on behalf of disadvantaged clientele. Traditionalists in the 1940s not only undermined the Farm Security Administration but also exacerbated the congressional problems of the progressive Bureau of Agricultural Economics. Those who were not seen as part of the science of agricultural advancement were viewed as incorrect, wrong, or misplaced. Thus, the USDA has for years been labeled a "stubborn bureaucracy and slow to change."[35]

34. Civil Rights Action Team, *Civil Rights at the United States Department of Agriculture*, 7–9, 11–14, 16, 46–50.

35. Gilbert, "Eastern Urban Liberals and Midwestern Agrarian Intellectuals," 180; Civil Rights Action Team, *Civil Rights at the United States Department of Agriculture*, 2.

All of these factors explain why the tenets and procedures of AAA program delivery prevailed. The Civil Rights Action Team criticized that legacy with yet another litany. As "hundreds of new personnel" and "hundreds of new programs" have been added to agricultural policy, local delivery and administration remained the norm. Farmer committees employed, and paid with USDA funds, their own directors to aid local deliberations. The addition of the Farmers Home Administration to the lending efforts of the USDA made greater involvement from local administrators, committeemen, and politicians an increased impediment to effective coordination. County committee systems locked out minority applicants and continued to fund the favored few, those who farmed the largest numbers of total acres.

Loan officers were rewarded for covering more acres with available funds, but not for encouraging diversity of participation. Almost all local committees were composed of white males, with no women or minorities. Only 36 of the 101 counties having the largest concentration of minority farmers had at least one minority farm committee member. Large-scale, landowning producers dominated committee ranks. Processing of minority loans took longer and, according to black farmer complaints, often arrived too late to be useful. Smaller average size of minority farms was a critical factor in explaining delays and rejections.[36]

This meant that effective management of farm program delivery remained impossible. Top-down administration just did not exist. In addition, the local decision-making committee units were composed of large-scale white farmers, gave more benefits first to large-scale farms, and followed the traditional logic of USDA service by prioritizing the most technologically proficient, modern, and market-oriented producers. There were no aberrations here. What was conceived in AAA continued unabated into the 1990s, even with extensive USDA reorganization and continued legislative modifications of price and loan policy. This was not a system in which black farmer problems would be given a priority. The death of the FSA ended assistance to black tenant farmers; the report of the Civil Rights Action Team gave them no mention.

36. Civil Rights Action Team, *Civil Rights at the United States Department of Agriculture,* 6–7, 8, 19–20, 21.

This was not acceptable oversight in that 36 percent of all African American farmers were still tenants in 1997. This compared to only 10 percent tenancy among all U.S. farmers. Moreover, the emphasis of agricultural policy on influencing prices through production-cutting policy meant that small-scale farmers were attended to last. This also was ignored in the report's explanation. Most black farms fell into that category and so policy-wise were not considered viable parts of U.S. commercial agriculture. African American farms were on average about 127 acres in 1997, with only 43 acres of harvested cropland. The rate for all U.S. farms was 488 total acres and 162 acres of harvested cropland.[37]

When USDA administrators were confronted with litigation concerning the consequences of what had become their modernization and development paradigm, the department was forced to face only its structural failure. Its intellectual failure was not in question, internally at least. Moreover, the USDA still acknowledged that actual change in its performance was quite problematic given the existing and entrenched farm committee structure. By 1998, the USDA was settling the legal claims of some black farmers who were partners to the two cases. In January of 1999, Secretary Glickman announced the final settlement in a consent decree between the USDA and "black farmers." Congress had, in 1999, waived the statute of limitations on claims. Cash payments and loan reviews were made available to all parties to the litigation. While these actions eased the plight of specific black farmers and former farmers, the end product was but a one-time infusion of cash to individuals, more than $368 million within nine months on the USDA's streamlined review track.[38] The settlement, however, did noth-

---

37. U.S. Department of Agriculture, *1997 Census of Agriculture*, vol. 1 (Washington, D.C.: U.S. Department of Agriculture, 1999), 24–25. These are hardly representative numbers since small hobby farms proliferate and far larger farms produce most of all commodities. Approximately 25 percent of producers grew nearly 90 percent of all commodities in recent years.

38. Civil Rights Action Team, *Civil Rights at the United States Department of Agriculture*, 57; Dan Glickman, "Remarks: Black Farmers Class Action Settlement Announcement" (Washington, D.C.: U.S. Department of Agriculture, January 5, 1999); Charisse Jones, "Black Farmers Say They've Been Cheated"; U.S. Department of Agriculture, *Pigford v. Glickman*, website, http://www.usda.gov/da/status .htm, October 2, 1990.

ing to change the institutional conditions that initially created discrimination. As such, the ultimate demise of an already economically and socially dead African American agriculture was all further assured.

African American freedmen were enticed by what they saw as promises of "40 acres and a mule."[39] For each one of them, that was the hope: a place to settle in rural tranquility. But for blacks, these promises proved to be only campaign slogans and the elaborate posturing of public officials. The failure of government to deliver the land and mules, however, was *not* the reason for black flight to the cities. Such small plots of land, with such limited capacity to farm, combined with a commitment to Jeffersonian logic and subsistence production would have forever left African American farmers out of the mainstream of a commercializing and consolidating U.S. agriculture. That would have been true if those conditions remained a constant.

What small-scale farmers faced was an evolving set of institutions and institutionally created circumstances that fostered and then always favored larger-scale producers. To develop the frontier, peasant-style European agriculture was not highly favored. Those institutions, started as they were in 1862, were indeed the stepchildren of different sectional interests. Eastern Republicans favored land grant proposals. Western Republicans feared that land grants would interfere with a Railroad Act and a Homestead Act, by giving too much western land to eastern states. Congress was similarly split in supporting the creation of the USDA. Many believed that any new department would be a home of patronage politics, merely more of what government had practiced since the Andrew Jackson administration. Supporters argued that it was time for men of agriculture to have an institutional voice in government, to ensure that the importance of farmers continued to be seen.[40]

In the end, all sections and partisans won. The forthcoming presi-

39. This was an order given by General William T. Sherman to the Union Army, mandating disbursement to former slaves. President Andrew Johnson immediately rescinded the order. But the slogan never goes away, most recently having been resurrected by proponents of reparations for the wrongs inflicted by southern slavery.

40. Sheingate, *The Rise of the Agricultural Welfare State*, 47–49.

dential election led Republicans to reluctantly gather behind homestead, railroading, and educational land grants. The party needed to prevent popular rejection in the midst of war. The creation of the USDA, without cabinet status, came from a realization that both politics and farm science would be important to the spread of economically viable and sustainable farmers as they moved west. With such mixed supporters, beneficiaries of the four acts worked only obliquely together. Yet together they fostered an institutional direction that would come to favor science, scientific research, and applied scientific outreach to farmers.[41] The politics finally rallied around the science, or at least its importance to advancing a nation.

This institutional culture reacted in favor of farmers who chose pathways to the commercial market and in opposition to subsistence farmers who merely (often against hope) wished to stay landed. And that culture reacted in favor of technologies that could help farmers grow more, with the same or even fewer efforts, and hopefully produce at lower prices. An increasing abundance of food products made it essential that consumers would consume more and that new consumers could be found.[42] By the time New Deal politics produced new public policies, the direction of favoring "big" farmers was set and followed. Big farmers were more than just the most willing listeners. Government was desperate to prop up prices, and only modernizing, large-scale farmers could make sufficient crop reductions to influence price factors. Large-scale farmers were also the ones most likely to be influential and respected in their local areas. This was important to a politically conscious USDA. AAA then found wide acceptance among Gilbert's politically astute "conservative agrarians" within the burgeoning Agricultural Establishment.

The FSA did not find this favor; indeed, it could not have since it ran contrary to prevailing institutional values, both in Congress and in administrative and scientific agriculture. The popularity of AAA price supports, loans, and farmer committees fed commercial agriculture.

41. Ibid., 49–50; Browne, *The Failure of National Rural Policy*, 37–49.
42. Schultz, *Agriculture in an Unstable Economy;* Robert Paarlberg and Don Paarlberg, "Agricultural Policy in the Twentieth Century," *Agricultural History* 74 (spring 2000): 140–42.

The FSA's failure doomed attention to farmers who were either tenants or who were falling behind large-scale farmers in production efficiency. Exits in the sector most affected these disadvantaged growers—the have-nots—but institutions continued to give greatest attention to the haves of an ever-modernizing but always economically stressed agriculture.[43]

Blacks, who were largely tenants and mostly small-scale producers, suffered the malignant and deadly consequences of what were benignly intended institutions, to be used for developing a nation through agriculture. Forty acres and a mule, even times thousands of farms, could not have brought black farmer survival for the masses. Their farms, like those of small-scale white farmers, would have been taken over by more market-minded, expansionist commercial farmers, either black or white. This was the pattern that beset all of rural America, consolidation after consolidation. Cities, as a result, would still have been places of black destinations, their unwitting orientations of choice in the middle and late twentieth century.

43. Paarlberg and Paarlberg, "Agricultural Policy in the Twentieth Century," 142–45.

&

"I Have Been through Fire"

Black Agricultural Extension Agents
and the Politics of Negotiation

JEANNIE WHAYNE

In June 1916, Otis O'Neal, a black specialist working in an "experimental" Agricultural Extension program in Georgia, wrote a report to the state director that dramatically captured the difficulties under which such federal agents worked.[1] The program was weighing whether to use black agents to reach black farmers in the South. The issue was whether whites would tolerate their presence and whether blacks would accept them. O'Neal reported that as an agent he had "been through fire," and that "dark clouds of disappointment have obstructed my path. More than once my life has been at stake."

His report was more than a mere rant about the problems confronting him. It was designed to demonstrate how much he had accomplished. Though he admitted that he "could not have said this at first," he was now able to assert that "I do not have a single enemy in the State." By 1920 O'Neal would be reassigned to serve as a county agent for Houston County, and in that role he functioned as the principal intermediary standing between the Cooperative Extension Service on the one hand and the black farmer on the other. His position was an acutely problematic one in that he had many masters. He reported not only to the state director of Extension, a white man, but also was ac-

1. Otis O'Neal, special Extension agent, to J. Phil Campbell, director of Extension in Georgia, June 9, 1916, p. 3. O'Neal indicates in his opening paragraph that he had been asked to submit a report on his "extension work with Negro farmers since I have been in Georgia," and that his report covered the period from October 1, 1914, to June 1, 1916, in General Correspondence, Office of the Secretary of Agriculture, Negroes, box 1, RG 16, National Archives Two, College Park, Maryland (hereafter OSA papers).

countable to a black district agent. It was his obligation to present the Extension program, as fashioned by white agricultural bureaucrats and interpreted by black bureaucrats, to black farmers, most of whom were sharecroppers. Because both he and his potential clients existed within a sociopolitical culture that was volatile and racist, he dared not present his program to black farmers without the permission of the planters for whom they worked.[2]

O'Neal and other black farm agents were charged with the responsibility of bringing scientific farming methods to African Americans, and they were seen as a key component of the U.S. Department of Agriculture's goal to stabilize the farm economy. The Cooperative Extension Service launched the experiment in black agricultural education shortly after the passage of the Smith-Lever Act in 1914, an act that created the agency. The ideas behind Smith-Lever evolved over the course of several decades of agricultural education experimentation, emanating from both white and black colleges. The Morrill Act of 1862 provided for the creation of agricultural and mechanical colleges, but the Civil War interfered with the process in the South until the early 1870s. Most southern states failed to create black colleges until the second Morrill Act of 1890, but certain private black colleges had assumed the responsibility for agricultural education, colleges such as Tuskegee Institute in Alabama and Hampton Institute in Virginia. The white colleges, however, had much better funding and were able to engage in more ambitious programs. They piloted the "demonstration" system, whereby farm agents working out of the agricultural colleges tested certain vari-

2. E. A. Williams, who had been an Extension specialist serving alongside O'Neal in 1916, was the African American state director of Extension working out of Georgia Industrial College in Savannah by 1920. In 1918 an additional layer of bureaucracy was created, putting a black field agent working out of Tuskegee Institute in charge of black Extension in Georgia and several other southern states. W. B. Mercier, "Extension Work among Negroes, 1920," U.S. Department of Agriculture, *Circular* 190 (Washington: Government Printing Office, 1921): 8–9, 21–22. Although black agents initially focused their efforts on black farm owners, it became clear that if southern agriculture was to be reformed, black sharecroppers had to be brought into the arena of agricultural education. O. S. O'Neal, special Extension agent, Georgia State Industrial College, Savannah, Ga., to J. Phil Campbell, director of Extension work, Athens, Ga., June 4, 1916, p. 3, box 1, OSA papers.

eties of seeds or demonstrated the use of fertilizers on a preselected plot of land owned by a farmer. Black colleges, meanwhile, focused on bringing black farmers to their premises to hold such demonstrations. In 1906 Tuskegee, with backing from the John F. Slater Fund, launched the "school on wheels," which was essentially a wagon loaded with demonstration materials that traveled across Alabama, reaching out to black farmers. In that same year, largely with funds from Slater and the Rockefeller Foundation, Tuskegee placed its first black agent in the field, Thomas M. Campbell. J. B. Pierce, working out of Hampton Institute, assumed the same responsibilities in Virginia a few months later.[3]

The passage of the Smith-Lever Act institutionalized both white and black agricultural education, and the Cooperative Extension Service began to create a structure and hierarchy. Under this system white farm agents were assigned to counties, with the expectation that the county would pay up to 50 percent of the cost of their salaries. The county agents reported to district agents, men who had responsibility for several counties, who then reported to the state director of Extension. That director was typically responsible to the dean of the agricultural and mechanical college within the state. Federal policy filtered through him down to the county agent.

The development of the black agent system paralleled that directed toward whites, although it was slower to emerge, in part because most county governments refused to provide funds. As the (white) vice director of Extension in Florida said, in responding to a survey in 1928, Florida centralized the distribution of all funds out of his office "be-

---

3. The Morrill Act of 1862 granted federal lands to states with the understanding that the proceeds from the sale of the land would be used to finance the creation of agricultural and mechanical colleges. In 1887 the Hatch Act provided funds to create experiment stations attached to agricultural colleges. Thomas T. Williams and Handy Williamson, Jr., "Teaching, Research, and Extension Programs at Historically Black (1890) Land-Grant Institutions," *Agricultural History* 62 (spring 1988): 244; Allen W. Jones, "The Role of Tuskegee Institute in the Education of Black Farmers," 263. For an examination of the difficulties confronted by the colleges founded by the 1890 legislation, see Robert L. Jenkins, "The Black Land-Grant Colleges in Their Formative Years, 1890–1920," *Agricultural History* 65 (winter 1991): 63–72; and Frederick S. Humphries, "1890 Land-Grant Institutions: Their Struggle for Survival and Equality," *Agricultural History* 65 (spring 1991): 3–11; Jones, "The Role of Tuskegee Institute," 264.

cause we feel it is best not to raise the question with a number of our Boards, and we think too that we secure about all the money that is available for Extension work in most of the counties, and we can probably distribute it better than if we would raise the question of asking them to pay a part of the negro agent's salary." The director of Extension in Georgia put it more bluntly, reporting in response to the same survey that they received "very little support locally for the negro county agents."[4] Although whites were initially unwilling to recognize the value of agricultural education for blacks, structurally the white and black programs were similar. White county agents reported to white district agents, black county agents reported to black district agents, and there appears to have been little contact between white and black agents of either category. Both white and black district agents reported to the white director of Extension. Nominally, however, authority over black Extension education was concentrated in three black institutions: Tuskegee, Hampton, and, for a brief period, Prairie View State Normal and Industrial College in Texas. In 1918 black field agents were put in charge of multi-state areas: Campbell was appointed the field agent working out of Tuskegee and had responsibility for the Gulf states. Pierce represented Hampton and had charge of the south Atlantic states. Until his death in 1919, E. L. Blackshear was the third field agent working out of Prairie View, and he had responsibility for three westernmost southern states. When Blackshear died, his territory was divided between that of Campbell and Pierce.[5]

4. A. P. Spencer, vice director, Florida Extension, February 18, 1928; J. Phil Campbell, director, Georgia Extension, February 16, 1928, both in box 355, Alabama Cooperative Extension Service Records, Auburn University (hereafter ACES).

5. Earl W. Crosby, "The Struggle for Existence: The Institutionalization of the Black County Agent System," 135. Blackshear originally had charge of three states, including Texas. After his death, Campbell was placed in charge of the so-called Gulf States of the South (Georgia, Florida, Alabama, Mississippi, Louisiana, Texas, and Oklahoma) while Pierce presided over the South Atlantic states (Maryland, Virginia, North Carolina, South Carolina, West Virginia, Kentucky, Tennessee, and Arkansas). Arkansas, Texas, and Oklahoma had previously been Blackshear's responsibility. See C. W. Warburton, director of Extension work, to Edward M. Lewis, Massachusetts Agricultural College, March 14, 1925, box 2, OSA papers.

Campbell and Pierce occupied important positions within the Extension program, but they worked in advisory capacities only and struggled throughout their long careers to exercise policy-making responsibility. Their greatest success was in expanding the black agent system, and they did so by establishing its importance to the primary goal of the Cooperative Extension program. This was not difficult to do. In order to bring scientific agriculture to the southern states, the plantation system had to be rescued from the brink of ruin, and black farmers were key to any solution. Planters had engaged in the overproduction of cotton since shortly after the Civil War and promoted an over-intensive cultivation of the soil so that decreased yields were an endemic problem. Black educators successfully argued that since black sharecroppers actually did most of the farming on plantations, they had to be reached if there was to be any hope of bringing modern farming methods to the southern plantation.[6] At the same time, even as Otis O'Neal was writing his report in 1915, rural African Americans were beginning to leave the South in large numbers. This trend accelerated during and after World War I as blacks moved to southern and, particularly, northern cities in search of industrial jobs. The federal farm loan programs implemented in the 1920s to address the problems confronting farmers did nothing to aid black farmers; the New Deal programs in the next decade served them no better. In fact, New Deal programs displaced the poorest southern farmers, both black and white. Before the New Deal programs introduced a labor surplus (by taking lands out of cultivation), the plantation system was labor intensive, and planters and policy makers alike grew increasingly alarmed about the exodus, forcing the Extension Service to begin to reinterpret its mission in the South. In addition to promoting new farming techniques, the service had to act to stem the flow of black agricultural labor. Some means had to be devised to make conditions better for blacks in the South while at the same time avoiding the appearance of challenging the racial status quo. White southerners would have rejected any program that threatened its rigid social structure, but blacks were leaving the South largely because of the limited opportunities open to them and

6. Departmental memo summarizing P. C. Parks to the president of the United States, January 1, 1913, box 1, OSA papers.

because of the violence and humiliation that awaited them at every turn. The Extension Service had to work around the edges of the problem, promoting the farm Extension program as one answer to the black exodus.

The black farm agents did not toil alone in this particular vineyard. They shared the stage with black Home Demonstration agents, women whose focus was on improving the conditions of the farm home and family. It was organized much like the farm program, with Home Demonstration agents assigned to counties and reporting to district agents. Eventually, as the program grew and matured, a state director of Home Demonstration was appointed and district agents reported to her. The white Home Demonstration agent had essentially the same responsibilities as black agents, but the black program took on a particular urgency because of the black exodus. World War I conscription, moreover, revealed a staggering deficiency in the southern diet, especially that of African Americans. A high percentage of potential military recruits had to be rejected for service because of diseases or physical deficiencies caused by poor diet. African American Home Demonstration agents were thus expected to do much more than simply help farm wives render the home more comfortable through better food preparation and mattress making. They were instructed in how to prevent both diet-related and other diseases, to introduce better sanitation practices, and to train farm women to appropriately care for the sick. While the Home Demonstration program made some effort to train farm women on how to contribute to farm income through gardening and marketing produce, most gardening projects focused on preserving foods for home consumption, particularly for black women. Canning projects became a chief focus of demonstrations, and lessons in preparing nutritious meals took on special significance.[7]

7. The county home agents reported to district agents who reported to state home agents. The state home agent reported to the director of Extension. Mercier, "Extension Work among Negroes, 1920," 13–15. Melissa Walker's study of the black Home Demonstration program in Tennessee suggests that while white women were oriented toward consumption and creating a "farm home based on the suburban white middle class model," the program for black women "rarely emphasized consumption." Walker's study focused on east Tennessee and elected to concentrate on farm-owning families. Melissa Walker, "Home Extension

The central dilemma for the Extension Service was how to make conditions better for blacks in the South without giving them the means of developing greater independence and thus freeing them from the dominance of plantation owners who desperately needed their labor and who exercised considerable influence within the USDA. It was up to black farm and Home Demonstration agents to work through this contradiction. Their position in this dilemma made them the perfect example of the "subaltern," the classic man or woman in the middle.

Subaltern studies originated as an analytical framework designed to examine the relationship between indigenous populations and imperial masters and, particularly, to locate "agency" in the actions of the colonial people. These theorists rejected the Cambridge School of colonial studies, which focused on the struggle between imperial and colonial elites and thus obscured the role of ordinary individuals and the culture within which they existed. The subaltern studies perspective might suggest that when it comes to the black Extension program, one must look beyond the struggle between Booker T. Washington and W. E. B. Du Bois over the most appropriate path for African Americans to take, economic or political, to grasp the experience of ordinary African Americans in the South. The Washington–Du Bois debate had little meaning or resonance, and, in a sense, not even an audience among the mass of African American farmers and their families.[8]

Work among African American Farm Women in East Tennessee, 1920–1939," 487–502. A South Carolina report written in 1918 included information about progress in the Home Demonstration program and provided some data on the "colored" program. While there were forty-four white home demonstrations in that state in 1918, nineteen black assistants (to the white agent) were appointed to work with African American farm women. It is unlikely that they worked together, however, as segregation practices dictated that white and black agents be housed separately. The document is a fragment, unfortunately, so a full citation is impossible to provide. It appears in the microfilm collection, Annual Narrative and Statistical Reports from State Offices and County Agents, the first reel on South Carolina. The microfilm series consists of more than seven thousand reels of microfilm covering all the states in the Union. They are organized by states, and the individual reels are organized alphabetically by county, although the district and state agent reports typically begin each year's account. The black agent reports are embedded within the white agent reports (hereafter ANSR microfilm).

8. Gyan Prakash, "Subaltern Studies as Postcolonial Criticism," *American His-*

One of the ways subaltern studies might aid us in understanding the experience of Extension agents' black constituency lies in their appreciation of the centrality of religion in the lives of African Americans. Subaltern studies rejects the Marxist approach, arguing that it misunderstood or misrepresented "the religious idiom of the rebels or viewed it as a mere form and a stage in the development of revolutionary consciousness."[9] Few American historians have made the mistake of underestimating the importance of the church in black life. Certainly, a close reading of the record would reveal the folly of ignoring the central role that the black church and black preachers played. In 1911, for example, one black South Carolina county agent, R. S. Murphy, reported that "the negro rural church and the negro preacher constitutes the two important factors in the negro's social and economic development, therefore, wherever feasible, farms have been selected [for demonstration] near churches and the negro preacher."[10] Murphy understood black rural culture well enough to appreciate the importance of religion and used that knowledge to best advantage as he sought to find support for the Extension program.

Subaltern studies theorists would recognize Murphy's strategy as similar to the maneuvers of indigenous officials of the imperial regime as they used their knowledge of the colonial culture to gain acceptance of imperial policies. The methodology has found its highest expression in the study of such relationships in India, Africa, and Latin America,

---

torical Review 99 (December 1994): 1477. Rebecca Ferguson's "Caught in 'No Man's Land': The Negro Cooperative Demonstration Service and the Ideology of Booker T. Washington, 1900–1918," 33–54, avoids the trap of focusing too narrowly on Washington by examining the response of black farmers to the efforts of black agents. Most of her information comes from the Booker T. Washington Papers and from the papers of Thomas M. Campbell of Tuskegee. Indeed, it was Ferguson's conceptualization of the dilemma facing the black Extension program that encouraged the development of the ideas outlined in this essay. The dilemma Ferguson concentrated on was the difficulty of convincing black farmers to accept the accommodationist program of Washington when what they needed was something far more revolutionary.

9. Ferguson, "Caught in 'No Man's Land.'"

10. R. S. Murphy, Kershaw County Negro agent, South Carolina, to Ira W. Williams, state agent, U.S. Farm Demonstration Work, Columbia, South Carolina, n.d. [but attached to Williams' 1911 report], p. 2, ANSR microfilm.

but it also opens a window on the world of the African American Extension agent in the South. The subaltern practices the art of negotiation, both rationalizing and justifying the agenda of the dominant partner in the relationship but in such a way as to transform it into a form of resistance. Black Extension agents clearly occupied the subaltern position and served the interests of white agricultural policy makers, yet they continually negotiated the specifics of the program. Subalterns in colonial societies, however, were much more successful in resisting the incursion of the imperial power.[11] The ability of colonial subalterns to play a role in negotiating the demise of imperial authority stands in direct contradiction to the failure of black subalterns in the Extension Service to play a similar role in the South. In the former, the crumbling of the imperial powers in the aftermath of World War II set the stage for a different historical outcome. In contrast, the federal bureaucracy in the United States increased in authority and power in the 1930s and 1940s and successfully negotiated the modernization of southern agriculture. As modernization swept over the South, black farmers departed by the tens of thousands. Their culture, their society, their entire way of life was abandoned as they sought a new life in an urban setting. It is arguable, however, that while black agents failed to bring a program to black farmers that either kept them in the South or substantially improved their lives, they provided them with the wherewithal to imagine something better for themselves.

Working in the space between larger impersonal historic forces and the realities of daily life, black agents sought to bring programs to black farmers and their families that would ameliorate the appalling impoverishment that was their lot. In recommending accommodation instead of militancy, farm agents were certainly working to counter any threat to the status quo, but this must be understood in its context. Violence awaited farmers who challenged planters for a fair settlement of the crop, whether black farmers acted individually or collectively. Those who would suggest that black farmers should have taken such a course of action rather than accept accommodation fail to appreciate that such heroics would have likely been suicidal. Indeed, the struggle to provide

---

11. For the role of the subaltern in colonial cultures, see Edward W. Said, *Culture and Imperialism* (New York: Alfred A. Knopf, 1993).

for and protect one's family took precedence in the minds of most ordinary men and women. They sought to achieve a level of comfort and
stability in a dangerous and volatile setting, and any program that
would have put their tenuous stability at risk would likely have been rejected. The most they would have been receptive to were the programs
offered by Extension agents. These programs were hardly radical, but
they provided actual material benefit to black farm families.

Rather than rallying them to challenge the white power structure politically, black agents provided their clients with advice on how to improve their daily lives, and while this mundane and pedestrian endeav-
or smacks of accommodation, it must be emphasized that most African
Americans lived outside the view of whites. Their hour-by-hour experiences were what occupied their greatest attention and determined
their basic level of personal comfort. Thus black farmers were more receptive to the Extension agent's demonstrations on how to clear stumps
from the land, build terraces, and make compost than they would have
been to rousing speeches about racial injustices. Farm women would
have recognized the value of demonstrations on how to grow and preserve vegetables and fruits, how to care for the sick and injured, and
how to make their homes more comfortable for their husbands and
children.[12] Their own preoccupation with the commonplace necessi-

---

12. The annual reports of black agents catalog the many demonstrations they
engaged in. P. H. Stone, the state agent for Negro work in Georgia, provides an
excellent example of these programs in 1926. There his farm agents gave demonstrations on building or repairing tool sheds, repairing schoolhouses, clearing
stumps, digging ditches, building or repairing terraces, breaking land, using barnyard manure on plats, composting, starting gardens, planting truck crops, testing
seed corn, selecting strawberries, pruning orchards, building hot beds, building
fire-heated potato beds, setting pecan trees, butchering pork, treating hogs for
cholera, purchasing purebred boars and sows, constructing poultry houses, purchasing baby chicks, establishing permanent pastures, building sanitary toilets,
whitewashing dwellings and outbuildings, and boring wells. His report also included a section on Home Demonstration work. Black home Extension workers
gave demonstrations on food production, cooking, and conservation. They reported 185 new gardens planted, 500 stalks of sugar cane planted, 7,000 cabbage
plants set out, 25 pecan trees and 4 grape vines set out, and 16 hot beds made.
They reported progress in home dairying, poultry, and home marketing. They
held demonstrations in cooking vegetables, breads, and pastry, and in preserving

ties of life restrained them from challenging the status quo and made them receptive to the black Extension program.

From the beginning the goals of the Department of Agriculture and the interests of white planters were at variance with the needs of black farmers and their families. Rescuing the southern agricultural economy through the promotion of better farming methods and bringing greater profits to landowners were the two most important objectives of the Extension program in the South. Agents like O'Neal and Murphy had the difficult task of transforming that program into something that black farmers would welcome without altering it in such a way as to make it unpalatable to planters or unrecognizable to the white agricultural bureaucracy.

Agent Murphy's 1911 report throws light on the difficult sociopolitical atmosphere on southern farms: "Sometimes your agent came across sharecroppers in good locations who felt unable to take up the work because the farm had to be run according to the ideas of the landlord." By 1916, when O'Neal was working in Georgia, the war and the black exodus had begun to shake some planters from their reluctance to support black Extension. O'Neal's report suggests that he encountered problems in gaining black acceptance of the program, implies that he experienced difficulties with whites on the local level, and, ultimately, reflects his success in negotiating that often treacherous terrain. "I have found the majority of people who oppose you, think, and if you can succeed in making them think in the right direction, that you come into a community to build up rather than tear down, you have found in them the warmest and best of friends."[13]

In other words, O'Neal succeeded in gaining black acceptance of his program and also convinced local whites that he posed no threat, that

---

fruit and vegetables. They helped their clients cure 2,500 pounds of hog meat and prepare 375 pounds of lard. They also gave demonstrations on preparing "healthful school lunches," sewing everything from dresses, coats, and undergarments to towels, sheets, and curtains. They helped black farm women to beautify both the interior and exterior of their homes. They devoted considerable attention to sanitation and health, giving "health" talks and instructing clients how to care for and feed patients. P. H. Stone, state agent for Negro work, Narrative Report, Men's Work, pp. 1–2; Negro Home Demonstration Work, pp. 1–3, box 2, OSA papers.

13. Murphy report, p. 2, ANSR microfilm.

his program served their interests. Drawing on the Department of Agriculture's justification for funding black Extension, O'Neal would likely have argued that teaching black farmers better farming methods would promote higher yields and better conserve the soil. Subaltern studies theorists would characterize the twin goals of profiting planters and reviving the southern agricultural economy as the "dominant culture value" of the Department of Agriculture and the white power structure in the South. By adopting a creative interpretation of the primary goals of the program and by pursuing certain secondary objectives, the black Extension workers, like subalterns in colonial situations, revalued the dominant culture value and used the program to challenge one important aspect of the plantation system: the economic dependence of black farmers.

Black Extension workers would not have to struggle very much to refashion the Extension program. Improving the productivity of the soil necessarily increased yields and thus augmented profits for both planters and sharecroppers (provided prices did not fall and that planters passed along increased profits to sharecroppers). But a labor scarcity prevailed in much of the South, and most white planters relied on the impoverishment and dependence of black farmers in order to maintain an adequate supply of labor. Black sharecroppers tended to become deeply indebted to the planters for whom they worked, and through the system of debt peonage, many found themselves unable to leave their places of employment without first paying off that debt, something that became increasingly difficult to do.[14] By encouraging better farming methods and helping black sharecroppers to secure greater profits, black Extension agents were undermining one important component of the southern plantation system: indebtedness. An important secondary goal of the Extension Service even more directly addressed the issue of black poverty and dependence. Extension workers attempted to educate black farmers to be more fiscally responsible and to avoid the chronic indebtedness that was characteristic of the

14. The standard work on debt peonage is Daniel's *Shadow of Slavery.* For a discussion of the legal aspects of debt peonage, see Harold Woodman, "Post Civil War Agriculture and the Law," *Journal of Southern History* 45 (August 1979): 319–37.

sharecropping system.[15] In addition to promoting better financial management, agents also encouraged black farm wives to maintain vegetable gardens, milk cows, and poultry, all of which would have made it less necessary for them to secure food from the plantation commissary. By encouraging the greater economic independence of black sharecroppers, Extension agents were laying the groundwork for freedom from the dominance of planters.

The refashioning of the dominant culture value, of course, was a process that evolved incrementally during the first five decades of the twentieth century. Simultaneously, the response of the Agricultural Extension Service to the maneuvers of black agents unfolded. Subaltern studies theorists would characterize this response as the counterinsurgency of the dominant elites, the attempt to reassert control over the program, reaffirm its goals, and, essentially, reinforce the dominant culture. Certain historical crises created opportunities for black agents to maneuver and encouraged the Extension Service to accommodate them when necessary and to contain and control them where possible. The exodus of African Americans from the rural South, which greatly alarmed planters; the need to produce agricultural commodities during World War I; the disastrous Mississippi River flood of 1927 that threatened both the labor supply and the profit margin; the emergence of New Deal programs that both supported and challenged the plantation system; and then the coming of World War II—all contributed their own part to this dynamic interaction. Even as the agency renewed its control and reaffirmed the primary goals of the program when each immediate crisis passed, many of the gains made by black agents remained in place. For example, the number of black agents increased as each crisis presented itself, and although the expansion was slow and halting, to be sure, it did not reverse itself. The number of black agents continued to increase into the post–World War II period, and while this worked to the advantage of planters and contributed to agricultural modernization, it also brought material benefits to black farmers.

The negotiation process between agents and local populations described by O'Neal in 1916 also continued and evolved throughout the first half of the twentieth century. Black agents occasionally tested the

15. Mercier, "Extension Work among Negroes, 1920," 11.

limits of their authority, pushing the perimeters as far as they could and then backing off when required to do so. This worked across all levels, from the lowliest county agent working in Georgia, South Carolina, or Arkansas to the district agents to whom they reported. Even the two principal field agents who oversaw the entire program and worked out of Hampton and Tuskegee played the role of the subaltern. Of course, the district agents and, particularly, the field agents, in occupying supervisory positions, were required to implement the white Extension program and sometimes discipline black agents who went beyond their bounds. Their subaltern negotiation, therefore, was at once more complex because their contact with white policy makers was greater and less complicated because they rarely worked directly with black farmers and their families and thus did not have to face some of the inherent contradictions in the program itself.

The negotiation between the subaltern and the dominant partner, between the black Extension worker and Department of Agriculture, represented something more than a struggle over the goals of agricultural policy. The entire exchange—during which the black Extension workers refashioned the program to fit the needs of African Americans and the agency repeatedly reimposed and reinforced its control and the goals of the Extension program—challenged another dominant culture precept. Black Extension workers, in contributing to the black struggle for a safe and comfortable life in the rural South, implicitly challenged another fundamental dominant culture value, the racial status quo.

Although explicitly charged with avoiding any appearance of interfering with the racial status quo, black Extension workers were expected to help ameliorate tensions and antagonisms between whites and blacks. Because they worked exclusively with black farmers and had little contact with whites, their message would have been delivered to black farmers, and it was a cautionary one: do not disturb the racial status quo. The Extension Service program, therefore, provided yet another school for socializing blacks to accept an inferior place within southern society. But planted deep within the lessons taught by black agents were the seeds of revolution: independence, self-respect, and an expectation of greater things to come through hard work and sacrifice. After World War II, blacks left the rural South in far greater numbers, and while many of them headed North in search of industrial employment, tens of thousands also settled in southern cities (as Louis Kyriakoudes has discussed), forming the critical mass necessary for the emergence of the Civil Rights movement. The hope and expectation engendered in the ideas promulgated by Extension Service representatives were a necessary step in the evolution of the thinking of rural African Americans. The move to an urban setting, where they were exposed to more radical ideas and the influence of a remarkable group of black leaders, was the next step, the step that launched the massive struggle for civil rights in the 1950s.[16]

In March 1919, just nine months before his death, E. L. Blackshear summarized the difficulties faced by black agents as they sought to establish their program in the South and deal with the delicate issue of race relations. It had come to his attention that "a political group in Texas has criticized the colored Government workers in the south, declaring they were only a political machine working in the interest of the North." The letter was directed toward black agents and urged them to be careful "in all our public utterances not to give ground for the charge that we are mixing other problems with the extension work that have no official connection with it." Just as they should not mix religion with Extension work, they should avoid challenging racial attitudes of whites. He implied in this admonition, however, that he had his own opinions on the subject of race. In a carefully coded statement, he said, "I have no right to make any sectarian statements, and the same rule applies to the race problem. Our opinions are doubtless identical on this problem, but there is a large body of citizens who do not think on this problem as we do, hence when we refer to the race problem it should be done judiciously and in a way to make peace between the races and not discord." His intriguing comment, "my own opinion," which he believed his colleagues shared, bears scrutiny. It embodies one of the central mysteries of the program. To what extent did black agents differ from white policy makers in their conception of the appropriate "place" for black farmers in the South's social structure? The remark could be interpreted to mean that Blackshear was distinguishing his

16. Prakash, "Subaltern Studies," 1476.

opinion on the race question from that of whites, suggesting that he did not agree with the racial status quo but believed that it was necessary to adhere to it for practical reasons. On the other hand, he might have been referring to the difference between his opinion and that of black farmers who had little patience with the accommodationist approach. After all, black agents did not work with whites; they worked with blacks, and thus would have had little contact with whites. The "large body of citizens who do not think on this problem as we do," who might have been subject to their influence, would have had to have been black. He went on to argue that if whites chose to agitate on the question, they were in a much better position of "awaking antagonism against us and backing it up then [*sic*] we are of making any success in our own efforts to create antagonism on the part of our race as against the white people of the community."[17] An alternative reading of Blackshear's letter suggests the intriguing possibility that, understanding he was writing this letter for two audiences—black agents working with and under him, and white supervisors to whom he reported—Blackshear's message had a double meaning, one that could be interpreted in different ways by different audiences. The notion that there existed a militancy among black farmers would play to the fears of white bureaucrats, and the idea that black agents could control that militancy would work to the benefit of black Extension. The perfect subaltern, Blackshear understood the ambivalence of his own subordinates but also appreciated the need to reassure and placate white leaders.

Blackshear's letter ultimately reached the secretary of agriculture, passing through the hands of Bradford Knapp, chief of the Extension Service at that time. While the letter reveals much about the problems facing black agents, Knapp's reaction throws additional light on the reason the white Extension Service appointed Blackshear, Campbell, and Pierce to their positions. In a note to the secretary of agriculture, Knapp enclosed Blackshear's letter and remarked: "The three negroes whom we appointed last January to deal with the negro problems in the South are doing fine work."[18] The implication is that the three men were

17. E. L. Blackshear to "colleagues," March 23, 1919, box 1, OSA papers.
18. "Memorandum for the Secretary," from Bradford Knapp, April 25, 1919, box 1, OSA papers.

hired not so much because of their expertise with Extension work but because of their ability to deal with the delicate race issue. Significantly, while Campbell and Pierce had long experience in the Extension Service, Blackshear's background was far different. He had been a leading black educator, working in the elementary and secondary school systems in Texas as a teacher and administrator before becoming the principal of Prairie View State Normal and Industrial College in 1906. He made the political mistake of supporting a prohibitionist candidate for governor in 1914 who lost to James E. "Pa" Ferguson. Ferguson replaced him in 1915, and he then became principal of Emancipation Park Elementary School in Houston.[19]

Blackshear likely came to Knapp's attention because of his actions during the Houston Riot in 1917, a riot involving black soldiers and white civilians. Blackshear was one of a number of black leaders called upon to calm the waters of racial unrest by addressing the black population. In that capacity, he made remarks that are entirely consistent with the position outlined in his 1919 letter, that violence on the part of blacks is to be avoided. In the cover letter that Knapp included with the 1919 Blackshear letter, Knapp remarked, "his letter is characteristic, yet I believe it to be pretty good advice." As Knapp put it, "He is attempting to keep down the racial agitation which seems to be running all through the south, by insisting that the negro extension workers do not discuss that question."[20]

The Houston Riot was not the last time that difficulties would arise between black soldiers and whites, prompting white officials to seek black intermediaries. The acting director of white Extension in Texas in December 1918 clearly saw an opportunity to use Blackshear and other black agents in an attempt to reeducate black soldiers. In a letter to Bradford Knapp, he suggested that "if arrangements could be made

19. May Schmidt, "Edward Lavoisier Blackshear," in *The New Handbook of Texas,* vol. 1 (Austin: Texas State Historical Association, 1996), 573–74.

20. Robert V. Haynes, *A Night of Violence: The Houston Riot of 1917* (Baton Rouge: Louisiana State University Press, 1976), 202–3. May Schmidt's biographical sketch suggests that he was already in charge of Extension at Prairie View in 1917, but that is clearly incorrect. That appointment was not made until 1918. "Memorandum for the Secretary," from Bradford Knapp, April 25, 1919, box 1, OSA papers.

through the War Department for the right kind of negroes to meet negro soldiers at points of demobilization and talk with them both in public and private, much might be accomplished that way." He clearly envisioned using black Extension agents in this capacity, and he went on to refer to Blackshear's assistance in Houston after the riot there in 1917. "If some plan could be worked out by which men like Blackshear and others of his race could present their views to returning negro soldiers, it would surely prevent some serious difficulties that are likely to occur unless some such step is taken."[21] No formal means of employing black agents in this task was implemented, but certainly black agents cautioned blacks to be circumspect and deferential in their relationships with whites.

Black agents were more directly involved in addressing the question of encouraging black farmers to produce sufficient agricultural commodities in support of the war effort. This took on greater urgency because of the black exodus, an exodus that began in approximately 1914 and accelerated during the war. While white leaders pondered what to do, black leaders from a variety of locations and perspectives began to press for varying remedies. A committee representing the Virginia Agricultural and Industrial Institute suggested that a Negro Department of Statistics, Resources and Commodities be created to "induce the Negro man and woman who has left the agricultural section of the South to return." Significantly, they suggested that a black man be placed in charge of the bureau and that the office be located in Richmond. Meanwhile, various other black individuals and groups began to press for the creation of a new division within the Department of Agriculture, also headed by an African American, not simply to produce for the war or stem the exodus but to "look after their [black farmers] needs."[22]

White officials refrained from establishing a bureau in Richmond or

21. F. O. Walton to Bradford Knapp, December 18, 1918, pp. 1–2, box 1, OSA Papers.

22. To the president of the United States from H. H. Price and S. S. Baker, April 23, 1917, box 1, OSA papers. The last quote appears in W. T. Andrews, editor, *The Daily Herald,* Baltimore, Maryland, to Clarence Ousley, assistant secretary, Department of Agriculture, June 28, 1918, p. 2. See also Memorandum for Mr. Harrison from R. A. Pearson (assistant secretary of agriculture), May 24, 1917; and file memorandum, June 18, 1918, all in box 1, OSA papers.

creating a new division within the department devoted to African Americans, but they did not ignore the letters and queries from black leaders. While they politely acknowledged their requests and called attention to the work of black Extension agents in the South, they also began to expand the black agent program by increasing the number of county agents and creating the district agent system through which county agents reported to district agents. When B. F. Hubert, the director of the Department of Agriculture at Tuskegee, in 1921 suggested that there existed the need for a comprehensive government program to deal "more broadly with the problems of negro farming people," Secretary of Agriculture Henry Wallace deflected the question by praising the progress made by the black Extension program, indicating that "when conditions permit, it may be possible to enlarge the work materially." In other words, he appropriated one strategy of black leaders—the effort to expand black Extension—in an effort to dismiss the suggestion that blacks be placed in policy-making positions. Later interoffice memos suggest that most white department officials were content to deal politely with the demands of black leaders, but were not prepared to move beyond systematizing and expanding the black agent system.[23]

Black leaders were not dissuaded in their efforts to secure a USDA appointment. Thomas Campbell made certain that white officials remained aware of the problems the black exodus presented to southern agriculture. Having established the importance of the black Extension program in keeping blacks from migrating away from the plantations—something it was, in fact, never able to accomplish—he alerted department officials to the threat posed by the "Back to Africa Movement." While in Washington in early 1923 reading through the narrative reports of black agents, Campbell came across one that he used to good advantage in keeping the issue before white administrators. Ac-

23. Giles B. Jackson to R. A. Pearson, assistant to the secretary, Department of Agriculture, May 10, 1917; D. F. Houston, secretary of agriculture, to Tom D. McKeown, House of Representatives, February 26, 1918; Bradford Knapp to F. R. Harrison, assistant to the secretary, USDA, December 16, 1918, all in box 1, OSA papers. Henry A. Wallace to B. F. Hubert, April 8, 1921, box 1, OSA papers. From the secretary to the president, April 11, 1921; memorandum for Mr. Jump from A. C. True (director of State Relations), April 20, 1921, both in box 1, OSA papers.

cording to the narrative report of an unidentified county agent, the movement was responsible for the failure of four community farmers' clubs in that agent's county. "This movement brought a great setback to these communities, as many of the farmers did nothing but walk around and talk about going to Africa and made no effort to progress as farmers. Not one of these farmers ever left, but they lost the year talking about it." Campbell's motivation perhaps went beyond merely informing the USDA that the movement competed with the Extension Service for the attention and loyalty of African American farmers. He seemed to wish to keep the issue of the appointment of an African American at a higher level, a policy-making level, within the USDA bureaucracy before them. Included in this effort was a lengthy report covering the period November 11 through December 15, 1923, and while it focused on the problems African Americans who left the South and settled in certain northern cities faced, it also shed light on why many of them left.[24] One man told Campbell that

> it was his intention never to live in the South again; that he was making every effort possible to move his family away as soon as he secured work. He further stated that a Negro in the South is born down and the white people keep him down. "If you want to get along with the white man, when you meet him in the road, kinda tip your hat. If you know his name, say Howdy do, Mr.————. If you don't know his name, say Howdy, 'Cap.' In either case be sure to speak to him whether you know him or not. Failure to do this is sure to gain for the party the reputation of a 'biggety Nigger.'"[25]

Other blacks informed Campbell that they came north in search of a safer environment, but some came in order to pursue greater economic opportunities, especially given the sharp downturn in the agricultural economy in the South that began after World War I. Indeed, Campbell's report challenged the notion that only the "uneducated and shiftless Negro was migrating to the North." Rather, "a large number

24. Unsigned but on USDA letterhead to L. N. Duncan, director of Extension, Alabama Polytechnic Institute, February 5, 1923, box 1, OSA papers. "Report of Investigation On Negro Migration, November 11 to December, 1923," T. M. Campbell, box 1, OSA Papers.

25. "Report of Investigation On Negro Migration, November 11 to December, 1923," T. M. Campbell, p. 2, box 1, OSA Papers.

of intelligent Negroes" had chosen to migrate in order to find opportunity unavailable to them in the South.[26]

Campbell was careful to make the point that regardless of their reasons for leaving the South, they faced many problems in the North: discrimination, job insecurity, housing shortages, and the emergence of Ku Klux Klan activities in northern cities. In other words, the exodus was not only creating problems for southern agriculture but also causing difficulties in the North as well. In 1924 Campbell wrote the director that "southern agriculture is affected by Negro migration and is no longer a sectional but rather a national problem."[27] An internal report generated within the USDA indicated that Campbell's warning was not without an audience. Referring to the Cotton Belt within Alabama, Georgia, Florida, Mississippi, Louisiana, Texas, and Oklahoma—Campbell's territory—the report acknowledged:

> This whole area is at present undergoing an almost radical change in agricultural practice due in part to the ravages of the cotton boll-weevil and the bid for Negro labor. In short, the battle is waged between southern agriculture and northern and southern industry. The great question now is, who will win? Much depends on who reaches the Negro farmer first as to whether or not he remains on the farm—the Negro extension agent or the industrial labor agent.[28]

While black leaders were able to keep the department aware of and concerned about the impact of the black exodus on agriculture in the South, their efforts to secure appointment of a black official in charge of black Extension within the USDA continued to be frustrated. In March 1925, Edward M. Lewis, acting president of Massachusetts Agricultural College, wrote the secretary of agriculture recommending Benjamin Hubert for an appointment as assistant secretary. Lewis was under the mistaken impression that the appointment of a black assistant within the department was under consideration. Lewis's letter was passed on to the director of Extension, C. W. Warburton, who quickly

26. Ibid., 7, 4.

27. T. M. Campbell to C. W. Warburton, June 21, 1924, Office of the Secretary of Agriculture, box 2, OSA papers.

28. Memorandum on letterhead, USDA, Office of the Cooperative Extension Service, Washington, D.C., n.d. but located within closest proximity to 1924 materials, box 2, OSA papers.

disabused Lewis of such a notion and indicated that he assumed that Lewis was simply "not fully informed with reference to agricultural extension work which is being done in the Southern states by and for negroes." In other words, he reiterated the department's position that the creation of an African American position within the USDA was not necessary.[29]

While Campbell and Hubert were engaging the USDA and the Extension Service on one level, county agents were working on another front. They were securing the support of local planters and county officials for black Extension. Christopher Haraway, the African American farm agent serving Mississippi County, Arkansas, indicated in his annual narrative report for 1926 that the county quorum court supported Extension work. One crucial supporter was R. E. Lee Wilson, a prominent planter of Wilson, Arkansas, who owned nearly seventy thousand acres of land and almost exclusively employed black sharecroppers. According to Haraway, Wilson was "not a member of the court but he is always on hand at court time to sponsor county agent work, and to say what ever he can for this phase of work." A perusal of Haraway's report and the emphasis he placed on increasing cotton yields suggests why Wilson was so enthusiastic about the Extension program. In 1925 black farmers in Mississippi County had participated in a statewide cotton contest and learned the importance of using fertilizers to increase yields.[30]

Haraway was allowed to address the quorum court concerning the merits of the program among black farmers, but it was the black Home

29. C. W. Warburton to Edward M. Lewis, March 14, 1925, box 2, OSA papers. A similar letter was written to President Kenyon L. Butterfield of Michigan Agricultural College who had apparently also recommended Hubert for the phantom position. C. W. Warburton to Kenyon L. Butterfield, March 14, 1925, box 2, OSA papers.

30. Other prominent white men could also be counted upon to address the quorum court. "Mr. C. E. Sullenger, lawyer is always on the alert for all the work in the county. . . . Mr. W. Ferguson, Marie Arkansas, who is chairman of the appropriation committee, is a loyal supporter." C. C. Haraway, Annual Narrative Report of County Extension Workers, Negro Extension Work, December 1, 1925, to November 30, 1926, p. 21, ANSR reel. C. C. Haraway, Narrative Report of County Extension Workers, Negro Extension Work, December 1, 1924, to December 1, 1925, p. 9, ANSR reel.

Demonstration agent's presentation to the court that captured the most attention in 1925. Mary J. McCain's elaborate demonstration included examples of the products produced by club members in various categories, many of which had won prizes at county and state fairs. A newspaper article reporting on that session of the quorum court indicated that she made a "most credible" impression and "made a big hit with the justices." She showed "samples of canned goods of every description and while she had the floor she was given the closest attention for her work has been truly remarkable."[31] The mention of canned goods speaks to the emphasis placed on home gardens, gardens that would produce food for home consumption and would likely guarantee a plantation labor force free of pellagra, a dietary deficiency caused by a lack of fresh vegetables. Lee Wilson and his farm managers were well known for not only providing small garden plots for their sharecroppers but also actually inspecting such gardens themselves. Wilson operated in a county that was bringing previously wooded and swampy land into cultivation and thus was more than ordinarily concerned about securing and maintaining an adequate supply of labor. He took great pains to provide good housing, better than average educational facilities, and medical care for his black sharecroppers. His attention to the garden plots of his sharecroppers was in part a reflection of his particular paternalistic attitude and his preoccupation with maintaining his labor force. In any case, the goals of extension, the needs of black farmers and their families, and the interests of Lee Wilson combined to create a harmonious arrangement.

In spite of McCain's "credible" performance at the county quorum court meeting, she and other black Extension workers were not only housed separately from white agents but also had little contact with them. Other states followed the same pattern. A 1928 survey conducted on behalf of the white director of the Extension Service in Auburn, Alabama, revealed that white and black agents tended to be segregated from one another and that black agents were not allowed to make requests for appropriations from county quorum courts. Directors of Extension in ten states responded to the survey and provided information

31. Mary J. McCain, Narrative Report of County Extension Workers, Negro Extension Work, December 1, 1924, to December 1, 1925, 12, ANSR reel.

about the relationship between black and white Extension workers and the circumscribed manner in which black agents operated. Haraway and McCain's appearance at the Mississippi County quorum court notwithstanding, according to Dan T. Gray, dean and director of the College of Agriculture at the University of Arkansas, "our white district men and women agents transact all the business with the county officials in making arrangements for appropriations for negro agents." Gray did not allow either the black county agents or the black district agents to "approach the county about appropriations."[32]

While black agents worked under this handicap, they were able to exercise considerable autonomy and freedom from white interference. D. P. Trent, director of Extension in Oklahoma, indicated that they had "considered the possibility of eliminating the negro district agent and having all the work supervised by the white district agents." But Trent seemed to be influenced by the fact that Thomas Campbell of Tuskegee "had always been very much in favor of maintaining the negro supervisor for negro work." Although Trent admitted that he thought black supervisors were preferable, he regretted that "one of the difficulties which I have found to the negro supervisor is the fact that all negroes are inclined to shield each other and that it is difficult to get the negro district agent to furnish information that may be unfavorable to other negro workers." He further indicated that they had been able to resolve this issue by securing information from the white supervisors (agents?) in the counties.[33] While it is unclear who his white informants were, whether he meant the white county agents or the district agents, he was describing the subaltern relationship at work, whether he knew it or not. Black district agents shielded the black county agents with whom

32. Dan T. Gray to L. N. Duncan, February 17, 1928, box 355, ACES. The other respondents were A. P. Spencer, vice director, Florida Extension, February 18, 1928; J. Campbell, director, Georgia Extension, February 16, 1928; W. R. Perkins, director, Louisiana Extension, February 17, 1928; R. S. Wilson, director, Mississippi Extension, February 16, 1928; I. O. Schaub, director, North Carolina Extension, February 15, 1928; D. P. Trent, director, Oklahoma Extension, February 24, 1928; D. W. Watkins, assistant director, South Carolina Extension, February 15, 1928; C. E. Brehm, assistant director, Tennessee Extension, February 16, 1928; and J. R. Hutcheson, director, Virginia Extension, February 16, 1928, all in box 355, ACES.

33. D. P. Trent, director of Extension, Oklahoma Agricultural and Mechanical College, to L. N. Duncan, February 24, 1928, p. 2, ACES.

they worked. John Redd Hutcheson, the white director of Extension at Virginia Polytechnic Institute, put another spin on the desirability of having blacks report to black district agents. "My experience leads me to believe that it is better to have the negro work directly supervised by negroes, but the general policies determined by white men. In other words, put a good negro in charge and keep in close enough touch with him to see that he does the right kind of work." These remarks are all the more interesting because Hutcheson spoke highly of J. B. Pierce, the field agent who worked out of Hampton Institute and supervised the black Extension force in the South Atlantic states. He characterized Pierce as a "reliable and efficient" man, who "still has general supervision over our negro work" even though he had been given authority over a "group of southern states."[34] In other words, Pierce did exercise supervisory authority over Virginia's black Extension workers, but as far as Hutcheson was concerned, he was not to be entrusted with formulating policy. That responsibility belonged in the hands of a white man.

By this point in time the flood of 1927 had given black Extension workers in some southern states the opportunity to prove their value to the Extension program. They played an important role in helping to manage blacks in the Red Cross refugee camps and, lacking a centralized system of command—something Campbell, Hubert, and other prominent blacks had been promoting for more than a decade—a Colored Advisory Commission was created to aid in organizing and directing the black Extension force. The commission included several Tuskegee officials, including the principal, Robert R. Moton, who chaired the commission, and Thomas Campbell, who served as a member. Another prominent member was the director of the Associated Negro Press, Claude A. Barnett. Other black organizations having representation on the board included the National Negro Business League, the National Urban League, the National Medical Association, and the Methodist Episcopal Church (North). Notably absent from this collection of black organizations was the National Association for the Advancement of Colored People (NAACP), an organization considered too radical by white agricultural bureaucrats.[35]

34. J. R. Hutcheson to L. N. Duncan, February 16, 1928, ACES.
35. The list of officers and members of the Colored Advisory Commission

The flood gave these black organizations the opportunity to exercise some influence, but it also revealed the way that black agents on the ground in the stricken states could be used to meet the needs of planters. Hiram C. Ray, one of two black district agents working in Arkansas in 1927, was appointed a special adviser for relief work among blacks in that state, and he used the opportunity of a captive audience of black refugees to provide Extension instruction. But the camps became notorious when it was made known that the Red Cross had acquiesced to planter demands that blacks not be allowed to depart without being signed out by the planters for whom they worked. Ray failed to mention that problem in his annual narrative report for 1927 and instead celebrated the fact that many dilapidated tenant houses and outbuildings had been washed away by the flood. He also expressed satisfaction that a certain element among the tenant classes had been forced from the area, and he hoped they would not return: "The bottoms have always been over-run with an abundance of cheap and inefficient labor."[36]

The statement that an excess of labor had "over-run" the bottoms is

---

read in this order: Dr. Robert A. Morton, chairman, principal of Tuskegee Institute; Bishop R. E. Jones, vice chairman, in charge of the Southwestern District of the Methodist Episcopal Church; Albon L. Holsey, secretary to Moton and secretary of the National Negro Business League; J. S. Clark, treasurer, president of Southern University; Eugene K. Jones, executive secretary, National Urban League; Jesse O. Thomas, southern field secretary, National Urban League; Mrs. John Hope, director of the Atlanta Neighborhood Union; Eva D. Bowles, executive secretary, Y.W.C.A.; Claude A. Barnett, director, Associated Negro Press; Roscoe C. Brown, assistant secretary, National Medical Association (and former field worker for the U.S. Public Health Service); Mary E. Williams, public health nurse under the Tuskegee chapter (the only Negro chapter) of the American Red Cross; Robert R. Taylor, vice-principal and director of Mechanical Industries at Tuskegee Institute; L. M. McCoy, president of Rust College, Holly Springs, Mississippi; J. B. Martin, regional director, National Negro Business League; B. M. Roody, vice president, National Negro Business League; S. D. Redmond, large landowner in Mississippi and a leader in civic and business affairs there; and T. M. Campbell, field representative, U.S. Department of Agriculture. "The Final Report of the Colored Advisory Commission, Mississippi Valley Flood Disaster, 1927," (Washington, D.C: American Red Cross).

36. H. C. Ray, Annual Narrative Report of District Extension Workers, Negro Extension Work, December 1, 1926, to November 30, 1927, p. 6, ANSR reel.

clearly at odds with reality. Planters in Arkansas and elsewhere had engaged in a public dialogue about the threat to the scarce black labor force that the flood presented. Ray, who had worked for Extension in Arkansas since the beginning and had helped found the Arkansas Negro State Farmers Association in 1920, was a particularly knowledgeable agent. He was not ignorant of the facts, but clearly found it to his best interest, and to that of black Extension, to characterize the situation in a manner that did not reflect poorly on white planters. But Ray received something in exchange for his accommodation. He was able to use his time in the refugee camps to push his rural uplift philosophy, something that the black Extension force had always promoted but which white bureaucrats had come to reluctantly.[37]

Ray was typical of many black agents working with Extension in the South. A 1913 graduate of Tuskegee Institute who worked briefly as assistant director in the agriculture department at Langston University in Oklahoma, he moved to Pulaski County in 1915 to serve as the first black agent in Arkansas. Since the black agent system was launched on an experimental basis and because "its success depended as much upon the interests of white landowners as upon Negro activities," his work was "very closely supervised."[38] He knew and understood from the very beginning the necessity of accommodating the interests of white bureaucrats and planters. His training at Tuskegee oriented him toward the idea of rural uplift, and he was determined to bring enlightenment to the black farm families he served. Many agents, fired with the ideas of rural uplift, approached their responsibilities with the zeal of the missionary and worked tirelessly to bring "enlightenment" to African American farm families. Like many other black farm agents, Ray frequently betrayed a class bias of his own in his reports. Most county agents were from the upper strata of black rural society and were

37. Gary Zellar, "H. C. Ray and Racial Politics in the African American Extension Service Program in Arkansas, 1915–1929," 434. For mention of the rural uplift philosophy and the USDA's attitude toward it, see Memorandum for the Secretary (Henry Wallace) from E. D. Ball, assistant secretary, March 24, 1921; Henry Wallace to B. F. Hubert, April 8, 1921, box 1, ANSR.

38. Mena Hogan, "A History of the Agricultural Extension Service in Arkansas" (master's thesis, University of Wisconsin, 1915), 140.

steeped in the philosophy espoused at both Tuskegee and Hampton. They were embarrassed by the poverty and illiteracy of the African American population, and their reports reflected this point of view. At the same time, they understood that their reports were being scrutinized by white bureaucrats, and black agents were careful to express ideas that conformed to white prejudices. Not only were their own jobs at stake, but they also had a sense that the black Extension program itself was vulnerable to a white backlash should agents overstep their bounds.

Thus black agents made accommodations during the flood of 1927 in the interest of promoting their own version of the Extension program. If they were complicit in the situation occurring in the Red Cross camps in 1927, they were even more so during the plow-up campaign of 1933. By the time of Franklin Delano Roosevelt's inauguration early that year, the entire world economy was in shambles. The farm economy had barely survived the disastrous 1920s, and most farm owners found they could not produce crops at a profit. In the plantation belt this drove even prominent planters to the brink of bankruptcy, but the consequences for black sharecroppers and tenants were even more tragic. Always living on the margin and constantly in danger of suffering from diseases caused by dietary deficiency, the worsening economic conditions reduced them to a poverty of shocking dimensions. Planters who had previously "furnished" their sharecroppers through the lean winter months were themselves at the mercy of creditors demanding payments that could not be met. Thus sharecroppers were left to their own meager resources, and starvation was near at hand. In this context, those who had followed the advice of farm agents and grown kitchen gardens and canned vegetables were in a better position. The shocking level of destitution that faced many farmers brings into stark relief the appeal of a program that focused on showing farmers how to provide for themselves the basic necessities.

By the time that Franklin Roosevelt took office in 1933, most southern planters were receptive to remedies they had rejected in the previous decade. Roosevelt's focus was on saving southern agriculture as a whole, and together with his advisers he quickly settled on a solution that had been maturing for some years: reduce acreage in order to cause a shortage in certain overproduced crops, thus encouraging prices to rise. They created the Agricultural Adjustment Administration (AAA), which was authorized to administer the remedy. Legislators and AAA officials understood that in order to convince farmers to participate, they needed to give them generous incentives, so they offered to "rent" up to 30 percent of the acres farmers had in production and then, to add even more incentive, provided for an additional parity payment if the prices they received for their crops did not reach a certain level. Because farmers had already planted their acreage by the time the legislation was passed in 1933, however, it was necessary to "plow up" the rented acres for the first year of the AAA program.

While African American county and district agents uniformly reported that blacks were beneficiaries of the plow-up program inaugurated by New Deal administrators in 1933, an independent report on conditions in the Mississippi Delta established that there was widespread discontent among African American farmers, principally because of the refusal of planters to share the plow-up proceeds with them. The report was careful to maintain anonymity, referring to plantations A through N. On Plantation K "all [sharecroppers] plowed up from 8 to 10 acres. He [the planter] had them to sign in such a way as to have the checks all come to him. Not a family has seen or heard of a check or any money." Some sharecroppers were able to secure something in return for plowing up their cotton, however. An entry in the report describing Plantation G read as follows: "About forty families. All made fine crops this year. Plowed up deal of cotton. When it was seen that they were going to clear something, he told them if they would just waiver their claims to their checks he would give them a clear receipt and 50 cents to pick cotton. All the money they got was for picking and a clear receipt for their debts."[39]

So widespread was the sense of discontent that a group of disgruntled sharecroppers and tenants founded the Southern Tenant Farmers' Union in 1934 in Poinsett County, Arkansas. It was unique in that it was an integrated union. White and black sharecroppers secured advice and

---

39. It is unclear who wrote this report or how it found its way into Department of Agriculture files. "General Conditions in the Mississippi Delta with Special Reference to Plowing Up Cotton Crops," n.d. but in 1933 file, pp. 3–4, box 2 , OSA.

support from two young local socialists who advised them to form a union to force planters to share crop subsidy payments with them and to protest the tendency of some to evict extraneous sharecroppers and tenants. With 25 to 30 percent of their acreage now no longer being devoted to the labor-intensive cotton crop, some planters determined to economize by ridding themselves of labor they no longer needed. The STFU was able to raise awareness of the situation confronting tenants and sharecroppers, capturing international attention and securing the creation of a Tenancy Commission. Black and white Extension agents alike were curiously silent on the existence of the union, even in the county in which it was founded. This silence is all the more telling because white Extension agents played a pivotal role in the administration of the AAA program—they were the ones who appointed the AAA county and township committees and supervised the plow-up and later the crop reduction programs. The white agent was the major player and, indeed, the black agent found himself more closely tied than ever to the program's primary agenda: saving southern agriculture. Black agents worked more closely with white agents to carry out the AAA program and lost some of their autonomy in the process. This loss of autonomy on the part of black agents did not translate into any expressions of sympathy for black farmers who were being evicted from plantations. The direct and confrontational approach of the STFU was at odds with the philosophy and program sponsored by the Extension Service. Black agents in particular had too much time and energy invested in that approach to be sidetracked.[40] By the 1930s the black agents were so emersed in their subaltern positions that their natural response would be antagonistic to the STFU. Their notion of what was appropriate behavior for black sharecroppers was distinctly different from that of union activists. The black agents had become captives of the bureaucracy they worked within. This was the nadir, in a sense, of the black agent system.

40. David Conrad, *The Forgotten Farmers: The Story of Sharecroppers in the New Deal* (Urbana: University of Illinois Press, 1965); Grubbs, *Cry from the Cotton*; H. L. Mitchell, *Mean Things Happening in This Land: The Life and Times of H. L. Mitchell, Co-Founder of the Southern Tenant Farmers Union* (Montclair, N.J.: Allenheld, Osmun and Co., 1979).

On the other hand, Thomas Campbell, who continued to occupy his position as a special field agent, wrote a report in 1937 that revealed that the black Extension program had not abandoned black sharecroppers. Campbell's report was designed to present the black perspective on the government farm tenancy program being launched by the federal tenancy commission. Implicit within the report, however, were criticisms of New Deal agricultural programs. Campbell incorporated excerpts from the reports of various black agents in the South, quoting one who criticized the Rural Rehabilitation program. In that excerpt, an unnamed black agent argued that "out of thirty-odd cases in Bibb County [Georgia], I know of only three that are materially better off." While the report did not directly discuss the evictions and the failure to share crop subsidy payments that accompanied the implementation of the crop reduction program, it indirectly addressed the issue by focusing on solutions to the displacement of tenants. Campbell praised the Resettlement Administration's decision to put displaced tenants in resettlement communities with a view to smoothing a path to land ownership, and he sought to make certain that blacks found a place within these communities. Campbell argued that the "Resettlement Administration offers a very sane way out of a very desperate and deplorable condition." He provided detailed information on the difficulties facing black tenants who had attempted to move into land ownership in the past, and he included information that was critical of some of the resettlement communities, communities where "some of the supervisors used on these projects practice the same methods of foreclosing tenants that the landlords have used heretofore, without giving them a fair chance to succeed." Unsurprisingly, he recommended the use of "colored supervisors" in the black resettlement communities. In the end, these communities offered little long-term benefit to either black or white displaced tenants.[41]

41. "What Negroes Think about the Government Farm Tenancy Program," Negro Leaders in Agriculture, Home Economics and Rural Life Express their Views on the Southern Farm Tenancy Situation, January 1937. This report was marked "strictly confidential" and found in box 22, pp. 1, 3, 18, Thomas M. Campbell Papers, Tuskegee Institute, Tuskegee, Alabama. For a viewpoint on the ineffectiveness of the resettlement communities, see Donald Holley, *Uncle Sam's Farm-*

The creation of the Agricultural Adjustment Administration, the agency that oversaw the plow-up and later the crop reduction program, did provide for the employment of blacks at a higher administrative level than ever before. The AAA hired three African Americans, James P. Davis, A. L. Holsey, and Jennie B. Moton, to "interpret our program" to "the colored race." The black Extension force continued to be organized as it had been in the past, with Campbell and Pierce working out of Tuskegee and Hampton respectively and serving as the highest-level black Extension officials.[42]

If the New Deal did not present a clear opportunity for blacks at either the higher echelons or on the ground within the southern states, World War II opened up a new world of possibilities. Because of the need to produce for the war, the black agent system was vastly expanded. Again black leaders pressed for representation within the USDA, and this time two assistants were hired on a temporary basis to work with African Americans to promote efforts at producing farm products in support of the war effort. Hubert, now president of Georgia State Industrial College, pressed for the appointment of James P. Davis, who was still at work for the Agricultural Adjustment Administration. But the USDA selected Claude A. Barnett, director of the Associated Negro Press, who had been a member of the Colored Advisory Commission during the 1927 flood, and F. D. Patterson, president of Tuskegee Institute, as special assistants charged with the responsibility of issuing a report on how to maximize farm production among African Americans. They issued a report urging a vast expansion of the black Extension workforce. They proposed adding 293 farm agents, 327 Home Demonstration agents, 29 state and district supervisors, 16 state assistants for 4-H work, 2 regional farm assistants, 2 regional home

---

ers: The New Deal Communities in the Lower Mississippi Valley (Urbana: University of Illinois Press, 1975).

42. Memorandum to Mr. J. D. LeCron from Alfred D. Stedman, assistant administration, Agricultural Adjustment Administration, December 13, 1937. J. D. LeCron, assistant to the secretary, to Charles S. Brown, December 16, 1937. The secretary of agriculture had apparently received a request for information from Mr. Brown, secured information from the AAA, and had Mr. LeCron respond; box 2, OSA papers.

demonstration agents, and a national agriculturalist with a permanent position within the USDA. The expansion was projected to cost more than one and a half million dollars. If the proposal had been implemented, it would have doubled the number of farm agents and more than doubled the number of Home Demonstration agents in the black Extension program.[43]

Although the Extension force did not increase to the extent Barnett suggested, a considerable expansion occurred, and one additional factor operating to encourage this development was the acceleration of the black exodus from rural areas. Just as the war created the need to produce more food crops, it also generated a demand for labor in defense industries that was difficult for rural Americans, black or white, to resist. Reminiscent of the opinions expressed during and immediately after World War I, policy makers began to see the efficacy of improving conditions for African American farm families, and the crucial player here was the Home Demonstration agent.

Support for the war, whether through service in the military or contributions made on the home front, created new possibilities for African Americans across the country to assert their rights to full citizenship. It also emboldened African American Home Demonstration agents in unprecedented ways. Called upon to help farm women in a variety of war production efforts, they were reminded of the importance of providing education on proper nutrition and sanitation. The high incidence of rejection for military service, mostly because of diseases related to nutritional deficiencies, reflected the poverty of the rural population. The optimism and enthusiasm of African American Home Demonstration

---

43. Claude A. Barnett and F. D. Patterson to Claude R. Wickard, secretary of agriculture, June 26, 1942, box 2, OSA papers. The initial report to the secretary of agriculture merely outlined the need for an increase in the Extension workforce. A later report included the details concerning numbers and costs. Claude A. Barnett and F. D. Patterson to Claude R. Wickard, secretary of agriculture, June 26, 1942; Claude A. Barnett to S. B. Bledsoe, assistant to the secretary of agriculture, October 31, 1942, box 3, OSA papers. The Extension force in 1940 included 293 farm and 236 Home Demonstration workers. J. D. LeCron, Assistant to the Secretary, to C. C. Spaulding, president, North Carolina Mutual Life Insurance Company, June 27, 1940. LeCron was responding to a letter from Spaulding urging the appointment of a black man in the USDA, box 3, OSA papers.

supervisors and agents was apparent in the annual narrative report for 1944 of the state supervisor for the program in South Carolina, Marian B. Paul. She declared that her agents were "valiant home front soldiers" who undertook the responsibility to "increase food and feed production, to create patriotic and patient attitudes, to sustain and raise morale, and to disseminate helpful information," despite "inadequate salaries paid our workers, the unsatisfactory working conditions, the racial injustices and the ignorance of the rural people." The mention of racial injustices by an Extension supervisor in a state that had been lagging in support for the Home Demonstration program reflects the new assertiveness that contributions to the war effort encouraged. In 1940 only fifteen Home Demonstration agents were employed in all of South Carolina, a state with one of the highest concentrations of African Americans. By 1945 their numbers had increased to thirty. Fortified by this expansion in their ranks, Paul revealed that black agents "feel now that their efforts are wider in scope than merely helping the Negroes of South Carolina, but that their influences will affect all mankind and make the entire world a better place in which to live."[44] Despite her remarks about racial injustices and the many problems that her force of Extension workers faced, her message was "patience," suggesting a continuation of the black Extension program's official adherence to the racial status quo. While blacks elsewhere in America were espousing the "Double V" philosophy—victory abroad against fascism, victory at home against racism—Paul and other black Extension workers continued to espouse the accommodationist approach. Yet they were ready to begin to move into a discussion of racial injustices. While this was far short of what other African Americans were demanding, this incremental step was consistent with the subaltern approach. The war presented another opportunity to push at the perimeters.

Also embedded within Paul's report was an admission of certain tensions between black and white Extension workers. She began by praising white officials, reporting that the African American Home Demonstration agent was seen as a leader who was "highly respected and receives cooperation from high and low." White officials on the local level were

44. Marian B. Paul, state supervisor Negro Home Demonstration Work, Narrative Annual Report, 1944, 1, 3, ANSR reel.

"most cooperative" and there existed a "closer and more wholesome relationship between the white and Negro Extension workers." At the
same time that Paul celebrated what amounted to interracial cooperation, she also suggested a certain reluctance on the part of African American Extension workers to accept direction from whites. The Home
Demonstration program, more than the farm program, had operated
almost wholly independently of white supervision. Paul wrote, "white
county agents, specialists and state officials are more cooperative and
interested, and the Negro workers are more tolerant." Thus, it seems,
greater interest on the part of the white community came with a price.
Their attention was something that black workers had to tolerate.[45]

Paul's optimism notwithstanding, black workers would move into the
postwar period with a number of burdens to bear. The exodus, which
had accelerated during the war, was by no means about to reverse itself.
A fundamental transition in southern agriculture was already under way:
a shift to a capital-intensive rather than labor-intensive system. The Post
War Planning Commission, established during the war to address how
to readjust to a peacetime economy, predicted this development, although even they could not have known just how massive the transformation would be or how quickly the mechanical cotton picker would
render the sharecropping system obsolete. Claude Barnett, writing in
October 1944 about the migration of rural African Americans to the
West Coast, focused on how they might be absorbed into the agricultural
economies of the western states to which they had migrated. He made
no mention of any possible return to the South once the war was over.[46]

Even though blacks continued to leave the rural South in record
numbers after the war, the black Extension service maintained its expanded workforce and even made some gains in equalization of salaries
paid white and black workers. In part this was the result of the realization that the black population had been underserved by the Extension
Service prior to World War II, but it also reflected an effort to create
better conditions within the South so that blacks would not flock to urban areas in such large numbers. In a very real sense, American policy

---

45. Ibid., 57.
46. Claude Barnett to Claude R. Wickard, secretary of agriculture, October 18,
1944, box 3, OSA papers.

makers faced an impossible conundrum. They understood that the rural South would no longer need the vast amounts of agricultural labor that had traditionally been required, but they also well knew that industry in the North and on the West Coast could not absorb the massive migration that was likely to materialize.

World War II and the immediate postwar period were the "high tide" of the black Extension program. Marian Paul's brand of militancy was as far as most Extension workers would be allowed to go. Neither white nor black agricultural bureaucrats would tolerate anything more, and when the occasional black Extension worker attempted to press too hard for change, he or she was dismissed or disciplined. For example, in the late 1940s a black Extension worker in Alabama who had shown early promise and been praised by Campbell and other officials was fired after too stridently making salary demands for an organization of Extension workers. In Arkansas in 1955, a black Home Demonstration worker was reprimanded for an alleged connection to the NAACP.[47] In both cases, black officials were involved in the discussions over the behavior of their subordinates, but white officials made the ultimate decision. As far as the black Extension program had traveled in the first five decades of the twentieth century, it continued to function as an adjunct to the white program and, aside from Barnett's tenure in the USDA during the war, it never secured the kind of direct access to the secretary of agriculture that it long demanded.

In the end, black Extension workers served the interests of agricultural modernization and undermined black rural society and culture. This was not the goal they envisioned for themselves. Indeed, they worked to improve conditions for black farm families and hoped to stem the tide of black migration. Their success in the former merely raised the expectations of black farmers beyond what they were capable of realizing in the South and possibly encouraged them toward joining the exodus. As each historical crisis presented itself, the black Extension worker used the opportunity to demonstrate how the program

47. Jeannie Whayne, "Black Farmers and the Agricultural Cooperative Extension Service: The Alabama Experience, 1945–1965," 539; Whayne, *A New Plantation South,* 230.

could serve the interests of white policy makers and planters and at the same time worked assiduously to pursue objectives that were designed to improve the lives of black farm families. White policy makers, meanwhile, transformed what might have been a challenge to their authority into an opportunity to bring scientific methods to southern agriculture. The black farmer became increasingly expendable and, ironically, the black Extension agent himself/ herself fell victim to the Civil Rights movement. When the agency was integrated in 1965, black agents lost all autonomy, became assistant agents to the white county agents, and over the next decades saw their ranks depleted even as black farmers continued to depart the South. By the end of the twentieth century, black farmers stood at an abyss, lacking sufficient access to government programs that might enable them to reverse the depletion of their numbers in the southern farm economy. In this context, the efforts of Thomas Campbell and other black agricultural bureaucrats to secure appointment of blacks to policy-making positions take on greater significance. Despite the limitations of the black Extension program as it operated in the first half of the twentieth century, the logic of their pursuance of a place at the policy-making table cannot now be denied.

I wish to thank my colleagues at the University of Arkansas for their thoughtful comments concerning this essay. Will B. Gatewood, Elliot West, Patrick Williams, Charles Robinson, and Bryan McCann provided excellent advice and criticisms. I also want to acknowledge the contribution of Gerlad Shenk, who first presented the idea of using the subaltern studies methodology in the southern context.

Exit, Voice, and Loyalty

African American Strategies for Day-to-Day Existence / Resistance in the Early-Twentieth-Century Rural South

PETER COCLANIS AND BRYANT SIMON

Crucibles. Betrayals. Nadirs. Dark journeys. Troubles in mind. These are just a few of the vivid phrases and images scholars have employed over the years in attempting to capture the Conradian horrors associated with many aspects of life for African Americans in the early-twentieth-century South. Nowhere were conditions for African Americans more difficult during this period than in rural parts of the region. Speaking broadly, we have no major quarrel with the depiction of black rural life suggested by these phrases and images. Indeed, in some ways conditions for blacks in the rural South seem almost as frightening as those in brutalized parts of Africa and Asia during the same period, the forgotten histories of which have recently been memorialized by Mark Cocker in *Rivers of Blood, Rivers of Gold*. Rather, what we propose to do here is to *frame* the picture of the rural South a bit differently by employing certain insights—and, yes, phrases and images—developed thirty-odd years ago by economist Albert O. Hirschman in his brilliant little book *Exit, Voice, and Loyalty: Responses to Decline in Firms, Organizations, and States.*[1] Once set in a different frame, certain key themes in the picture of African American rural life are at once clarified, highlighted, and brought out.

Hirschman's work is widely respected by social scientists, though like many eclectic and iconoclastic thinkers, he has had more admirers

---

1. Mark Cocker, *Rivers of Blood, Rivers of Gold* (London: J. Cape, 1998). See also Jan Breman, *Taming the Coolie Beast: Plantation Society and the Colonial Order in Southeast Asia* (Delhi: Oxford University Press, 1989). Albert O. Hirschman, *Exit, Voice, and Loyalty: Responses to Decline in Firms, Organizations, and States.*

than disciples. Historians have not been affected much at all by Hirschman's scholarship: a number of economic historians have picked up on the themes he laid out in his 1958 study *The Strategy of Economic Development*—"linkages" and "unbalanced growth" in particular—and some historians of early American political thought have appropriated aspects of the clever argument he mounted in *The Passions and the Interests*, published in 1977.[2] Hirschman's other books and essays have received less attention by historians, which is surprising, given that he has long been a member of what is arguably the most prestigious rung on the American academic ladder: the Institute of Advanced Study in Princeton, New Jersey. Whether it is his intellectual independence or the fact that he has been known to employ the occasional equation in his work, historians have been respectful but distant to Hirschman, acknowledging him more than reading him.

In *Exit, Voice, and Loyalty*, Hirschman, true to form, sets his sights on rather unusual intellectual quarry: "lapses from efficient, rational, law-abiding, virtuous, or otherwise functional behavior" on the part of individuals, business firms, organizations, or even states, and the patterned way(s) in which others—individuals, clients, patients, customers, subjects, or citizens—respond to such lapses. Today this "unpremeditated book"—rather more an extended essay, actually—is considered one of the pioneering works in the increasingly influential neo-institutional school of economics.[3] In the book Hirschman demonstrates inter alia how real-world outcomes are shaped, if not determined, by dense interactions among relevant parties, interactions which are themselves affected by various forms of "friction," such as transaction costs, that preclude perfect rationality. If satisfactory (and more or less efficient) outcomes *can* result from such interactions, it is generally through a complex process of give and take, feedback loops, calls, and responses.

2. Albert O. Hirschman, *The Strategy of Economic Development* (New Haven, Conn.: Yale University Press, 1958); Albert O. Hirschman, *The Passions and the Interests: Political Arguments for Capitalism before Its Triumph* (Princeton, N.J.: Princeton University Press, 1977).

3. Hirschman, *Exit, Voice, and Loyalty*, 1, vii. On Hirschman's place in this school, see, for example, Eirik G. Furubotn and Rudolf Richter, *Institutions and Economic Theory: The Contribution of the New Institutional Economics* (Ann Arbor: University of Michigan Press, 1998), 272–78.

The main title of Hirschman's study captures much of its essence: *Exit, Voice, and Loyalty*. Indeed, in many ways the study can be seen as an intricate and nuanced elaboration on the range of possible responses by "customers" to a deterioration in the "saleable outputs" available to the same. One should note that Hirschman fully intended his argument to embrace cases involving "customers" consuming public goods, including the rights of citizenship. In applying Hirschman's argument to African Americans in the rural South, we do, however, relax one of his underlying suppositions: the idea that the deterioration in the "firm's" performance is due to "unspecified, random causes which are neither so compelling nor so durable as to prevent a return to previous performance levels, provided managers direct their attention and energy to that task."[4] Obviously, the "saleable output"—in this case, the economic opportunities and normative political rights, privileges, and immunities—made available by the state to rural blacks in the Jim Crow South did not decline because of "unspecified, random causes." Equally obvious is the fact that the decline in said "output" was both "compelling" and "durable," and that for much of the twentieth century state "managers" in the South were hardly inclined to "direct their attention and energy" to remediation of the same. Nonetheless, in our view Hirschman's conceptual schema is sufficiently intriguing and his insights on human behavior sufficiently powerful to not only survive but also yield robust results even after suppositional relaxation. Once one accepts Hirschman's general approach, the options available to black "consumers" of inferior state outputs—with or without said relaxation—were pretty much the same.

Hirschman lays out and develops a deceptively simple two-option response scheme in his "unpremeditated book." In actuality, Hirschman's parsimonious frame is both subtle and rigorous, allowing for many different strategic scenarios. We, too, aspire toward interpretive rigor even as we shade, modulate, and graduate in employing the same scheme with regard to the experience of African Americans in the rural South. Before going any further, though, let us turn our attention briefly to Hirschman's two primary strategic options.

4. On Hirshman's use of the term "saleable outputs," see *Exit, Voice, and Loyalty*, 3–4.

The "exit" response is perhaps the more straightforward of the two possibilities laid out by Hirschman, which is not to say that one can readily apprehend, much less grasp completely, all of its implications and feedback effects at first glance. Only with this important proviso in mind can we legitimately proceed. The exit option, broadly speaking, can take several forms: one can stop buying a firm's products, for example, or quit an organization. In each case, the option, considered as an "endogenous force . . . of recovery" is intended, if only implicitly, to impel management to correct the problems that led to the exercise of the exit option in the first place.[5]

Here, we socialize and amplify Hirschman's concept, employing it to bring greater analytical structure and meaning to several exit strategies pursued by African Americans in the rural South, including one of the most momentous "exits" in modern history: the "Great Migration" of rural African Americans to the urban North in the twentieth century. This migration occurred in two more or less discrete waves, of course, one beginning in the 1910s and peaking in the 1920s, and a second running from the Second World War through the mid-1960s. We shall concentrate here on the first of these waves, though the response from "management"—the white South—was so slow and timorous that our comments regarding the "exit" option by African Americans, alas, are relevant to a considerable degree to the second migration wave as well.

If exit is first and foremost an economic option, "voice" is best viewed in political terms, that is, as means by which a firm's customers or members of an organization express grievances to management (or to third parties, public or private) in order to bring redress. Such expressions of voice can take many forms, "all the way from faint grumbling to violent protest" in Hirschman's words.[6]

We shall employ the concept here to encompass the full panoply of African American political expression in the rural South in the twentieth century. In so doing, we perforce extend the bounds of Hirschman's conceit in certain ways. To Hirschman, writing more than thirty years ago, "voice" implied "articulation of one's critical opinions rather than

5. Ibid., 4, 15.
6. Ibid., 4, 16.

a private, 'secret' vote in the anonymity of a supermarket." Moreover, to Hirschman, voice "is direct and straightforward rather than round-about." In fine, "[v]oice is political action par excellence."[7]

Voice is all of this—and more. Clearly, in the early decades of the twentieth century *some* rural African Americans expressed their political voice(s) at the civil level in public and straightforward ways, while others—arguably, most—chose other means and other levels to express themselves politically. In order to capture such means and such levels, we shall employ several insights and concepts developed by the political scientist James C. Scott subsequent to the publication of *Exit, Voice, and Loyalty,* most notably, Scott's concept of infrapolitics, consisting of what he has (famously) labeled "weapons of the weak" and "hidden transcripts."[8]

At the most general level, then, exit and voice are the options possible in Hirschman's schema. But at the margin, how does a customer, a club member, a citizen, or even a denizen choose between them? In the face of deteriorating output of some private or public good, why do some people remain loyal while others do not? When, as Hirschman puts it, is loyalty functional and when is it not?[9]

These are complex problems to model, and even Hirschman is often left nonplussed by them. This said, such problems are perhaps even more difficult to grasp empirically, as we shall see in examining the densely layered, multivalent commitments and loyalties rural African Americans had to—or at least *in*—the South. If such commitments and loyalties sometimes held exit at bay and sometimes activated voice—responses Hirschman would understand well—such commitments and loyalties sometimes led someplace else.

Exit derives from the Latin participle *exire* (to go out), literally, "he/she/it goes out." Things get a bit more complicated in English: to go out, to go away, to depart, even to die. Then there is a noun form too.

7. Ibid., 16.

8. James C. Scott, *Weapons of the Weak: Everyday Forms of Peasant Resistance* (New Haven, Conn.: Yale University Press, 1985); James C. Scott, *Domination and the Arts of Resistance: Hidden Transcripts* (New Haven, Conn.: Yale University Press, 1990).

9. On these concerns, see Hirschman, *Exit, Voice, and Loyalty,* 76–105.

As regards African Americans in the rural South, we will limit the meaning to departures other than from life itself, but, even so, interpreting and understanding is not easy. There are exits and there are *exits*, as it were, and there are pushes and there are pulls promoting the same.

Looking at the early-twentieth-century South, it is not hard to come up with a list of push and pull factors promoting exit options among rural African Americans; indeed, it is in some ways more difficult to explain the forces that kept even more rural African Americans from departing, going out, or going away. In a civil sense, for example, the "saleable outputs" made available to rural blacks—the dearth of basic political and human rights, the abundance of daily humiliations, and the "oversupply" of intimidation, terror, and coercion—pressed, if not propelled, many toward exits of one type or another. Economic problems, whether endemic or episodic, added thrust. Rural underdevelopment, with its attendant misfortunes—poverty, ill health, undereducation, chronic debt—framed the experience of many African American farmers in the South in the early twentieth century, and "facts on the ground" such as soil exhaustion, the boll weevil, disastrous floods, and the pernicious if perhaps unintentional effects of New Deal agricultural policies bore down hard on individual farmers in discrete locales.[10] Such push forces were coupled with, and complemented by, assorted tugs and pulls. Dreams of starting over, however unrealistic, motivated many to exercise the exit option, as did the seductive allure of bright lights, big cities, and most important, unskilled factory jobs. And all the time, of course, news, gossip, rumor, and spin were helping to reduce drag: better land in the next county, a better cropping arrangement with farmer Smith, a better "settle" with furnishing merchant Jones, and better pay at a Chicago packinghouse even working under foreman O'Hara, Obradovich, or Kohl. Whether true or not was

10. On the rural South in the twentieth century, see, for example, Fite, *Cotton Fields No More*; Daniel, *Breaking the Land*; Wright, *Old South, New South*; Kirby, *Rural Worlds Lost*; R. Douglas Hurt, ed., *The Rural South since World War II* (Baton Rouge: Louisiana State University Press, 1998). On the position of African Americans specifically in southern agriculture between 1877 and 1945, see the special issue of *Agricultural History* 72 (spring 1998). See also Peter A. Coclanis, "In Retrospect: Ransom and Sutch's *One Kind of Freedom*," *Reviews in American History* 28 (September 2000): 478–89.

almost, but not quite, immaterial. In economic terms, exit functioned as both a bargaining strategy and an attempt to gain better access to desired "outputs." In personal terms, of course, exit promised something else: a chance at reinvention, if not redemption.

Thus, throughout the early twentieth century we see rural African Americans on the move. Although we would not deny that peonage existed in the South, we are struck more by the mobility of rural African Americans than by legal fetters and constraints limiting the same. To be sure, the extent of mobility was often modest, to which point the famous life history of Ned Cobb/Nate Shaw attests. Systematic data assembled by sociologist Stewart Tolnay (and by Louis M. Kyriakoudes in the first essay in this collection) offer further evidence thereto: according to Tolnay, African American tenants and sharecroppers moved frequently, but not very far, most often from one farm site to another within the same county. The need for farm credit makes movement of this type quite understandable. As Gavin Wright has argued, rural credit markets were organized along lines of familiarity and trust, and in such markets so-called reputational effects were often profound, setting strict limits on the geographical horizons of many "exiting" African Americans.[11] If there were plenty of reasons for "walkin'," and if many rural African Americans (in addition to Robert Johnson) may have had "ramblin'" on their minds, most (Johnson included) were never able to move very far.

Intracounty farm-to-farm exits could make marginal differences in the "saleable outputs" extended to individual African American households, but other types of exits affected both the southern agricultural economy and African Americans as a group more profoundly. Considerable numbers of black farmers in the South quit the rural sector altogether, opting for exit to one or another of the region's growing cities

11. On the persistence of the migration/mobility theme in African American culture, see, for example, Levine, *Black Culture and Black Consciousness*, 263. Rosengarten, *All God's Dangers*; Stewart E. Tolnay, *The Bottom Rung: African American Family Life on Southern Farms*, 134; Gavin Wright, "Freedom and the Southern Economy," in Gary M. Walton and James F. Shepherd, eds., *Market Institutions and Economic Progress in the New South 1865–1900: Essays Stimulated by "One Kind of Freedom: The Economic Consequences of Emancipation"* (New York: Academic Press, 1981), 85–102; Wright, *Old South, New South*, 52–60, 81–123.

and towns, places such as Norfolk, Memphis, Atlanta, and Birmingham. Although urban population and levels of urbanization in the South lagged behind those in other sections of the U.S., both rose significantly in the early twentieth century, in part through in-migration of African Americans from the farm sector.[12]

Another related type of exit—the Great Migration of rural blacks to the urban North and, later and to a lesser extent, to the urban West— was at once more dramatic and ultimately more powerful in its effects on and implications for "management" in the South. The drama of this exodus has been captured and captured well by scholars, writers, and artists, nowhere better than in painter Jacob Lawrence's *Migration* series (1940–1941) and in the FSA photographs included in Richard Wright's *12 Million Black Voices*.[13] The effects and implications of this exodus for white "management" in the South have (perhaps understandably) received less treatment over the years.

As suggested earlier, the Great Migration proceeded in two waves, the beginning of each of which was co-synchronous with, though not merely a corollary to or a function of, war. Indeed, in many ways World Wars I and II, *guerres père et fils,* so to speak, were precipitating and in-

12. Tolnay, *The Bottom Rung,* 120–42. See also David F. Sly, "Migration," in Dudley L. Poston, Jr., and Robert H. Weller, eds., *The Population of the South: Structure and Change in Social Demographic Context* (Austin: University of Texas Press, 1981), 109–36, esp. 128–34; Harvey S. Perloff et al., *Regions, Resources, and Economic Growth* (Baltimore: Published for Resources for the Future by the Johns Hopkins University Press, 1960), table 4, p. 19; U.S. Department of Commerce, Bureau of the Census, *Historical Statistics of the United States: Colonial Times to 1970,* 2 vols. (Washington, D.C.: U.S. Government Printing Office, 1975), vol. 1, 22–37, 93–96; "The Great Migration," in Kwame Anthony Appiah and Henry Louis Gates, eds., *Africana: The Encyclopedia of the African and African American Experience* (New York: Basic Books, 1999), 869–72 (especially map on 870). Note that the African American population of St. Louis, which for some purposes can be considered a "southern" city, also grew rapidly in the early twentieth century.

13. The literature on the "Great Migration" is voluminous, and includes many excellent cases of black migration to specific urban destinations in the North and West. For the basic contours of the phenomenon, see the works cited in footnote 19. See also Fligstein, *Going North,* and Robert Estall, *Population Change: The American South* (London: John Murray, 1989). Richard Wright, *12 Million Black Voices.* Note that the FSA photographs included in this work were selected by Edwin Rosskam.

tervening variables, underpinned and reinforced by more powerful independent variables, most notably industrialization, concomitant job opportunities, and the perceived call (however faint and untrue) of freedom. The first wave, lasting from the 1910s through the 1930s, resulted in a net population outflow from the South of almost two million African Americans, most from rural areas. As a result of this wave, so-called Bronzevilles were created in most large northern cities: New York, Chicago, Philadelphia, Detroit, and Cleveland, most notably. During the second wave, encompassing the period from the 1940s through the 1960s, another four million African Americans (net) pursued this strategic option. The redistributive (and social) effects of this migration were profound: whereas about 90 percent of the total number of African Americans in the United States lived in the South in 1900, roughly 75 percent lived in the region in 1940, and only about 50 percent did in 1970.[14]

After the 1960s, interregional migration patterns reversed, and the South registered a positive inflow of African Americans from other regions.[15] Had African Americans developed or renewed a sense of loyalty to the South? If yes, why? Had the exit strategy, in fact, worked? If so, had it worked alone or in combination with other strategies, such as voice, for example? Had the "saleable outputs"—whether measured via economic opportunities, degrees of discrimination, levels of political participation, or, more broadly, "margins of hope"—available to and within effective market reach of African Americans in the South grown and improved in quality over time? Or, conversely, had the "outputs" available to African Americans elsewhere declined in relative terms vis-à-vis the South? We could answer all of these questions, at least provisionally, right now, but before we do, let us turn to the second of Hirschman's options, which is to say, let us consider *voice*.

Voice, writes Hirschman, is "any attempt at all to change, rather than to escape from, an objectionable state of affairs, whether through indi-

14. U.S. Department of Commerce, Bureau of the Census, *Historical Statistics*, vol. 1, 23.

15. See the works cited in footnote 12. The numbers in the text are derived from Sly, "Migration," 125. Note that Tolnay's estimate of black outmigration in the 1930s is higher than Sly's. See Tolnay, *The Bottom Rung*, 117.

vidual or collective petition to the management directly in charge, through appeal to a higher authority with the intention of forcing a change in management, or through various types of actions and protests including those that are meant to mobilize public opinion." According to Hirschman, "the realm of politics" represents the most "characteristic province of voice."[16]

Of course, Jim Crow, a system built in part to limit black access to politics, ruled the South in the early twentieth century. Aided by the poll tax, the understanding clause, and the grandfather clause, white southerners—typically the richest ones—disenfranchised most African Americans and a large number of poor whites. When legal subterfuge did not work, elites turned to fraud and intimidation. Remarkably, however, a number of black southerners still managed to make themselves heard in this most characteristic province of voice in the 1930s. Throughout the decade, there remained mostly in the region's urban areas dedicated cadres of African American Republicans. Most often, these preachers, insurance salesmen, and undertakers voted in general elections, controlled a few patronage posts, and attended a convention here and there, but they generally spoke in soft, nonthreatening tones.

Louder still were the efforts of middle-class and working-class blacks to gain a voice in the Democratic party—the only party that really mattered in the Jim Crow South. At the decade's close, for instance, South Carolina schoolteacher Lottie P. Gaffney along with four other women and two ministers went at the designated time to the designated place to register to vote. They knocked hard on the door. Nothing happened. They knocked again. Finally, the registrar looked out and could not believe it. "Darkies," he said to Gaffney, more shocked than mad, "have never registered in the South and especially in Cherokee County." Then he slammed the door in their faces. They kept knocking all afternoon, but the registrar would not answer. African Americans in Columbia, Greenville, Charleston, Cheraw, and Spartanburg, South Carolina, followed in Gaffney's footsteps and tried to register to vote. Very few people were to gain their voting rights. Most were treated like the Spartanburg man who was told that if he continued to ask to have his name

---

16. Hirshman, *Exit, Voice, and Loyalty,* 30.

placed on the voting roll his house would be torched and he would be "scalped." But still African Americans in other places continued to try to gain a voice in politics. In Louisiana, black women and men publicly called for the end of the poll tax, while in Georgia they revived old chapters of the National Association for the Advancement of Colored People. But African Americans remained stuck in the South's political quicksand. Without the vote few listened, and with no one listening, it was hard to get the vote.[17]

Most black southerners estimated that the costs of raising their voices in the "most characteristic" of places—that is, electoral politics—were not worth the potential risks. Silence at the registrar's office and polling station, however, did not mean that African Americans were necessarily loyal to the system or determined to stay in the region. Instead, their silence reflected a clear understanding of the calculus of power. Everyone in the black community knew about Reconstruction; they knew how white men stole their rights. They had heard chilling tales of lynching, murder, fraud, and intimidation. Hearing these gruesome stories did not silence African Americans, but it did make many—even the most disgruntled—cautious. Still, not everyone remained quiet or resorted to exit. Throughout the 1930s, African Americans spoke out in many political languages and in multiple political settings against the social and economic injustices of the Jim Crow order and the sharecropping regime.

Some rural blacks, as Robin Kelley and Nate Shaw have explained,

---

17. On patterns of black voting see Nancy Weiss, *Farewell to the Party of Lincoln: Black Politics in the Age of F.D.R.* (Princeton, N.J.: Princeton University Press, 1993); and Glenda Elizabeth Gilmore, "False Friends and Avowed Enemies: Southern African Americans and Party Allegiances in the 1920s," in Jane Dailey, Glenda Elizabeth Gilmore, and Bryant Simon, eds., *Jumpin' Jim Crow: Southern Politics from Civil War to Civil Rights* (Princeton, N.J.: Princeton University Press, 2000), 219–38. Mrs. Lottie P. Gaffney to the NAACP, August 25, 1940, November 7, 1940; and NAACP Press Release, May 29, 1941, Voting Rights Campaign, pt. 4, Reel 10, NAACP Papers; Ralph Bunche, *The Political Status of the Negro in the Age of FDR* (Chicago: University of Chicago Press, 1973), 238–47, 425–27. For more on the activities in Louisiana and Georgia see also Adam Fairclough, *Race and Democracy: The Civil Rights Struggle in Louisiana, 1915–1972* (Athens: University of Georgia Press, 1995), 23–25; and Patricia Sullivan, *Days of Hope: Race and Democracy in the New Deal Era* (Chapel Hill: University of North Carolina Press, 1996), 105–6.

pledged their allegiance to the Communist party.[18] Even more famously, others joined the Southern Tenant Farmers' Union (STFU). Founded in 1934, the biracial union of black and white tenants staged cotton pickers strikes in 1935 and 1936, protested against government policy, demanded direct payments under the New Deal's Agricultural Adjustment Act, and rallied to stave off evictions. Strongest in Arkansas and Oklahoma, the STFU claimed more than thirty thousand members in seven southern states by 1937. A Holly Grove, Arkansas, sharecropper complained that "De landlord is landlord, de politicians is landlord, de judge is landlord, de shurf is landlord, ever'body is landlord." But she said, "de Tenant Farmers' Union put up a kick. En now dey send *us* de checks (for crop reduction payments)." Voice, she argued in other words, paid off in this case.[19]

Despite the STFU's efforts, the majority of rural African Americans judged the costs of such public forms of voice to be too risky and too great, so they spoke in other political ways. Every day from March 1933 onwards, President Franklin D. Roosevelt received hundreds of letters from black southerners. Some wrote to praise the chief executive. Others delivered detailed reports on local conditions. Even more asked Roosevelt for something. A man from Vicksburg, Mississippi, wanted "food and Cloths." "A Colored Friend down in Tupelo Miss" wrote looking for some money to pay his bills and keep his creditors at bay. A Huntsville, Alabama, man asked for help to get him and his family of seven through the winter. Others wanted relief jobs or pension money they thought was due to them. Still others voiced demands. When they did, they made clear that they saw themselves as American citizens, as members of the national political community even as state and local officials in the South

18. For more on this see Nell Irvin Painter, *The Narrative of Hosea Hudson: His Life as a Negro Communist in the South* (Cambridge, Mass.: Harvard University Press, 1979); Rosengarten, *All God's Dangers,* and Kelley, *Hammer and Hoe.*

19. On the Southern Tenant Farmers' Union, see Mitchell, *Mean Things Happening in This Land,* and Grubbs, *Cry from the Cotton.* For an overview of the union, see Tom E. Terrill and Jerrold Hirsch, *Such as Us: Southern Voices of the Thirties* (Chapel Hill: University of North Carolina Press), 56; and Pete Daniel, *Standing at the Crossroads: Southern Life since 1900,* 121–22. For the voices of participants, see Howard Kester, *Revolt among the Sharecroppers* (Knoxville: University of Tennessee Press, 1997), and Rosengarten, *All God's Dangers.*

denied them these very same rights. Explaining that she was on the verge of starvation, a "naket half clad's" woman told the president that "Mississippi is made her own laws an don't treat her destuted as her Pres has laid the plans for us to live." A man from a nearby town was sure Roosevelt would not stand for local officials giving "all the work to white people and . . . us nothing." A Marion, Arkansas, man called on FDR to "helpe the poor negrous and stop them peoples at the cort house frome Robing the government." Like most of Roosevelt's black correspondents, this man did not sign his letter. "These white people will kill all the Negroes," he believed if local whites found out that he wrote the president. A Reidsville, Georgia, man told the chief executive, "cant sign my name . . . they will beat me up and run me away from here and this is my home."[20] In a world like this where writing a letter could lead to murder or maiming, voice obviously had to be exercised with extreme care.

Realizing this, many African American sharecroppers and cotton pickers spoke with their feet. The rural South of the early twentieth century was a world of constant motion. Always on the lookout for a better deal, farm laborers moved from town to town, landlord to landlord. Grace Turner spent her entire life on the move. Over a twenty-year period, she relocated seven or eight times. When North Carolina's Hattie Duncan felt like she got a bad deal from her landlord, she started, according her neighbor, Mary Matthews, a "row wid him." "We knowned, we wouldn't git nothin' dat way," explained Matthews. So instead of fighting with her boss, she and her husband picked up and moved on to work for another landlord.[21] There is no way to tell if Matthews was the only one to move or if Mr. Jones—the original landlord—started to treat his sharecroppers better, but he might have gotten the message. When prices rose or cotton needed to be picked, Mr. Jones had to have workers. In order to get them, he had to listen to them. Either he raised wages and improved conditions, or his cotton rotted in the field. As a kind of collective voice, then, moving could be an effective instrument, especially during good times, but there were few good times in the rural South in the 1930s.

20. Robert McElvaine, *Down and Out in the Great Depression: Letters from the Forgotten Man* (Chapel Hill: University of North Carolina Press), 81–94.
21. Terrill and Hirsch, *Such as Us,* 87–89.

When rural laborers stayed put, they often used the quieter, harder to track voice of "infra-politics" to address their grievances.[22] Beneath the top layer of political life, which is to say the open, public layer, there is, according to James Scott, another layer or level in which subordinate groups the world over historically have operated with or without the knowledge and/or acquiescence of their superordinates. This is the layer or realm of infrapolitical life. Again, according to Scott, subordinates—slaves, serfs, oppressed and low-caste groups—have long recognized that extant power asymmetries would likely render open political expression, much less opposition or dissidence, futile, if not suicidal. As a result, they have characteristically registered their political voice not in public, transparent ways, but in masked form in "everyday acts of resistance." At the material level, such resistance has often taken the form of noncompliance, petty theft, dissimulation, or feigned ignorance. At the ideological level, resistance is often revealed in "hidden transcripts" such as rumors, gossip, jokes, gestures, songs, folktales, and the like.[23]

To be sure, too much can be made of Scott's conceptual conceits. At times, imaginative scholars have created acts of resistance out of whole cloth. Scott himself cautioned against such overreaching. Just as a necktie is sometimes only a necktie, sometimes a fart—Scott's famous illustration notwithstanding—is only a fart.[24] Nonetheless, in our view one misses something important about the voice of rural African Americans in the South if one limits one's gaze to the top layer, the transparent, the "public transcript," as it were. By employing Scott, and thus an enhanced conceptualization of the political, it is much easier to hear the full range of the "vocal" behavior of rural African Americans and the forces that ultimately compelled or at least promoted positive political feedback responses by "management," that is, the white South.

Like their enslaved ancestors, early-twentieth-century African Americans therefore had a "voice." They had the ability to shape the quality and direction of their lives and to resist the demands of the powerful. Sharecroppers and tenants stole what they needed from landlords and

22. Scott, *Weapons of the Weak;* Scott, *Domination and the Arts of Resistance.*
23. Scott, *Weapons of the Weak;* Scott, *Domination and the Arts of Resistance.*
24. Scott, *Domination and the Arts of Resistance,* v.

employers. They skipped work, faked illnesses, dragged their feet on the job, and sabotaged machinery. They organized slowdowns and strikes. They did their own work on company time with company tools and materials and sometimes they lied, cheated, and dissimulated.[25] Overall, rural black laborers used what little power they had to work as little as possible and get as much as they could out of their bosses.

On the streets and in town, African Americans launched other kinds of protests against the South's racial order. From the white perspective, Jim Crow was a carefully choreographed affair. Everyone had a part to play and every line and every gesture was scripted. African Americans were supposed to be poor and look like it; they were told to remove their hats whenever they spoke to a white man; they were taught to move off sidewalks when whites passed; they were told to use the back door of white homes, never the front; and they were instructed to address whites as Boss or Mr. or Mrs. Deploying the weapons of the weak, African Americans defied these unwritten but still closely adhered to rules. They went out in public in fancy clothes, "accidentally" bumped into whites on sidewalks, and called themselves Mr. and Mrs. One family named their daughter "Mis Julia" reportedly to make sure that whites would address her with polite respect.[26]

Black agricultural workers protested away from work and away from the streets as well. Employers and landlords struggled to turn share-croppers, tenants, and laborers into sober, efficient, and disciplined laborers. To do this, they sought to control workers both on and off the job. On Saturday nights, however, black women and men took control over their time and their bodies. At rural bars, juke joints, and house parties they shook, sang, danced, gambled, drank, and boogied. Through these movements and sounds, African American laborers

25. Kelley, *Hammer and Hoe;* Kelley, "'We Are Not What We Seem': Rethinking Black Working-Class Opposition in the Jim Crow South," *Journal of American History* 80 (June 1993): 75–112. For other examples of everyday resistance, see Tera Hunter, *To 'Joy My Freedom: Southern Black Women's Lives and Labors after the Civil War* (Cambridge, Mass.: Harvard University Press, 1997); and Elsa Barkley Brown, "Negotiating and Transforming the Public Sphere: African American Political Life in the Transition from Slavery to Freedom," *Public Culture* 7 (fall 1994): 107–46.

26. J. William Harris, "Etiquette, Lynching, and Racial Boundaries in Southern History: A Mississippi Example"; Cobb, *The Most Southern Place on Earth,* 163.

claimed control over their bodies. What's more, they rejected—at least symbolically—the values of their white employers. Yet again they claimed a voice in the affairs of the Southland.

The music playing at full blast at the juke joints and bars served as another realm of voice for black working people. The blues in particular provided African Americans with a way to speak about the world around them. To be black and a sharecropper or a tenant living in the southern countryside in the first part of the twentieth century meant to be shut off from the most official forms of communication: formal politics, the media, and literature. Through the blues, African Americans found a voice. While the music was often deeply personal, reporting on love and sex lost and found, it also took the form of social commentary. Like contemporary rap, blues was a kind of street newspaper, a combination of grassroots ethnography and oral documentary.[27]

Musicologist William Barlow argues that the blues provide a "ground-level view of southern society." The singers reported on the price of cotton, dark winds, the boll weevil, and the landlord. They talked about poverty and hard times. But as Barlow points out, they also sang about politics. "An ethos of revolt," he detects, infused the music.[28] Sometimes, as others have shown, the music was explicitly political. Brownie McGhee complained that Herbert Hoover "[t]ook us off a Camel cigarettes and put us on Golden Grain." (Golden Grain was a cheap, often sour-tasting rolling tobacco.) Franklin Roosevelt, not surprisingly, won the praise of a number of bluesmen. Six months after FDR told the nation it had "nothing to fear but fear itself," Jack Kelley recorded "President Blues." Roosevelt, he sang, woke up one morning, thinking of "his poor people" and vowing to "fight on" and "make everything all right." Joe Pullum echoed Kelly's words in his 1934 song, "CWA Blues." (The Civil Works Administration was a New Deal agency that employed at its height more than four million persons.)[29] Praising the president, Pullum declared:

27. Kelley, *Race Rebels,* 190.
28. Barlow quoted by Cobb, *The Most Southern Place on Earth,* 282–83. See also Levine, *Black Culture and Black Consciousness;* and Robert Palmer, *Deep Blues: A Musical and Cultural History of the Mississippi Delta* (New York: Viking Press, 1981).
29. On the CWA, see William E. Leuchtenburg, *Franklin Roosevelt and the New Deal, 1932–1940* (New York: Harper and Row, 1963), 121.

CWA, look what you done for me:
You brought my good gal back, and lifted Depression off-a-me.

Others bluesmen pointed to the limits of Roosevelt's policies. Carl Martin complained, "I sittin' right here waitin', on that Brand New Deal."[30]

Blues singers at times spoke in more violent, even apocalyptic, political voices. The appropriately named Furry Lewis raged:

I believe I'll buy me a graveyard of my own;
I'm goin' kill everybody that have done me wrong.

Another Deep South musician added:

I feel my hell a-risin' every day.
Someday it'll burst this levee and wash the whole wide world away.[31]

Whatever the message of individual songs, the blues, and for that matter gospel and rhythm-and-blues, were perhaps the most unmediated form of voice available to African Americans in the rural South in the 1930s. Here was a space that whites barely touched. African Americans could, therefore, speak honestly and voice their pain, their bitterness, and their hopes for escaping from and staying in the South.

Loyalty, Hirschman writes, "holds exit at bay and activates voice." Talking about the function of loyalty, he adds, "The importance of loyalty . . . is that it can neutralize within certain limits the tendency of the most quality customers or members to be the first to exit." Among other things, loyalty, therefore, kept people from leaving. To put this another way, by staying, women and men demonstrated their loyalty.[32]

Much like Hirschman, William Alexander Percy, scion of the powerful Mississippi planter family, interpreted staying as loyalty. Looking at aging African Americans on his family's plantation, he saw loyal

30. Guido Van Rijn, *Roosevelt Blues: African-American Blues and Gospel Songs on FDR* (Jackson: University Press of Mississippi, 1997), 66–67, 69–70, 76–77.

31. Cobb, *The Most Southern Place on Earth*, 295.

32. Hirschman, *Exit, Voice, and Loyalty*, 78, 79.

hands, black men so deeply attached to their white bosses that they could not imagine a life without them.[33]

This is Percy's illusion. This was also WPA worker Mary Chappel's illusion. Reared in the country, Katy Brumby came to Birmingham after World War I. For seventeen years, she cooked and cleaned for Chappel's family. "Katy," Mary Chappel wrote, "is loyal above all." She continued, "She is not only a friend, but a member of the family, which, despite the accusation of 'paternalism,' is the only way to describe a relationship at once so intricate and so simple."[34]

Perhaps some African Americans in the South were loyal to their bosses and to the Jim Crow regime in the ways that their bosses imagined. Some told stories—to white interviewers—of following their "old mistis and old marsters." Mary Johnson, for example, told Ina B. Hawkes a long and meandering story about how much her African American parents loved the white folks who owned them. Before Hawkes left her house, she asked her, in Hawkes's words, "to go to the welfare people for me and tell dem I sho needs a coat an' some dresses 'cause I sho is necked." Loyalty, in this case and a lot of others, was probably an act—a weapon of the weak—a strategy of coping with periodic violence and crushing poverty. Black farm workers and sharecroppers doffed their hats, looked down, smiled, and said all kinds of "Yes Sirs" and "Yes Maams" in hopes of getting a better deal from landlords.[35] Obsequiousness was a way of trying to create reciprocity. Given their conditions, black families gambled that if they played the parts whites wanted them to play—the part of Sambo, that is—then they might be able to gain an advantage or two. Maybe "loyal" blacks figured that white women and men would repay them for their loyalty with some extra money, a better plot of land, help during hard times, and a chance for their children to get ahead. Again, loyalty was probably most often an act, a choice, a carefully considered gambit, one that

33. Percy, *Lanterns on the Levee.*

34. "The Story of Katy Brumby," www.memory.loc.gov.

35. Federal Writers' Project, *These Are Our Lives: As Told by the People and Written by Members of the Federal Writers' Project of the Works Progress Administration in North Tennessee, and Georgia* (Chapel Hill: University of North Carolina Press, 1939), 28; "Negro Life on a Farm," www.memory.loc.gov; Kelley, *Race Rebels,* 21–22.

carried with it the potential for deep psychic scars, but in the end, still a rational calculation.

Mississippi native and blues legend Muddy Waters once sang: "Gotta mind to move, a mind to settle down."[36] Certainly tens of thousands of African Americans shared Water's ambivalence about their homelands and the new worlds in the North. Tens of thousands "exited" the South in the first half of the twentieth century. Like Waters, they took the train to Chicago, or to Cleveland, Detroit, Pittsburgh, and hundreds of other places with factory jobs and emerging ghettos. But obviously just as many, if not more, African Americans stayed put in the land of their parents. Landlords like Percy regarded this staying as loyalty, and it was loyalty, but not to Jim Crow and the benevolent boss.

Sharecroppers stayed in Greenwood, Mississippi, Percy's home, and elsewhere because they could not leave. Turnover rates for tenant farmers and sharecroppers in the Delta, to look at one place, fell sharply during the 1930s. Of course as the Great Migrations of the 1920s and 1940s suggest, the depression and limited options, more than loyalty, account for these figures. At the same time, some southern blacks had already gotten reports from up north telling them it was not really the promised land after all. Some others stayed because they were attached to the land and the rhythms of rural life. "Farmin' all I ever done, all I can do, all I want to do," one man said, adding sadly, "And I can't make a livin' at it." But still he stayed on the land. Another man went to New York to visit a friend and concluded he could not live there. Life in the country was the only life for him.[37] Most stayed because they were loyal to place. They were loyal to family, to friends, to church, and of course to the land. Clearly, loyalty was important to African Americans living in the rural South, but it was loyalty to the patterns of day-to-day life, to the past, and to each other, not to old man Jim Crow.

Toward the end of *Black Boy*—that classic and searing memoir of growing up in and on the fringes of the rural South in the early twen-

36. Cobb, *The Most Southern Place on Earth,* 285. For more on Waters and his southern-ness and northern-ness, see Robert Gordon, *Can't Be Satisfied: The Life and Times of Muddy Waters* (New York: Little, Brown, and Co., 2002).

37. J. William Harris, *Deep Souths: Delta, Piedmont, and Sea Island Society in the Age of Segregation,* 305; *These Are Our Lives,* 30, 52–53.

tieth century—Richard Wright sounds at times a bit like Albert Hirsch-man. "I could," he writes from the perspective of a young man, "cal-culate my chances for life in the South as a Negro fairly clearly now." One option, he figured, was to "fight southern whites by organizing with other Negroes." Wright, however, rejected using this most explic-it form of "voice." "Outright black rebellion," he wearily concluded, "could never win." It would lead to certain death, and he declared, "I did not want to die." Yet loyalty—not even the self-conscious dance of loyalty performed by Shorty, his onetime co-worker—was an option to Wright. "I could not submit and live the life of genial slave," he wrote.[38] All he could do, then, was leave the South.

Of course that is what Wright did. He pursued the exit option, fleeing from Mississippi to Memphis and then north to Chicago. When he found there the horrors of a "native son," he redid the math, in Herschman-like way, and decided to exit once again, this time to Paris. That is where he stayed, and that is where he died—in exile. But Wright knew, as he wrote in *Black Boy*, that no matter where he went, "deep down . . . I could never leave the South."[39]

Beginning in the 1970s, African Americans have begun to recalculate the equation of exit, voice, and loyalty. Wright's spiritual ancestors— the women and men who fled the South—are coming back to the re-gion, not in droves, but in slow, steady streams. Pointing to a row of empty bar stools, Ben Hampton, a Greenwood, Mississippi, native and manager of the legendary Chicago blues club The Checkerboard Lounge, explained, "A lot of people I know have gone back south."[40] They have crossed back over the Mason Dixon line to where the "col-ored" signs have come down off the walls of restaurants and bus ter-minal waiting rooms and where the polling stations are open to all cit-izens. But they also exited from the crime, drugs, and violence that

38. Wright, *Black Boy* (reprt., New York: Harper Perennial, 1966), 282–83. In his new book, Adam Fairclough makes a somewhat similar argument about the dim prospects for rebellion in the early-twentieth-century South. Fairclough, *"Bet-ter Day Coming": Blacks and Equality, 1890–2000*, 41–65.

39. Wright, *Black Boy*. 284.

40. Hampton quoted by Carlo Rotello, *Good with Their Hands: Boxers, Bluesmen and Other Characters from the Rust Belt* (Berkeley: University of California Press, 2002), 70.

cripple many corners of urban America. They have escaped to where the jobs are now. They have returned to the South because the promise of voice—of a political voice—did not, in the end, make that much of a difference, at least to some. And many have come "home" because they longed for the places of their grandparents and great-grandparents. Whether that place exists or floats in a kind of hazy nostalgia for Sunday dinners after church and ordered communities hardly matters.

African Americans have come back to the South and claimed it as their own. Now a new test of loyalty will take place. The multivariant calculations Hirschman wrote about so clearly and crisply never end. They are what public and economic lives are all about.[41]

41. On "coming home," see Stack, *Call to Home,* and James C. Cobb, "Searching for Southerness: Community and Identity in the Contemporary South," in Cobb, ed., *Defining Southern Culture: Mind and Identity in the Modern South* (Athens: University of Georgia Press, 1999), 125–49, 237–40.

Suggested Readings

"African Americans in Southern Agriculture, 1877–1945." *Agricultural History* 72 (spring 1998). Special Issue.

Aiken, Charles S. *The Cotton Plantation South: Since the Civil War.* Baltimore: Johns Hopkins University Press, 1998.

———. "The Rural South: A Historical View." In Emery N. Castle, ed., *The Changing Countryside: Rural People and Places* (Lawrence: University Press of Kansas, 1995), 318–38.

Andrews, William L., ed. *African-American Autobiography: Essays Theoretical and Critical.* Englewood Cliffs, N.J.: Prentice Hall, 1993.

———. *To Tell a Free Story: The First Century of Afro-American Autobiography.* Urbana: University of Illinois Press, 1986.

Angelou, Maya. *I Know Why the Caged Bird Sings.* New York: Bantam Books, 1968.

Archer, Chalmers, Jr. *Growing Up Black in Rural Mississippi: Memories of a Family, Heritage of a Place.* New York: Walker and Co., 1992.

Ayers, Edward L. *The Promise of the New South: Life after Reconstruction.* New York: Oxford University Press, 1992.

Baer, Hans A., and Merrill Singer. *African-American Religion in the Twentieth Century: Varieties of Protest and Accommodation.* Knoxville: University of Tennessee Press, 1992.

Baker, Houston A., Jr. *Long Black Song: Essays in Black American Literature and Culture.* Charlottesville: University Press of Virginia, 1972.

Beaulieu, Lionel J., ed. *The Rural South in Crisis: Challenges for the Future.* Boulder, Colo.: Westview Press, 1988.

Blight, David W. "W. E. B. Dubois and the Struggle for American Historical Memory." In Genevieve Fabre and Robert O'Meally, eds., *History and Memory in African-American Culture* (New York: Oxford University Press, 1994), 45–71.

Braxton, Joanne M. *Black Women Writing Autobiography: A Tradition within a Tradition.* Philadelphia: Temple University Press, 1989.

Brundage, W. Fitzhugh. *Lynching in the New South: Georgia and Virginia, 1880–1930*. Urbana: University of Illinois Press, 1993.

Burton, Orville Vernon. "Race Relations in the South since 1945." In R. Douglas Hurt, ed., *The Rural South since World War II* (Baton Rouge: Louisiana State University Press, 1998), 28–58.

Cobb, James C. *The Most Southern Place on Earth: The Mississippi Delta and the Roots of Regional Identity*. New York: Oxford University Press, 1992.

———. "'Somebody Done Nailed Us on the Cross': Federal Farm Welfare Policy and the Civil Rights Movement in the Mississippi Delta." *Journal of American History* 77 (December 1990): 912–36.

Cohen, William. *At Freedom's Edge: Black Mobility and the Southern White Quest for Racial Control, 1861–1915*. Baton Rouge: Louisiana State University Press, 1991.

Collier-Thomas, Bettye. *Daughters of Thunder: Black Women Preachers and their Sermons*. San Francisco: Jossey-Bass, 1998.

Crosby, Earl W. "The Roots of Black Agricultural Extension Work." *Historian* 39 (February 1977): 228–47.

———. "The Struggle for Existence: The Institutionalization of the Black County Agent System." *Agricultural History* 60 (spring 1986): 123–36.

Daniel, Pete. *Breaking the Land: The Transformation of Cotton, Tobacco, and Rice Cultures since 1880*. Urbana: University of Illinois Press, 1985.

———. "Going among Strangers: Southern Reactions to World War II." *Journal of American History* 77 (December 1990): 886–911.

———. *Lost Revolutions: The South in the 1950s*. Chapel Hill: University of North Carolina Press, 2000.

———. *The Shadow of Slavery: Peonage in the South, 1901–1969*. Urbana: University of Illinois Press, 1972.

———. *Standing at the Crossroads: Southern Life since 1900*. New York: Hill and Wang, 1986.

Dittmer, John. *Local People: The Struggle for Civil Rights in Mississippi*. Urbana: University of Illinois Press, 1994.

Dorr, Lisa Lindquist. "Black-on-White Rape and Retribution in Twentieth-Century Virginia: 'Men, Even Negroes, Must Have Some Protection.'" *Journal of Southern History* 66 (November 2000): 711–48.

Du Bois, W. E. B. *Dusk of Dawn: An Essay toward and Autobiography of a Race Concept*. New York: Harcourt Brace and Co., 1940.

Dudley, David L. *My Father's Shadow: Intergenerational Conflict in African American Men's Autobiography*. Philadelphia: University of Pennsylvania Press, 1991.

Dvorak, Katherine L. *An African-American Exodus: The Segregation of the Southern Churches*. Brooklyn, N.Y.: Carlson Publishing, 1991.

Ellenberg, George B. "African Americans, Mules, and the Southern Mindscape, 1850–1950." *Agricultural History* 72 (spring 1998): 381–98.

Fairclough, Adam. *"Better Day Coming": Blacks and Equality, 1890–2000*. New York: Viking, 2001.

Ferguson, Karen J. "Caught in 'No Man's Land': The Negro Cooperative Demonstration Service and the Ideology of Booker T. Washington, 1900–1918." *Agricultural History* 72 (winter 1998): 33–54.

Fite, Gilbert C. *Cotton Fields No More: Southern Agriculture 1865–1980*. Lexington: University of Press of Kentucky, 1984.

Fligstein, Neil. *Going North: Migration of Blacks and Whites from the South, 1900–1950*. New York: Academic Press, 1981.

Foley, Neil. *The White Scourge: Mexicans, Blacks, and Poor Whites in Texas Cotton Culture*. Berkeley: University of California Press, 1997.

Franklin, V. P. *Living Our Stories, Telling Our Truths: Autobiography and the Making of the African-American Intellectual Tradition*. New York: Oxford University Press, 1995.

Gates, Henry Lewis, ed. *Bearing Witness: Selections from African-American Autobiography*. New York: Pantheon Books, 1991.

Gordon, Louise. *Caste and Class: The Black Experience in Arkansas, 1880–1920*. Athens: University of Georgia Press, 1995.

Gottlieb, Peter. *Making Their Own Way: Southern Blacks' Migration to Pittsburgh, 1916–1930*. Urbana: University of Illinois Press, 1987.

Gray, Richard. *Southern Aberrations: Writers of the American South and the Problem of Regionalism*. Baton Rouge: Louisiana State University Press, 2000.

———. *Writing the South: Ideas of an American Region, with a New Afterward*. Baton Rouge: Louisiana State University Press, 1997.

Grim, Valerie. "The Politics of Inclusion: Black Farmers and the Quest for Agribusiness Participation." *Agricultural History* 69 (spring 1995): 257–71.

Grossman, James R. *Land of Hope: Chicago and the Great Migration.* Chicago: University of Chicago Press, 1989.

Hahamovitch, Cindy. *The Fruits of Their Labor: Atlantic Coast Farmworkers and the Making of Migrant Poverty, 1870–1945.* Chapel Hill: University of North Carolina Press, 1997.

Hale, Grace Elizabeth. *Making Whiteness: The Culture of Segregation in the South, 1890–1940.* New York: Pantheon, 1998.

Hargis, Peggy G. "Beyond the Marginality Thesis: The Acquisition and Loss of Land by African Americans in Georgia." *Agricultural History* 72 (spring 1998): 241–62.

Harris, J. William. *Deep Souths: Delta, Piedmont, and Sea Island Society in the Age of Segregation.* Baltimore: Johns Hopkins University Press, 2001.

———. "Etiquette, Lynching, and Racial Boundaries in Southern History: A Mississippi Example." *American Historical Review* 100 (April 1995): 387–410.

Harrison, Alferdteen, ed. *Black Exodus: The Great Migration from the American South.* Jackson: University Press of Mississippi, 1991.

Heyrman, Christine Leigh. *Southern Cross: The Beginnings of the Bible Belt.* New York: Alfred A. Knopf, 1997.

Hickey, Jo Ann S., and Anthony Andrew Hickey. "Black Farmers in Virginia, 1930–1978: An Analysis of the Social Organization of Agriculture." *Rural Sociology* 52, no. 1 (1987): 75–88.

Higginbotham, Evelyn Brooks. *Righteous Discontent: The Black Women's Movement in the Black Baptist Church, 1880–1920.* Cambridge, Mass.: Harvard University Press, 1993.

Higgs, Robert. "The Boll Weevil, the Cotton Economy, and Black Migration." *Agricultural History* 50 (April 1976): 335–50.

Hirschman, Albert O. *Exit, Voice, and Loyalty: Responses to Decline in Firms, Organizations, and States.* Cambridge, Mass.: Harvard University Press, 1970.

Hullinger, Edwin Ware. *Plowing Through: The Story of the Negro in Agriculture.* New York: Morrow, 1940.

Hurston, Zora Neale. *Dust Tracks on a Road.* 2d ed. Edited by Robert E. Memenway. Urbana: University of Illinois Press, 1984.

Johnston, Ruby Funchess. *The Religion of Negro Protestants: Changing Religious Attitudes and Practices.* New York: Philosophical Library, 1956.

Jones, Allen W. "The Role of Tuskegee Institute in the Education of Black Farmers." *Journal of Negro History* 60 (April 1975): 252–67.

Jones, Jacqueline. *Labor of Love, Labor of Sorrow: Black Women, Work and the Family from Slavery to the Present.* New York: Basic Books, 1985.

Kirby, Jack Temple. *Rural Worlds Lost: The American South, 1920–1960.* Baton Rouge: Louisiana State University Press, 1987.

Lemann, Nicholas. *The Promised Land: The Great Black Migration and How It Changed America.* New York: Alfred A. Knopf, 1991.

Levine, Lawrence W. *Black Culture and Black Consciousness: Afro-American Folk Thought from Slavery to Freedom.* New York: Oxford University Press, 1977.

Lewis, Earl. *In Their Own Interests: Race, Class, and Power in Twentieth-Century Norfolk, Virginia.* Berkeley: University of California Press, 1991.

———. "To Turn as on a Pivot: Writing African Americans into a History of Overlapping Diasporas." *American Historical Review* 100 (June 1995): 765–87.

McMillen, Neil R. *Dark Journey: Black Mississippians in the Age of Jim Crow.* Urbana: University of Illinois Press, 1989.

McMillen, Sally. "No Easy Time: Rural Women, 1940–1990." In R. Douglas Hurt, ed., *The Rural South since World War II* (Baton Rouge: Louisiana State University Press, 1998), 59–94.

Marks, Carole. *Farewell—We're Good and Gone: The Great Black Migration.* Bloomington: Indiana University Press, 1989.

Matthews, Donald H. *Honoring the Ancestors: An African Cultural Interpretation of Black Religion and Literature.* New York: Oxford University Press, 1998.

Maxwell, William J. *New Negro, Old Left: African-American Writing and Communism between the Wars.* New York: Columbia University Press, 1999.

Montgomery, William E. *Under Their Own Vine and Fig Tree: The African-American Church in the South, 1865–1900.* Baton Rouge: Louisiana State University Press, 1993.

Moody, Anne. *Coming of Age in Mississippi.* New York: Bantam Doubleday Dell, 1968.

Myrdal, Gunnar. *An American Dilemma: The Negro Problem and Modern Democracy.* New York: Harper and Brothers, 1944.

Olney, James. "Autobiographical Traditions Black and White." In J. Bill Berry, ed., *Located Lives: Place and Idea in Southern Autobiography* (Athens: University of Georgia Press, 1990), 66–77.

Ownby, Ted. "Struggling to Be Old-Fashioned: Evangelical Religion in the Modern Rural South." In R. Douglas Hurt, ed., *The Rural South since World War II* (Baton Rouge: Louisiana State University Press, 1998), 122–48.

Percy, William. *Lanterns on the Levee: Recollections of a Planter's Son.* Baton Rouge: Louisiana State University Press, 1973.

Phillips, Kimberley L. *Alabama North: African-American Migrants, Community, and Working-Class Activism in Cleveland, 1915–45.* Urbana: University of Illinois Press, 1999.

Pitts, Walter F. *Old Ship of Zion: The Afro-Baptist Ritual in the African Diaspora.* New York: Oxford University Press, 1993.

Raboteau, Albert H. *Canaan Land: A Religious History of African Americans.* New York: Oxford University Press, 2001.

Ransom, Roger, and Richard Sutch. *One Kind of Freedom: The Economic Consequences of Emancipation.* Cambridge, England: Cambridge University Press, 1977.

Raper, Arthur F. *Preface to Peasantry: A Tale of Two Black Belt Counties.* Chapel Hill: University of North Carolina Press, 1936.

Rosengarten, Ted. *All God's Dangers: The Life of Nate Shaw.* New York: Alfred A. Knopf, 1974.

Schultz, Mark R. "The Dream Realized: African American Landownership in Central Georgia between Reconstruction and World War II." *Agricultural History* 72 (spring 1998): 298–312.

Schweninger, Loren. *Black Property Owners in the South, 1790–1915.* Urbana: University of Illinois Press, 1990.

Sharpless, Rebecca. *Fertile Ground, Narrow Choices: Women on Texas Cotton Farms, 1900–1940.* Chapel Hill: University of North Carolina Press, 1999.

Stack, Carol. *Call to Home: African Americans Reclaim the Rural South.* New York: Putnam, 1996.

Stimpson, Eddie. *I Remembers: A Black Sharecroppers' Recollections of the Depression.* Denton: University of North Texas Press, 1996.

Tolnay, Stewart E. *The Bottom Rung: African American Family Life on Southern Farms.* Urbana: University of Illinois Press, 1999.

————, and E. M. Beck. "Racial Violence and Black Migration in the American South, 1910 to 1930." *American Sociological Review* 57 (February 1992): 103–16.

Trotter, Joe William, Jr., ed. *The Great Migration in Historical Perspective: New Dimensions of Race, Class, and Gender* (Bloomington: Indiana University Press, 1991).

Walker, Melissa. *All We Knew Was to Farm: Rural Women in the Upcountry South, 1919–1941*. Baltimore: Johns Hopkins University Press, 2000.

————. "Home Extension Work among African American Farm Women in East Tennessee, 1920–1939." *Agricultural History* 70 (autumn 1996): 487–502.

Washington, Booker T. *Up from Slavery*. New York: Dell, 1965.

Whayne, Jeannie M. "Black Farmers and the Agricultural Cooperative Extension Service: The Arkansas Experience, 1945–1965." *Agricultural History* 2 (summer 1998): 523–51.

————. *A New Plantation South: Land, Labor, and Federal Favor in Twentieth Century Arkansas*. Charlottesville: University Press of Virginia, 1996.

————, ed. *Shadows over Sunnyside: An Arkansas Plantation in Transition, 1831–1945*. Fayetteville: University of Arkansas Press, 1993.

————, and Willard B. Gatewood, eds. *The Arkansas Delta: Land of Paradox*. Fayetteville: University of Arkansas Press, 1993.

Williams, Bruce B., and Bonnie Thornton Dill. "African-Americans in the Rural South: The Persistence of Racism and Poverty." In Emery N. Castle, ed., *The Changing Countryside: Rural People and Places* (Lawrence: University Press of Kansas, 1995), 339–51.

Williamson, Joel. *Rage for Order: Black-White Relations in the American South since Emancipation*. New York: Oxford University Press, 1986.

Winters, Donald L. "Agriculture in the Post–World War II South." In R. Douglas Hurt, ed., *The Rural South since World War II* (Baton Rouge: Louisiana State University Press, 1998), 8–27.

Woodman, Harold D. *New South—New Law: The Legal Foundations of Credit and Labor Relations in the Postbellum Agricultural South*. Baton Rouge: Louisiana State University Press, 1995.

Woofter, Thomas Jackson. *Negro Migration: Changes in Rural Organization and Population in the Cotton Belt*. New York: Negro Universities Press, 1969.

Wright, Gavin. *Old South, New South: Revolutions in the Southern Economy since the Civil War.* New York: Basic Books, 1986.

Wright, Richard. *Black Boy.* New York: Harper Perennial, 1993.

Yaeger, Patricia. *Dirt and Desire: Reconstructing Southern Women's Writing.* Chicago: University of Chicago Press, 2000.

Zellar, Gary. "H. C. Ray and Racial Politics in the African American Extension Service Program in Arkansas, 1915–1929." *Agricultural History* 72 (spring 1998): 429–45.

꧁꧂

Contributors

R. DOUGLAS HURT is professor of history and director of the Graduate Program in Agricultural History and Rural Studies at Iowa State University. He also serves as editor of *Agricultural History,* the international journal of record for the field, and he is a past president of the Agricultural History Society.

WILLIAM P. BROWNE is professor of political science at Central Michigan University. Among his publications are: *Cultivating Congress: Constituents, Issues and Interests in Agricultural Policy Making* (Lawrence: University Press of Kansas, 1995); *Sacred Cows and Hot Potatoes: Agrarian Myths in Agricultural Policy* (Boulder, Colo.: Westview Press, 1992); and *The Failure of National Rural Policy: Institutions and Interests* (Washington, D.C.: Georgetown University Press, 2001).

PETER A. COCLANIS is professor of history and chair of the Department of History at the University of North Carolina at Chapel Hill. He is the author of *The Shadow of a Dream: Economic Life and Death in the South Carolina Low Country, 1670–1920* (New York: Oxford University Press, 1989), and he has edited *Ideas, Ideologies, and Social Movements: The United States Experience Since 1800* (Columbia: University of South Carolina Press, 1999). He is a past president of the Agricultural History Society.

VALERIE GRIM is an associate professor in the Department of African American and Africa Diaspora Studies at the University of Indiana. She specializes in the history of black communities in the South, and she has published extensively on African American agricultural and rural life in Mississippi.

LOUIS KYRIAKOUDES is a National Institute of Child Health and Human Development Postdoctoral Research Fellow at the Carolina Population Center at the University of North Carolina at Chapel Hill and associate professor of history at the University of Southern Mississippi. He has published articles in *Agricultural History* and *Social Science History*. His forthcoming book is entitled *The Social Origins of the Urban South: Race, Gender and Migration in Nashville and Middle Tennessee, 1890–1930* (Chapel Hill: University of North Carolina Press).

LOIS E. MYERS is associate director and senior lecturer at the Baylor University Institute for Oral History. She is the author of *Letters by Lamplight: A Woman's View of Everyday Life in South Texas, 1873–1883* (Waco, Texas: Baylor University Press, 1991), and the co-author with Rebecca Sharpless and Clark Baker of the forthcoming book *Rock Beneath the Sand: Country Churches in Texas* (College Station: Texas A&M University Press).

TED OWNBY is professor of history and southern studies at the University of Mississippi. Among his publications on southern history are: *American Dreams in Mississippi: Consumers, Poverty, and Culture, 1830–1998* (Chapel Hill: University of North Carolina Press, 1999); *Subduing Satan: Religion, Recreation, and Manhood in the Rural South, 1865–1920* (Chapel Hill: University of North Carolina Press, 1990); and he has edited *Black and White Cultural Interaction in the Antebellum South* (Jackson: University Press of Mississippi, 1993) and *The Role of Ideas in the Civil Rights South* (Jackson: University Press of Mississippi, 2002).

REBECCA SHARPLESS is director and senior lecturer at the Baylor University Institute for Oral History. She is the author of *Fertile Ground, Narrow Choices: Women on Texas Cotton Farms, 1900–1940* (Chapel Hill: University of North Carolina Press, 1999) and with Lois E. Myers and Clark Baker the forthcoming *Rock Beneath the Sand: Country Churchs in Texas* (College Station: Texas A&M University Press).

BRYANT SIMON is associate professor of history at the University of Georgia. He has published *A Fabric of Defeat: The Politics of South Carolina Textile Workers, 1918–1948* (Chapel Hill: University of North Carolina Press, 1998), and he has edited a forthcoming volume entitled *"Jumpin' Jim Crow": The New Political History of the New South* (Princeton, N.J.: Princeton University Press).

MELISSA WALKER is associate professor of history at Converse College in South Carolina. She is the author of *All We Knew Was to Farm: Rural Women in the Upcountry South, 1919–1941* (Chapel Hill: University of North Carolina Press, 2000).

JEANNIE WHAYNE is professor of history and chair of the department of history at the University of Arkansas. She has published extensively on southern agricultural and rural history, including: *A New Plantation South: Land, Labor, and Federal Favor in Twentieth-Century Arkansas* (Charlottesville: University of Virginia Press, 1996) and *Arkansas: A Narrative History* (Fayetteville: University of Arkansas Press, 2002). She has edited *Shadows over Sunnyside: An Arkansas Plantation in Transition, 1830–1945* (Fayetteville: University of Arkansas Press, 1993), and edited, with Willard B. Gatewood, *The Arkansas Delta: Land of Paradox* (Fayetteville: University of Arkansas Press, 1993).

Index

ABOUT THE EDITOR

R. Douglas Hurt is Professor and Director of the Graduate Program in Agricultural History and Rural Studies at Iowa State University in Ames. He is the author of numerous books, including *Nathan Boone and the American Frontier* (University of Missouri Press).